SO MANY WAYS
TO HURT YOU

By Adrian Street

Contact Information:

U.S. Mailing Address:

Adrian Street
1496 Oak Drive
Gulf Breeze, FL 32563

Email: daffodil777@bellsouth.net

Website: http://www.bizarebazzar.com

ISBN-13: 978-1477613238
ISBN-10: 1477613234

Cover:
Just a few of my ever-growing collection of Ring Jackets.

DEDICATIONS:

To my Father & Arch Nemesis - Your constant opposition guaranteed my success.

To my Mother - Without you I may never have been born.

To My Sister Pamela's LOVE.

To My Brother Terence's LEFT FIST.

To Jean for producing such beautiful Kids.

To Adrian, Vince, Amanda, and Natasha - who are the beautiful Kids.

To Russell Plummer for your great stories in 'The Wrestler.'

To 'Wresting Heritage' & 'Wresting Furness' whose Great websites have immortalized 'THE GOLDEN AGE OF BRITISH WRESTLING'.

To Victor Rook whose advice and book 'Musings of a Dysfunctional Life' inspired me to complete my own stories.

I will be eternally grateful to those who told me I could do it. - And even more grateful to those who told me I couldn't.

I want to pay a SPECIAL tribute to every wrestler I shared the ring with. Friend or Enemy. You all taught me the lessons I needed to reach the top. I couldn't have done it without you.

INTRODUCTION

My book has been self written and self edited - there maybe mistakes - the only time I spent in Oxford or Cambridge was when I wrestled there. Throughout my life I have always done things one way - My way. - So for better or worse, This is my story.

SO MANY WAYS TO HURT YOU

My Theatres are the noisy halls with benches made of wood,
My audience eats popcorn while screaming out for blood.
When there are no more bones to break and no more skulls to crack,
I'll bow to my admirers at the end of every act.
I'm a Gladiator, who doesn't need a sword
I nominate myself, for an academy award.

Well I made my choice and that was to try once again to become what I had set my mind on becoming originally, but I have always wondered since that time what adventures, or misadventures I may have missed or avoided by making the decision to remain a wrestler and not attempt to become an Italian film star.

I would be leaving the independent circuit behind me and moving into the big time. I would also be leaving behind a few good friends and a few bad enemies. Foremost among the enemies was World Lightweight Champion, George Kidd and then ex World Junior-Heavyweight Champion, Mike Dimitri. George Kidd had been the top of my hate list. Why he hated me was still a mystery, but he had cost me lots of matches and a little money, as he had refused to appear on shows if I had been booked on them. Why Mike Dimitri hated me was also a mystery, he referred to me as a 'Walking, talking erection,' and claimed if I had been his son, he would have drowned me at birth, but at least he never cost me any money.

I had no sooner come to terms with my decision, when I received another letter from Dale Martin's Wrestling Promotions and this time it was signed by Jack Dale himself. I was invited to attend the gym in Dale Martin's offices on the next Sunday morning for a 'try out', which once again raised the question in my mind, as to whether I was at last going to wrestle for them after all - or not! I had always got on okay with Jack Dale, in spite of my consistent pestering for a start with his promotion, and his constant refusal. But I wondered after so many refusals, if he may have resented his partner Les Martin hiring me, and was now looking for an excuse to fire me before I even got started.

When I arrived at the gym, to my dismay it was already packed with young hopefuls like myself, and all brimming with identical aspirations. Jack Dale was standing next to the ring, and had just called a halt to a match in progress that a couple of wrestlers had been engaged in, and ordered another couple of wrestlers into the ring to replace them. I was still standing just inside the door watching them wrestling, when Jack Dale noticed me, and even though the last wrestlers to enter the ring had only been wrestling for a few minutes, Jack once again called a halt to the action and called me over,

"I want to see how you can shoot," he told me, then he called to another wrestler and said, "Alan, get in the ring with Adrian, I want to see if he can shoot." Shoot wrestling is not regular professional wrestling but the real thing, I was relieved, as that would take care of wondering what moves to perform in order to impress Jack Dale. Instead I could just concentrate on defending myself as best I could, while looking for an opening and to take advantage of whatever opportunity my opponent presented me with. I stepped into the ring and eyed my opponent,

'The first mistake he makes, I'll go on the attack big time,' I thought, 'this time I'm taking no prisoners – or chances, I've got my whole future riding on the next ten to fifteen minutes.' He was a few inches taller than me and almost thirty pounds heavier, but that didn't faze me in the least. I had wrestled with much larger men than the one who was facing me now. Butch, who I used to wrestle with in the Forester's for instance, he was a few inches taller, and probably outweighed me by 70 pounds or more, and I could handle him as though he were a Baby. The other man stepped slowly out of his corner and we began to circle each other, he seemed to move with almost exaggeratedly slow movements, and I found myself mimicking his pace. I thought I saw an opening and I dived for it, but my opponent accelerated into a blur – then the World turned upside-down and I landed heavily on my head, with the World exploding into my chest. I found myself flat on my back with the other wrestler covering me, but I fought like a Wildcat to prevent him controlling my mobility and keeping me there. I broke free, and in an instant found my feet, but in the next instant the World turned upside down again, and once again after crashing into the canvas I was struggling for my life to break free of his hold. Up I got again, and then back down, whatever he was doing to me, I had no answer for it. Even though I continued to break free and stand up, I was never on my feet long enough to draw a breath before – WHOOOPS! Here we go again! I lost count of how many action replays I suffered in the next 5 or 6 minutes, but as I found my feet for the umpteenth time, and once again bracing myself for another out of body experience, Jack Dale called a halt to the action.

"Okay! That's enough," he ordered, then, "Street – come with me!" I felt as though the World had fallen on me again, 'Well he's got his excuse,' I thought, 'I was hoping to make a great impression in front of Jack Dale, but instead I get the crap beaten out of me.' I followed him into the shower room; I was fully expecting the same tired old scenario – 'Come back when you're older, bigger and an amateur champion.' But instead,

"That was excellent, those Lancashire turns were terrific - I've never seen them done better!" I quickly glanced over my shoulder, as I thought he must be talking to someone else, 'Lancashire what?' I thought, 'what the fuck is he talking about - is he taking the piss or what?'

"Do you know who you were wrestling with?" he asked me. I shook my head.

"That was Alan Butts," he told me, and recognizing the blank expression on my face for what it was, added "Alan Butts – he represented Great Britain in Rome last year in the Olympic Games. If you can escape from him after he's thrown you down like he did, you must know what you're doing - those Lancashire turns were terrific."

'Lancashire turns my arse,' I thought, 'he could have called what I was doing what ever he wanted to call them, and I wouldn't have known the difference. What I did was a product of pure blind panic, fueled by a total ignorance of what the Hell was happening to me. My reaction would probably have been more accurately described as a drowning man clutching at straws. Nevertheless, fortunately for me it must have been the right reaction, as it seemed that I still had 8 matches for Dale Martin's for the month of August. Even better with Jack Dale's blessing. I must admit that I would have much preferred to have past my test in a more triumphant manner, but I consoled myself when I was told that Alan Butts had even beaten the very classy Tony Charles every time they had wrestled against each other in the amateurs. Alan for that reason was treated by Jack Dale as the Star of the try out, and as the best future prospect to be accepted that day by Dale Martin's Wrestling Promotions.

Out of the couple of scores of would be wrestlers present that Sunday Morning, only about one dozen of us were told that we had passed the try out. And that we were all to attend the gym again each and every Sunday morning, in order to hone our skills and be deemed worthy of wresting in the Dale Martin's Manner. We were also told that we would all be expected to sign a 7 year contract with a 'Mystery Manager' that we would be introduced to, when we arrived at the gym next Sunday. I remember being quite excited at the prospect of signing a 7 year contract, as that would mean that I would be sure of wrestling for Dale Martin's for at least 7 years. I was a little less excited when we were also told that we would be paying our Manager 10 percent of our future earnings.

At this stage I need to explain that in Britain, unlike Canada and North America at that time, we didn't have professional 'stage' managers who would do most of the talking. Or get involved in matches, and interfere when their wrestlers were appearing to be on the losing end and so on and so forth. Those managers were managers in name only. They had no contracts with the wrestlers, and were not employed by the wrestlers who they were 'supposed' to manage, but by the promoter. They were employed just to add another dimension-angle-controversy, or interest to the match that their so called charges were involved in. In Britain wrestlers didn't talk or have anyone else talk for them, they just wrestled. In order to fully understand the remainder of my story, now would also be a good time to explain the essence of professional wrestling. I'll begin by answering once and for all, the most asked question in our business at that time – 'Is professional wrestling real or is it fixed?' the answer to that question was yes.

I appreciate that what I have just stated is a contradiction. But then so was professional wrestling in Britain at that time when wrestling under the 'Joint Promotion's Banner'. When a wrestler arrived at a venue, he would be informed who he would be wrestling against that night, which match they would be performing in, and also who would win the match - 'well that's fixed' I hear you say. And I say 'yes and no,' another contradiction I admit. But even though wrestlers would be told who was to win and who was to lose, they were very rarely told exactly how they were to achieve that result. If a wrestler was told he was to lose, and he wasn't happy with those orders – and let's face it none of us were. He may go ahead and lose the match as he was told to do, but there were no rules or orders that would prevent him from totally domineering the match before he lost it - if he was capable of doing so. I was going to say that it is Human Nature to want to be a winner rather than a looser, but as we all know, a creature doesn't have to be human to possess that instinct, and every form of life from the highest to the lowest strive in their own way to be the best. In every form of sport it would be very rare for a consistent looser to become a Star, and it's the Stars who get the recognition, the attention, the glory and last but not least the money. Talking of other forms of sport, I've always thought that it was unfair for professional wrestling alone to bear the reputation of being fixed If there's money involved, there's an angle, whatever the sport may be. Shaving points, drugging horses, and I know for a fact that every conceivable method was used to enhance, or ruin the chances of a Greyhound winning a race from the time I spent with Uncle Fred and his pals. Also I would be the last person to argue that Mohammad Ali wasn't the greatest. But for anyone who believes that either of the matches he had with Sonny Liston were anywhere close to being on the level, then I've got a 20 story Igloo in Central Africa I'll sell you cheap. I don't want to ruin other people's enjoyment by knocking their favorite sports, and I very much enjoy watching Boxing myself, but remember the term 'taking a dive' is not a terminology we use in the Wrestling business. When Mohammad Ali took on Antonio Inoki in Japan, in a Boxer versus Wrestler match, Inoki was told in no uncertain terms that the match would end in a draw, and that if Inoki decided to attempt to win, or to injure their boy Ali, they would drop a bomb on Inoki that would make the ones dropped on Nagasaki and Hiroshima look like damp firecrackers. Okay, I've made my point, let's get back to wrestling.

Wrestlers from all over the World began invading Britain in increasing numbers, due to the tremendous surge in popularity. All of these wrestlers were determined to build a reputation at all costs, and British wrestlers were equally determined to deny them their ambition, in order to retain and/or build their own reputations. Reputations are best built on victories, but only one adversary in each encounter can be victorious.

There were wrestlers from India and Pakistan who were regarded as demigods in their own counties, and when they appeared in Britain they drew huge crowds of their own Nation's immigrants to watch them perform. This often resulted in triple jeopardy for an opponent; firstly a promoter would be highly unlikely to award a victory to the adversary of a wrestler who was responsible for putting so many arses on seats. Secondly wrestlers from these countries, who were used to such immense hero worship, were not content in just winning the match when they wrestled in front of their countrymen, they also wanted to totally dominate the match in the process. Thirdly, this often resulted in an Ethnic crowd's overreaction that would cause an adrenalin rush in their Hero, that made him extremely dangerous to share the ring with. The Hungarian Revolution in 1956 was in part responsible for the wave of great Greco-Roman Wrestlers from that country who invaded Britain as refugees. Many of whom settled permanently. Soviet Sambo Wrestlers, Turkish Oil Wrestlers, Persians who trained with giant clubs rather than barbells, nimble Frenchmen with their aerial, acrobatic maneuvers. Wrestlers from South America favoring their own style of Jujitsu. Arabs, Egyptians, Mongolians and a variety of Martial-Art Masters from all over the Orient brought with them their nation's pride, dreams of grappling stardom and a myriad of exotic wrestling styles and techniques. But - if you think that such a deluge of wrestling talent would be capable of overwhelming the wrestlers of Britain, you could not possibly be more mistaken. Tough Farmers and Miners from Yorkshire and Lancashire ruled the roost in Britain when it came to their own style of crippling submission wrestling. They brought the pride of their gyms and their own jealously nurtured reputations into the professional wrestling rings with them. And believe me if you were capable of hanging with any of them, you were well prepared for anything that the rest of the grappling World could throw at you.

Karel Istaz was not only a member of the 1948 Olympics, a 14 time Champion of his native Belgium, seven times in Greco-Roman style and seven times in Freestyle, but he was also the Champion of that country's dockland all-in anything goes fighting - head butt to the nose, thumb in the eye, knee to the groin, rip, tear, smash, kick and stomp kind of action. When he first arrived in Britain the very first thing he demanded to know was -

"Where is Riley's Gym?!" Billy Riley's Gym 'The Snake Pit' was in Wigan, a grimy, depressing Lancashire Coal Mining Town, and would have been typical of hundreds of other mining towns of Great Britain if it had not been for Billy Riley. The Man who's brutal style of Lancashire Catch-as-Catch-Can wrestling made Wigan, World famous, and the Mecca of Europe, if not the World for 'straight' submission wrestlers. After leaving a long trail of broken limbs in his wake, and winning the British Empire Championship from Jack Robinson in South Africa, Billy Riley toured the United States before returning to Wigan. Where he built his gym for the purpose of teaching what was soon to become regarded as the most lethal form of Martial Art in the World of Sport.

Karel Istaz, who was always on the lookout for real competition, couldn't wait to show his wares in the World famous 'Snake Pit.' He would show these Britishers what shooting, hooking and ripping was all about – and who knows maybe even pick up something new in the process. He was in for a very rude awakening, as even the lowliest member of Billy Riley's gym, proved to be more than a match for one of the best shoot wrestlers in Europe. So impressed was Karel, that he threw out everything that he thought he knew about wrestling, and started from the bottom learning the Wigan style of wrestling from the Master Billy Riley for the next 8 years. He changed his name to Karl Gotch after emigrating to the United States of America, and later became the foremost authority in shoot wrestling in Japan, where he was recruited to train their wrestlers. He became known in Japan as 'The God of Pro Wrestling.'

There were many of Billy Riley's veteran Shooters from 'The Snake-pit' who helped to swell the ranks of Joint promotions army of international wrestlers as each month more and more venues were added to the already very impressive list. These Wigan wrestlers were afraid of no man - in fact there was only one thing in the World that they were afraid of, and that didn't just scare them, it terrified them to death. That was the fear that the new huge wrestling bubble would eventually burst, and leave them jobless. Almost to a man these Wiganers had been Coal Miners, as most members of their male relatives were, and had been for more generations than even they were aware of. And for generations work was very hard to obtain in those areas, even in the pit. Payment for slogging their guts out in the very bowels of the Earth 6 days a week was pitiful and to quote my Father 'it was dirty, unhealthy, hard work, poorly paid and very dangerous.' Not only can I attest to that personally, but add that it was one of the very few things my Dad ever said that I did agree with. Most Wiganers had a reputation of being very frugal, if not downright mean, a meanness born of generations of barely being able to make ends meet. Many of them would bring a week's supply of jam sandwiches from home with them, when they came down from the north to wrestle for Dale Martin's as their only source of sustenance. The demand for wrestlers had gradually coaxed these tough miners to leave the pits in favor of full time employment. But they never seemed to loose their paranoia of suddenly finding themselves without work. A typical greeting from almost every one of these stalwart warriors was always followed by,

"How long do you think this business is gonna last then?" As tough as they were they seemed to need constant confirmation and reassurance that professional wrestling had a future. Whenever you wrestled with a product of 'The Snake Pit' you were always aware that your opponent imagined that The Great Man Billy Riley himself was sitting ringside sternly judging their performance. Of course when you wrestled with one of them on television, he was sternly watching their performance – and that could be fun!

The Promoters themselves were an enigma; in one breath they would tell you who was to win, in the next they'd tell you to keep it straight. Wrestling was booming like never before, money was rolling into their coffers like never before, and they became as paranoid as the Wiganers. That even the slightest hint that professional wrestling was not an honest, legitimate sport would collapse their immensely lucrative and ever expanding empire like a house of cards in a category 7 Hurricane. As a wrestler learning what you could do, or shouldn't do - what you might get away with, and what you couldn't. Was sometimes like doing a Highland-Fling, with sprained ankles, to rock 'n' roll music in a minefield, while juggling with the unexploded bombs I used to bring home when I was a kid. Bullying was not only condoned it was encouraged, and even rewarded - usually, but not always. There was a Hierarchy, the Top Dogs were untouchable and unbeatable - usually, but not always. There was much more to demonstrating the ability of dominating an opponent that you had been told to lose to, than just a flash of ego or resentment. Both adversaries were well aware of the fact that a wrestler who was capable of taking the Lion's share of a match, even in the face of defeat on one occasion, would probably be told to win on the next. Therefore it was up to each wrestler to strive to promote themselves at the expense of their opponents - usually, but not always. Positions could change like patterns in a kaleidoscope, as wrestlers strove to assert their wills by applying the gentle art of force, in their quest to reach the top of the ladder of success. But there was always a wrestler on the rung just above you, who would happily kick you in the face to prevent you catching him up. Just as there was always another wrestler on a rung below, who would happily kick your legs away, stab you in the back, or climb right over you to take your place. Jealousy was rampant, as most wrestlers considered being told to win or lose was a sign of approval or disapproval by the promoter that they wrestled for that night. And promoters being well aware of that fact, would enthusiastically fan those fires of resentment with every devious scenario they could conceive of. Wrestlers were also aware of the fact that if the wrestling bubble did burst, or even shrink, resulting in wrestlers being laid off. It would obviously be the losers rather than the winners who would be the first to lose their jobs. Even after months or years of brutally bullying his way to a higher position in the food chain, a wrestler could not afford to relax or become overly complacent. As they could suddenly be told to lose to an ultimate underdog, by a promoter who merely wanted to observe his reaction, or just to rattle his cage.

On the other hand there were also wrestlers, who in spite of being great athletes may have had very little ability regarding 'real/straight wrestling', but were capable of 'staging' a very convincing and exciting match. Some of these through their skill and charisma, became just as big main event 'Superstars' – or even bigger, than many of the genuine shooters. Nevertheless, whether you were a great straight wrestler, a super performer, somewhere in between, or both there was no counter against the most powerful weapon in Britain's Professional Wrestling Rings. The Much Dreaded 'Office Hold!' Whatever a wrestler's shooting ability, or lack thereof may have been, it would prove null and void if the wrestler proved to be a consistent 'Box Office Draw' – if they consistently put arses on seats they would be awarded what wrestlers referred to as the counter-proof Office-Hold. Box Office Draws would win every match which was designed to ensure that they remained crowd-pullers; they VERY rarely lost as the promoters wisely didn't believe in killing off the Golden Geese. If you were unwise enough to attempt to Bully or dominate a Golden Goose the promoters wouldn't necessarily fire you, they simply wouldn't match you with one again. If you wrestled a Golden Goose it would most probably be a main-event match - for a main event match there would be a little more money and a lot more prestige.

This little story places the Joint Promoter's mentality in a nutshell -

'Tiger' Jimmy Ryan had left his native Ireland at the age of seventeen to live and work in Birmingham; he wrestled first as an amateur and then part time for various independent promoters until 'The Big Bang.' He then began wrestling full time for Dale Martins, and decided to move the 100 miles from his home to live in London, in order to be closer to his employers. At first Tiger made a decent living, as he was averaging about 25 matches or more every month, but gradually the amount of matches he was getting began to dwindle, until he was lucky if he got only 10 a month. In desperation Tiger went to Dale Martin's Office to have a word about it with Jack Dale. After explaining his predicament to Jack Dale, Jack replied,

"Tiger, I'd like to help you out, but what can I do? You never win a match!"

In fairness to many of Joint's promoters, they were not asking - or should I say, telling their wrestlers to do anything they couldn't, or hadn't done themselves. Jack Dale had been a very rough, tough wrestler, as had Ted Beresford, George de Relwyskow senior and Jack Atherton, who was not only a great friend of Billy Riley, but also a product of Billy's 'Snake-Pit' in Wigan. Last but not least, Norman Morrell represented Britain in the 1936 Olympics in Berlin, where he claimed to have been introduced to 'Der Fuhrer' himself. Many wrestlers who knew Norman best claimed that much of Der Fuhrer's most endearing qualities may well have rubbed off!

The next Sunday morning after my tryout I once again attended Dale Martin's Offices to meet my mystery Manager and sign a contract with him, that would entitle him to 10-percent of my wrestling wages for the next 7 years. Although I had been in my new manager's company many times before, this would be the first time in my life that I would shake hands with or even speak more than one word to the ex Junior-Heavyweight Wrestling Champion of the World – Mike Dimitri.

THE FULL TIME PROFESSIONAL WRESTLER

"Will is stronger than fact, it can mold and overcome fact." - H.G. Wells.

I do not suggest for one second that my existence on this Earth, or my insatiable determination to become a full time professional wrestler made the tiniest microscopic amount of difference to the fact that Professional wrestling, had almost overnight sprang from near obscurity to major national awareness. But I had made my mind up at the age of thirteen, that I was going to become a full time professional wrestler, and even though no such animal existed at that time in Britain, I did not have the slightest doubt that that was what I was going to do with the rest of my life. So I must say that I do agree whole heartedly with H.G. Wells, and I firmly believe that Will is stronger than fact – and that it can mold and overcome fact, and I nominate myself as a case in point.

The first match I had for Dale Martin Promotions was at the seaside town of Weymouth, and was a Main Event contest against Jackie 'Mr. TV' Pallo. Jackie Pallo was already one of the biggest names in British pro wrestling, thanks to his TV debut when wrestling was first aired on the small screen. Although Jackie lost this match, he lost it in such a way that made him nationally famous overnight, and the most talked about wrestler in the whole of Great Britain. At the climax of his first televised match, Jackie hurled his opponent into the corner of the ring, and then dashed towards him in order to deliver an almighty dropkick, his opponent ducked at the last second, and Jackie sailed on past him. Jackie's legs splayed out either side of the corner post, which resulted in him smashing his Christmas crackers on it, before bouncing off the corner post onto the canvas where he writhed in agony serenaded by the referee delivering the ten count. In those days, nothing like that had ever been seen on television before, and even though Jackie was always the Bad guy, letters of sympathy and concern were sent to both Dale Martin's Offices and to the TV Station by the truckload. The promotion was not slow in capitalizing on the huge amount of publicity this incident generated, Jackie was put on the tube again, and this time awarded a win. First to show that he had fully recovered, and secondly to help boost the ratings of a Sport which was still in it's small screen infancy. Wrestling was only shown on television once a week, from 4 till 4.45 every Saturday afternoon, which generally consisted of just two matches. This resulted in the chance of an appearance being strictly rationed, but Jackie Pallo's spectacular debut resulted in him appearing on television on a very regular basis. Thus his new nickname – 'Mr. TV.' The regularity of Pallo's TV appearances elevated him in becoming the first of the new TV Superstars to become a household name. Jackie Pallo's real name was Jack Guthridge, his family was into Boxing and Jackie was expected to follow suit. But Jack being the contrary sod he was turned to wrestling instead. He told me before the match that he was 38 years old, although I believe he was probably older. Nevertheless, I remember wondering if I would still be wrestling when I was as ancient as my opponent was that night. I had never seen Jackie Pallo wrestle, not even the now famous and still much talked about TV debut. Owing to the fact that I didn't own a TV, and had rarely had the opportunity to watch one since before I left Wales 4 years earlier. Because I had never seen Jackie Pallo wrestle, I had no preconceived impression on what to expect. So I just got stuck right into him, completely ignoring his superstar status, which surprisingly resulted in us having a very good solid and exciting match. Back in the dressing room when the match was over, I told Jackie that his style reminded me very much of a wrestler named Carlton Smith, who I had watched wrestling many times in Cardiff. He confirmed my assessment. Carlton Smith he told me had since retired, and Jackie admitted that as a result of his retirement he had blatantly ripped off Carlton's style, and image to the very best of his ability. The next day I was unable to resist phoning 'Gentleman' Geoff Moran, my very first professional opponent, who a couple of years earlier had told me that I was not good enough to wrestle for Dale Martin Promotions, and predicted that I never would be. He had also asked me if I could ever imagine wrestling for Dale Martin's in a Main Event contest, as I had for him and Johnny Childs. My affirmative reply had caused his eyes to roll, while he sighed in pure exasperation at my gross naivety, ignorance and what he thought was lofty, overblown future wrestling aspirations.

My second match was in Watford Town Hall on the following Monday night, and my opponent would be a wrestler who I had very much admired since the first of the many times I saw him in action in Cardiff. He was none other than Alan Colbeck, the European Middleweight Wrestling Champion. Even though I had already been wrestling professionally for a few years, I have to admit that I was totally awestruck at the very thought of sharing the ring with a wrestler of Alan Colbeck's caliber. So much so, that I found myself taking stock of the situation by comparing his very impressive wrestling pedigree with my own. Alan was a large Middleweight, I was barely a pound or two over the lightweight limit. Alan had well over a decade more experience than I had, plus he was the European Champion. Dale Martins had even refused to recognize my dubious claim of the Welsh Welterweight Crown. On paper I considered myself the ultimate underdog in this encounter, so for the very first time in my short wrestling career, I managed to exercise immense restraint during the match. I only attempted to get away with as much as I thought an average wrestler could get away with, when pitted against the European Champion. Back in the dressing room when the match was over, I felt very smug in the fact that for once, I had succeeded in doing the right thing. When both Jack Dale who was present that night, and my opponent Alan Colbeck, congratulated me on having a good match. But later that week I also succeeded in giving Alan Colbeck, good reason to completely revise his original assessment of my performance against him. That Saturday night I wrestled in Maidstone, against my first opponent from Billy Riley's gym, 'The Snake Pit.' Melwyn Riss was not only one of the best Lightweights to graduate from the famous gym, but was also the undisputed, Admiral Lord Mount-Evans British Lightweight Wrestling Champion. Melwyn Riss was another wrestler I had never seen wrestling before, and I remember looking across the ring and sizing him up as we waited for the bell to ring to start our match. I estimated that he was probably slightly shorter and very slightly lighter than me; he also lacked my muscle-mass and muscular definition. At that time I had never heard of Billy Riley, or his Snake-Pit and was completely ignorant of the legendary wrestling capabilities of Wigan Wrestlers. So ignorance being bliss, when the bell rang I went after Melwyn like a hungry Leopard goes after a Baboon. Although it didn't take me too long to appreciate why Melwyn Riss was the undisputed British Champion. Nevertheless, I was determined to give a good account of myself, and leave no doubt in anyone's mind that I belonged in the ring with any Wrestling Champion the World had to offer. We had one Hell of a match, and the Maidstone Fan's loud appreciation repaid us in full measure. So loud was their applause, that on the way back to the dressing-room at the end of the match, I was gratified to see every one of the other wrestlers who were wrestling there that night standing outside the dressing-room door where they had been watching our match. Drawn out by the sheer volume of the crowds reaction. But - as I entered the dressing-room, I was immediately accosted by Alan Colbeck who was also wrestling that night, and he demanded almost angrily,

"Why didn't you wrestle me like that?!" At first I didn't understand what he meant, and seeing the look of bewilderment on my face he asked, "Why did you hold back Monday night? You should have wrestled like you did tonight." I attempted to explain how I had summed up what chance I thought a comparative lightweight novice, like myself. Would stand against a seasoned Middleweight European Champion like him, and I reminded him, that he had told me after our bout earlier that week that I had given him a good match. "It was a good match!" he confirmed, "but if you had wrestled me like you wrestled with Melwyn tonight, we would have had a great match! – I never dreamt that you were capable of being so aggressive." He added, "Next time you wrestle with me, wrestle like you did tonight it will be terrific." I just stood there blinking and nodding while attempting to absorb what Alan was telling me. "Would you prefer to remain a novice or would you prefer to be a Champion?" He asked me.

"A Champion of course." I replied.

"Well if you want to be a Champion - Wrestle like a Champion!" He told me.

I was soon to learn that all the advice given to you by more established wrestlers, was not necessarily given to you with your best interest in mind, but I took what Alan Colbeck told me that night very seriously, and it turned out to be great advice from a great wrestler. Although I wasn't thrilled by the fact that my mistake had succeeded in Pissing off my most illustrious opponent to date, I did appreciate that my mistake - as mistakes often do, had once again taught me a very valuable lesson.

When I opened the envelope containing my wages for the best professional wrestling match I had had so far in my life, it was my turn to be pissed off. Not that I had exactly been over the moon with the 5 pounds each, that I had received for the other two matches I'd had for Dale Martin's Promotions. Especially as 10 percent of that had to be paid to my Manager Mike Dimitri. At Maidstone that night my wage packet only contained 4 pounds. 'Well,' I thought, 'they've obviously made a mistake, I'll just have to go to Dale Martin's Offices on Monday morning and sort it out.'

And, that wasn't the only thing I needed to sort out; Les Martin had told me that he didn't like my professional wrestling name 'Kid Tarzan Jonathan.'

"It sounds more like an old Bare-knuckle Fighter than a wrestler." He told me.

I attempted to defend the name by lying about all the thousands of wrestling fans I had generated as a result of my 4 years wrestling as Kid Tarzan Jonathan for the Independent promotions. I then grabbed the excuse he gave me, to once again flash my many Bodybuilding magazines, with photos of 'Muscleman' Kid Tarzan Jonathan gracing their pages to reinforce my point. I had hoped that if I could persuade him that Kid Tarzan Jonathan had already gained too much fame to ignore or waste, he might reconsider. But Les seemed adamant and totally unimpressed by my boasting of my independent wrestling pedigree or my Bodybuilding fame. As our discussion had not really been resolved, or an alternative professional name suggested. I had been fairly confident that our disagreement would just blow over and I would continue to be billed as Kid

Tarzan Jonathan. But it didn't - and the first I knew of it was when I'd turned up at the first venue, and saw the wrestling posters outside the arena which announced – Main Event' – 'Mr. TV.' Jackie Pallo versus Adrian Stuart. I was not thrilled, in fact I was royally pissed off - I am Welsh and proud of it, and as far as I know Stuart is a Scottish name. Now I had nothing against the Scots in general, but thanks to the existence of World Lightweight Wrestling Champion, George Kidd, anything Scottish was the last thing I wanted attached to my professional wrestling name.

My journey to Dale Martin's Offices the next Monday morning resulted in a mixture of success and failure. But, unfortunately more failure than success. To begin with Kid Tarzan Jonathan would not be reinstated; I did however reach a compromise, if I couldn't use the name Kid Tarzan Jonathan then I would use my own name. Adrian Street and not, under any circumstances would I agree to Adrian Stuart. Although we reached agreement on that point, things were never the same between Les Martin and me again. I was to learn that if a promoter had an idea, it was not a good idea for a mere wrestler to contradict it. It had been Les Martin who had hired me in the first place, after Jack Dale's consistent reluctance to do so. But now it seemed that their roles were reversed. I sensed that I had lost much of Les Martin's support due to my going against his petty wishes, but had gained Jack Dale's support as a result of proving to him that I could wrestle and hold my own against anyone I was pitted against. At this stage of my career I was loathe to rub anyone up the wrong way, but if I had to choose who's approval I would prefer out of Les or Jack, then it would be Jack. Although Les Martin was one of my bosses, he was just a businessman and had never been a wrestler. Jack on the other hand had not only been a very tough competitor, earning the nickname of 'Elbows' Jack Dale in reference to his devastating overhand forearm smash. But had also enjoyed a 15 year reign as the undisputed Middleweight Wrestling Champion of Great Britain. When I tackled 'Elbows' Dale about my wages, I didn't fare much better than his old wrestling adversaries had in their quest to relieve him of his British title.

I marched straight into his office and got right to the point,

"Jack," I told him, "my wages were not correct at Maidstone last Saturday; I was shortchanged by one pound."

"Oh really," he replied, "How much did you get?"

"4 pounds." I answered.

"No you weren't shortchanged," he responded, "that is what you are supposed to get paid for each match."

"Well I got paid 5 pounds at Weymouth and 5 pounds at Watford Town Hall." I said.

"That's correct," He agreed, "You got an extra pound at Weymouth because you were Main Event, and you got paid an extra pound at Watford Town Hall to cover your train fare, as we don't provide the transport for our wrestlers to that venue."

"I always got 5 pounds a match for all the independent Promoters." I lied.

"Well, You'll get a lot more matches from Dale Martin Promotions," He argued, "so that will make up for it."

"I've only got 8 matches for you this month, I used to get a lot more than that from the independents," I lied again.

"Let me check and see what we've got for you in September." He replied.

I stood silently in front of his desk as he flipped through the pages of a large pad and poked at it with the stub of a pencil,

"There," He announced triumphantly, "You've got 12 matches for next month and you'll probably get more than that for October." He predicted with a smile.

Only with great effort did I succeed in subduing any sign of appeasement as I thanked him and walked out of Jack Dale's office in a daze. But even in a daze my mind was working overtime, as I began adding and subtracting. 12 matches in one month would average 3 matches a week. Even if I only received the minimum of 4 pounds a match that would amount to 12 pounds a week, minus 1 pound 4 shillings for the 10 percent I would have to pay Mike Dimitri, and that would leave me with 10 pounds, 16 shillings a week - more than I had ever earned at any regular job in my life. Then I took into account my ability to generate a little more income as a result of posing for bodybuilding magazines and my mind was made up.

I had two errands in mind, the first was to my employer 'Turriff's of London Water-Board' and then to pay a visit to

Giles and the rest of his gang.

After I left Turriff's offices I set off to find the gang. Giles' hateful glare as he recognized me approach was tinged with a question mark, as he realized I was wearing a smart suit instead of my usual scruffy working clothes.

"Where 'ave yer been?" he demanded, "You're gonna git yerself fuckin' fired."

"You can't fire me, you stupid old twat!" I replied sweetly, "I've just quit - I'm a full time professional wrestler now."

****

Even before my first professional match for Dale Martins Promotions, I had heard of Joint Promotions, but had thought that it was merely another name for the same company. I was to learn that Dale Martins was just one member of a number of Wrestling Promoters who together comprised of Joint Promotions. Dale Martins were the biggest, and with the exception of just a few venues, they promoted the whole of the South of England and South Wales. Devereaux Promotions also operated in the South. It had originally belonged to Charles Devereaux, but after his death it was inherited by his wife who employed Wrestler, Ken Joyce as Booker and Matchmaker. Later it was more or less absorbed into Dale Martin's Promotions but with Ken Joyce still at the helm. Later still Paul Lincoln sold out to Dale Martins and was absorbed in the same way. Norman Morrell Promotions was based in Bradford, Yorkshire, but he also ran Lime Grove Baths, in Shepherd's Bush, London and Portsmouth on the South Coast. Ted Beresford promoted out of Huddersfield, Yorkshire, Max Crabtree promoted Halifax, Yorkshire, plus a number of Scottish venues. Relwyskow and Green were based in Leeds, Yorkshire, but also had venues in Scotland and Belfast in Northern Ireland. Wryton Promotions of Manchester ran venues in Lancashire, North Wales and all over the Midlands. Jack Atherton and Frank Woodhouse, also from Manchester ran Lancashire, the Midlands, Scotland and Redruth in Cornwell. Billy Best from Southport, Lancashire ran Southport, Blackpool and Liverpool Stadium. While George Kidd promoted in his home town of Dundee, Scotland. Joint Promotions headquarters was in Leeds, Yorkshire.

Even though Jack Dale had promised me enough work each month to enable me to become a full time professional wrestler. I was still not satisfied with the amount of money I was receiving for each contest. Especially as I had to pay 10 percent of it to Mike Dimitri. With a couple more main events in August, to bring in a little more money my gross earnings for my first month was 36 pounds, out of that I paid Dimitri 3 pounds-12 shillings, which was exactly the amount I was left with each night after paying out 10 percent. So for every 8 to 10 matches I had, I felt that I was wrestling one of them for nothing. As I was not thrilled with my wages, and had not been able to get an increase myself, I thought that as I had been forced to employ a manager the least he could do was to do a bit of negotiating on my behalf.

"Mike, I'm not happy with my wages," I told him, "and as you are my manager I'd like you to get me an increase to at least 6 pounds a match."

"Now is not the right time," Mike told me, "it would be better to wait at least another 6 to 7 months or so, and see what business is like then."

"What do you mean it's not the right time?" I demanded, "Joint Promotions were only running a few hundred shows a year a few years back, now they are running 4,500 shows a year - if this isn't the right time, when is!?"

"They've got lots of wrestlers coming into the country from all over the World, and they are spending a fortune on fares," he replied, "it would be better to wait and see what happens over the next few months."

"Oh, so let me get this straight," I countered, "I'm expected to wrestle for less money, so that Dale Martins can afford to bring in more foreign wrestlers, whose only chance of becoming big stars and fulfilling the promoter's money making potential and make them a profit on their investment, is to beat British wrestlers like myself in my own back yard? That's a game I won't play Mike."

"Well they've got a lot of wrestlers who will." He told me.

"If I get an increase, then you'll get more money too." I pointed out.

"Now is not the right time." He insisted. The next time I bumped into Jack Dale I asked him exactly what my manager was for.

"Well he can teach you more about wrestling." He explained.

"What is he going to teach me that I don't already know?" I asked.

"He was Junior Heavyweight Wrestling Champion of the World," Jack replied, "He's a great submission wrestler too,"

'Okay,' I thought, 'I'd better check him out.'

As well as managing a dozen or more young wrestlers, Mike Dimitri was still wrestling for Dale Martin's Promotions; the next time we both appeared on the same wrestling show, was at The Seymour Hall in London, and I made sure I watched his every move from his ring entrance, to his exit. Mike was wrestling in the semi-main event match against South African Heavyweight Frickie Alberta, Frickie was a great guy, but to put it mildly, was the possessor of very questionable wrestling skills. Mike Dimitri in contrast had been a very skillful wrestler, but with very much emphasis on the 'Had been.' Not only was Mike extremely close to 60 years of age, but it was not a very well preserved 60 years of age. He had a lopsided posture, and a limp caused by a damaged hip that he had to have replaced for a plastic one just a few years later. He had also sustained so much damage over the years on his right shoulder, that the muscles in his deltoid and his right hand had shrunken, and weakened to such an extent that he could not even grip and lift a ten pound weight with it.

The match began, Mike was very slow, and every move he made looked as though he was causing himself more pain than he was his opponent. His opponent was also very slow, he looked totally bewildered most of the time. Every move he made was so poorly performed and ponderous, that it looked as though he was causing more pain to the spectators than he was to Mike Dimitri. At first the audience watched in silence, the only sound was the loud monotonous grunts made by both contestants as they pulled, pushed and struggled their way around the ring. It soon became obvious that the only thing that prevented the whole audience falling asleep, was the loud monotonous grunts. Soon the loud grunting sounds were drowned by the restless fans, as they began to shout,

"BOOOOOOOR-ING!!!"

"WHEN'S THE WRESTLIN' GONNA START?!!!"

"WE WANNA REFUND!!!"

"BORING – BORING – BORING!!!!"

"BOOOOOOOR-ING!!!" Poor Mike couldn't do anything about it, he was no longer physically equipped. Poor Frickie couldn't do anything about it either - he wasn't physically or mentally equipped. It seemed like a week later that the bell sounded to end round one. Both contestants must have been panic stricken as the seconds ticked away between round one and round two as the audience's heckling intensified. What the Hell were they going to do, to satisfy the bloodlust of the action starved wrestling fans? Both contestants seemed to have the very same idea at the very same time, as the bell rang to begin round two, they both dashed madly towards each other, as fast as each was able. Only to be stopped in their tracks by the voice of a big fat male spectator, who leaned towards them over the balcony, and screamed out in a loud soprano squawk,

"OOOW QUICK! SOMEBODY STOP THEM – THERE'S GONNA BE A FIGHT!" The whole audience exploded with laughter as Fatty's quip became the undisputed highlight of the entire wrestling match. Mike Dimitri was a very proud man, and I did sympathize with him very much for the frustrating ordeal he had just suffered. Nevertheless, later in the dressing-room, when there were no other wrestlers within earshot of our conversation, I said to him,

"Mike, I am not happy with my wages, and as you are my manager I would like you to get me an increase to at least 6 pounds a match."

"I don't think this is the right time to ask for more money." He replied.

"Jack Dale told me you were a great submission wrestler," I told him, "so if I'm paying you to be my manager - when do the submission lessons begin?"

I believe that I have made it clear by now, that I did resent paying anyone anything out of my meager wrestling earnings, especially as they didn't appear to be doing anything to earn it. Also another unpalatable aspect had arisen, as the 'rumor' began to circulate amongst the veteran wrestlers. It was rumored that Mike Dimitri had some special arrangement with Dale Martins concerning dozens of wrestlers who he was managing, and was adding to daily. Who were not only paying him 10 percent each out of their wages, but were wrestling for peanuts which undercut the more substantial wages that the veterans were receiving. Paranoia was rampant that these cheap wrestlers, or '10-percenters' as they were now being referred to, were being groomed to keep wages low, and maybe even replace seasoned wrestlers who were being paid a better wage. There may have been more than a little truth to that rumor, as it became a proven fact that it was a Joint Promotion's policy to keep wrestler's wages as low as possible. That policy was not just born out of the Promoter's chronic meanness. Although that was also a very valid aspect. Joint Promotion's policy was, that if you paid a wrestler too much they thought that the wrestler would become more independent. If he became more independent he would become harder to control, and control was something that Joint Promotions were determined not to relinquish to any degree under any circumstances. So it was not only possible - it was highly probable, that we 10-percenters were just another tool employed by the promoters to keep their wrestlers off balance and under their thumbs. To me the fact that Mike Dimitri insisted that now was not the right time to ask for more money confirmed it. The promoter's policy caused the wrestlers to adopt a policy of their own concerning 10-percenters. And that was, in order to keep the wages up, and to protect their own jobs, they would seek out the evil 10-percenters, and beat and bully them right out of the wrestling business.

I was traveling in one of Dale Martin's transport vans to a show one day, with about ten or so other wrestlers, when the subject of Mike Dimitri and his 10-percenters came up. For some reason I seemed to have slipped below their radar, and no one seemed to suspect that I was one of the very people they were planning to persecute, as they grizzled, grumbled and discussed their termination strategy. Although I realized that the other occupants of the van were oblivious of my status, I nevertheless resented the threats in their discussion, and could not resist the challenge to respond,

"I am one of Mike Dmitri's wrestlers," I declared. I was quizzed endlessly by the other wrestlers. I told them that it was by no means my choice, or the choice of any of the other 10-

percenters, to be one of Mike Dimitri's boys in the first place, and certainly not our choice to pay 10 percent of our earnings to someone else.

"What exactly was Mike Dimitri's deal with Dale Martins, and was he being used as a tool against the wrestlers?" They all wanted to know, I told them quite honestly,

"I wish I knew the answer to that one myself."

As you can imagine, I had already got plenty to contend with, just being a new boy in a new World. Wrestling almost every night, against different wrestlers. Many of whom I may have never wrestled before, or ever even seen before I stepped into the same ring. I was determined to make a name for myself, just as my opponents were. Every night was a new challenge, each wrestler I met had his own style. Some were fast, some were slow, some were very skilled, some were not, some were very strong. Some were very clumsy, awkward and stiff to wrestle with, others were smooth and more comfortable. Some spoke English some didn't, but all were ambitious! I was not complaining, this is the life I had dreamed of, and the life I was now living. But it was often impossible to gauge whether an opponent was naturally awkward and clumsy. Or was that black eye, bloody nose, or cut lip, I had just received an attempt to dominate the match - or even worse, to drive another 10-percenter with a bounty on his head out of the wrestling business for good. Well it seemed that the promoters had a policy to keep their wrestlers under control, and were using the 10-percenters to help them achieve their goal. The wrestlers as a result adopted their own policy of getting rid of the 10-percenters. - I as a result adopted my own policy, and I would no longer fret over the reason for a cut lip, bloody nose, or a black eye, or for any other excessive pain I might suffer at the hands of my nightly adversaries. My policy was very simple, from now on, whether it was through ambition, clumsiness, awkwardness, vindictiveness, jealousy or a simple accident. If my opponent hurt me, I would hurt them back, if he blackened my eye, I'd blacken his, if he cut my lip, I'd cut his and if he kicked me too hard, I would kick him harder, if he didn't attempt to damage me, I wouldn't try to damage him. It proved to be a good policy; I have exercised it throughout my entire career and still do.

****

The first time I met the Wigan 'Snake-Pit' graduate Billy Robinson, was when we were both appearing at St. Matthews Baths Hall in Ipswich. As I walked into the dressing room he accosted me before I had even had a chance to put down my kitbag,

"Are you Adrian Street?" he asked me, and after receiving my affirmative reply, he continued, "I'm Billy Robinson, secretary of the Wrestler's Union, are you a member of the union yet?"

'Oh Bollocks! Not again.' I thought. My mind immediately spun back to over 2 years earlier, when I was asked a similar question by that Cod eyed Irish creep, Pat Kloak when I had made my Tony DeMarto Promotions debut. My negative response on that occasion, had resulted in my complete banishment from professional wrestling for a few endless months. Without the knowledge as to when, or if ever, I would be reinstated. Even if you can imagine what an awful impact that had on a young teenager who had thought that at last he had began to make some serious headway into pursuing his dreams. You can't possibly contemplate what loosing it all now would mean to me. Not only would all my dreams, of finally wrestling full time for the big time promotions come crashing down on me. But I would now find myself out of wrestling, without a job again, in job starved London. Add to that, the fact that after living my dream for almost a couple of months, I was now completely spoiled forever in the desire to ever want to pursue any other career.

"No, I'm not a member of a wrestler's Union," I admitted reluctantly, "I didn't know there was one." Imagine now my utter relief when Billy responded with,

"Okay then, I'll sign you up right now," and as he produced a small red card and began to fill it in, he added, "That'll cost you one pound."

I had never been so happy to spend one pound in my life.

A couple of days later I bumped into Jack Dale as I arrived at the office to catch my ride to that night's venue, I couldn't wait to impart the tremendous news with him that I was now a very proud member of Joint Promotion's Wrestling Union.

"What did you do that for you bloody idiot?!!!!!!!" was his response. Was I taken aback? – You can say that again, I thought that by joining the wrestler's union that I would be adding to my professional legitimacy, now according to Jack, I'd fucked up.

"Why do you think you signed a contract with Dale's and Mike Dimitri?" he raved, "So you wouldn't have to have anything to do with those bloody fools and their bloody stupid union!" he added.

"Oh sorry Jack," I replied sheepishly, "I didn't know, nobody told me anything about a union until I was told I had to join it." A while later the wrestler's union approached 'Equity' the actors union in a quest to join up with them, and hopefully obtain the support of a much more powerful organization. It seemed that Equity was very responsive to their approach and that the wheels were now in motion for our enrollment. That was when Dale Martins, who were totally panic-stricken at the prospect, called for a big meeting that was held in the gym section of their Brixton Offices. With all their wrestlers crammed into the small gym, Jack, Les and Johnny Dale got right to the point,

"What the bloody Hell do you all want to join an actor's union for?" They wanted to know, "Do you want everyone to think you're all actors?!" Well no, we certainly didn't. There was nothing that pissed off a wrestler more in those days, than being called an actor - except maybe a Clown. Either way it amounted to the same thing, and that was the very suggestion that profession wrestling was not a straight, real, legitimate sport. Or to doubt our claim that we were all legitimate athletes and sportsmen and, not – definitely not, actors or clowns. An actor who almost fell foul of that fatal misassumption was the late, great Peter Ustinov; Peter was a huge fan of wrestling, and wouldn't miss the matches at Manchester's Belle-Vue, if his own very busy schedule would possibly allow him to attend. Being the huge celebrity that he was, Peter was allowed free of charge to stand backstage in the passageway used by the wrestlers when they entered the ring, and he would always be completely mesmerized by each and every match he witnessed.

Then one day on a TV interview, he was asked about the art

of acting,

"Professional Wrestlers, are the best actors in the World," Was his reply, "they enter the ring with no script, no rehearsals, and are able to inject drama, humor, anger and excitement into every contest. Their fight-scenes would be impossible for even the most skilled Hollywood stuntmen to duplicate. But the only people who don't seem to appreciate what great actors wrestlers are, are the wrestlers themselves." He added. What Peter said, he actually meant as a compliment and was attempting to pay them very much deserved credit. But as much as he may have admired professional wrestlers, he really could not have understood them. His compliment was regarded as the foulest, most slanderous insult, by each and every grappler, and even more so, by each and every grappling promoter. Paranoid that the slightest hint of fantasy or acting associated with their business, would cause it to slither back into the 'Dark-Ages' of pre-TV wrestling.

On the very next occasion when Peter attended the matches in Belle Vue, instead of being welcomed as was normal, when he entered the backstage entrance, he was unceremoniously told to 'fuck off' and to never come back. Then just after he left, a couple of wrestlers had to be restrained from following him, and staging a re-enactment of William Shakespeare's 'Julius Caesar.' With Peter playing the title role to the wrestlers playing Cassius and Brutus at the Senate steps on the Ides of March.

Unanimously the wrestlers who attended 'The Meeting' at Dale Martin's offices that day, voted to tell Equity the same thing that the promoter had told Peter Ustinov as he was being ejected from Belle Vue's backstage. So – once again the promoters had won the victory for full control over the wrestlers, and soon after that, the first wrestler's union that I was a member of disintegrated overnight. Although we had all voted against joining Equity, a few wrestlers secretly signed their forms and joined anyway. While most others, myself included, proudly tore up our enrollment forms into confetti – an 'act' that I would live to regret.

Within a few months there were only about 4 of Mike Dimitri's ten-percenters left, and the rest of them, mostly the victims of excessive violence were gone. Strangely, the first to quit was 'the star' of the first of the Dale Martin's tryouts, the

Olympic Wrestler that I had been paired with Alan Butts. Although it wasn't bullying by the other wrestlers that was the cause of ending Alan's professional wrestling career. Alan had quit before rumors of the 10-percenters even got started, a tragic victim of Dale Martin's Transport. The very first time we were both traveling to a show together, we had only ridden from Dale Martin's office to pick up a few more wrestlers from a restaurant called 'Martini's' where many of the Northern wrestlers stayed when they wrestled down South. Before we even arrived at the restaurant Alan began to show signs of distress. From Dale Martins to Martini's restaurant was probably no more than one mile, but by the time we stopped outside Martini's Alan leapt out of the van and lost his breakfast. With another 200 miles in front of us to the venue that night, you can just imagine the state poor Alan was in by the time we reached our destination. Not to mention the fact that he then had to wrestle, and after that ride another 200 miles back to London in that same dreadful van. Then the next day, and the next day, and the next day, he would have to do it all again. You can't imagine how tough a Man needs to be to become an Olympic Wrestler. The stress he puts his body through during his workouts are nothing less than brutal. Then the competition from other Olympic hopefuls during the elimination trials are insane. But even though Alan was tough enough for the 1960 Olympics, he wasn't tough enough to take Dale Martin's Transport.

Dale Martin's owned a small fleet of navy-blue colored vans that were used to transport the wrestlers from their offices back and forth to the various venues. The vans were old converted ambulances, and were stuffed with as many uncomfortable seats as could be forced into their confined interior. The vans had no suspension, if you hit a pebble you'd feel it, they had no heaters, in the winter you could freeze your arse off. They had no air conditioning, in the summer you could cook, and they had a top speed of about 45mph. Not that it would have mattered much if they had been capable of going twice that fast, as the roads in Britain in those days were really terrible and were not at all conducive with speed. I was also amazed by the number of professional wrestlers who smoked cigarettes in the van and in the dressing rooms. Then you would enter the ring in a blue haze from the cigarettes being smoked by about two thirds of the audience. If I ever had any children who wanted to follow in my footsteps, and I wanted to dissuade them from becoming wrestlers. I could just imagine myself repeating my Father's warning to my Brother, when he wanted to follow his footsteps into the pit,

"You won't like it," I'd tell them, "it's dirty, hard work, unhealthy, poorly paid and dangerous." Yes, wrestling was all those things and more in those days, but I loved it.

Dales also owned a number of large navy blue colored trucks that were used to transport their rings, and sometimes extra chairs to their many venues.

****

On the very day that I, along was all the other 10-percenters signed that dreaded contract, I knew I had an ace up my sleeve that none of the others possessed, and that none of the others, including Jack Dale, Les Martin, or Mike Dimitri seemed to be aware of. I was the youngest wrestler at that tryout, and at the contract signing. In fact at the age of 20 I was still too young to sign a legal contract. In order to make it legal it would have to be signed by a Parent or Guardian. I was well aware of that fact when I signed it myself, but refused to mention it for two reasons. First it may have jeopardized my chances of wrestling for Dale Martins, and secondly I knew that I would be in a better position to declare the contract null and void if it suited me to do so. But, only AFTER I had made a name for myself. As far as I was concerned my contract with Mike Dimitri had placed me in a very precarious position in regards to the very dangerous people I shared a wrestling ring with every night. But if Mike Dimitri was the cause of my problem, maybe he could also be the cure. The old saying goes, 'if you can't beat them, join them,' but what do you do if they won't let you join? To me the answer was obvious. If you can't join them, then you have to learn to beat them.' For that, I needed a lot more weapons than I was presently in possession of in order to protect myself from all those Headhunters. So the very next time I paid Mike Dimitri his 10 percent of my wrestling wages, I repeated my last question to him,

"Mike, when do the submission lessons begin?"

Through the remainder of August I wrestled matches against Mick McManus, Bob Archer O'Brien, Pasquale Salvo, plus another match each against Melwyn Riss and Alan Colbeck. In September I had matches against most of them again, plus Billy Stock, Monty Swann, Vic Faulkner, Eddie Saxon, Stefan Milla, Bobby Steel, Bob Anthony and Linde Caulder. Then the amount of matches increased dramatically, in October I had 27 matches, the same in November and 26 in December. After that it was very unusual for me to wrestle less than 30 times a month. Often I would wrestle in two towns in one day, or in tournaments, that could amount to as many as 3 times in a single night in one Arena. That could sometimes bring my score up to 40 matches in one month.

Traveling to a match in North-East London in early November, the bus I was on gradually ground to a halt and all passengers were informed that the public transport bus would not continue one more inch until visibility improved dramatically. The evening had began foggy, and had deteriorated more and more the closer I had got to the venue, it was now impossible to see more than a few feet.

'If we don't get going soon, I thought, I'm going to be really late.' I decided that it would be best to get off the bus and walk. It was very fortunate that this was the very same area that I had worked in with Bill Waller when employed by the Railway, so I did have some idea of where we were. It seemed to take forever, virtually feeling my way through the ever thickening fog, but eventually I arrived at the Hall. I found that in spite of the dreadful weather, the place was almost full of fans eager for a good night's wrestling. There was however a problem, due to the dreadful weather there were only 3 other preliminary wrestlers and a referee beside myself in the arena,

"How the hell are we going to be able to put on a show with only half the wrestlers required?" one of them asked.

"We could have a four man tournament." I suggested.

"That would still only make 3 matches instead of 4." They replied.

"Not if the two losers of the preliminary bouts wrestled each other before the two winners wrestled each other in the final," I countered. That's what we did and it turned out great. Especially as the fans were well aware of our problem and they really appreciated our effort in making sure that they got the 4 matches that they had expected and had paid for. At first I thought that someone else on the card must have taken credit for my idea, as I got no thanks or any reaction at all from Dale Martins for literally saving the show. But on my next date sheet I received my very first television match, which not only added considerably to my prestige, but also paid me a hefty 20 pound fee. The most money I had ever been paid for one match in my life so far. I did well on TV and began to enjoy appearances every few weeks. But, the only time I would wrestle in a Main Event contest, would be if I was wrestling against one of the Big Star Main Event wrestlers, and I would merely be regarded as an opponent. Normally very little notice was taken of preliminary wrestlers by the promoters, as all the publicity and emphasis was centered on their Main Event wrestlers, whose Super-Star status was responsible for filling their arenas. But away from office politics and the promoters control, the media would write about what caught their eye, or what they found most newsworthy when covering the wrestling scene. It seemed that Bill Jones's assessment had been correct, I did have something. Even though I was basically only a preliminary wrestler at that time, I already seemed to possess the power to attract a great deal of attention. This sort of coverage by local newspapers, where I became the main feature in spite of only being a preliminary wrestler soon became quite common,

LAST NIGHT'S WRESTLING.
FLYING DROP-KICK SENDS SANTOS CRASHING THROUGH THE ROPES TO DEFEAT.

There was plenty of variety at last night's wrestling at St. Matthew's Baths Hall, Ipswich, both in weight, styles and nationalities, with contestants from England, Wales, Argentina, Ireland, Spain and Russia taking part. In the opening bout Miguel Santos, from Argentina, was opposed to the young Welshman, Adrian Street, and it soon became evident the former was not above 'bending' the rules somewhat when it suited him, but some quick interventions by burly referee Johnny Peters soon restored order and the first two rounds although fluctuating were fairly even.

SPECTACULAR CLOSE.

Midway through round three a folding body-press put the Argentinean ahead, but Street brought the proceedings to a most spectacular close early in the last round, when a Flying Drop-kick sent Santos hurtling through the two top ropes to crash on to the floor of the hall wrecking the time-keeper's table in the process. The count of ten was a mere formality, for Santos was completely knocked out by Adrian Street and had to be half carried to the dressing-room where he recovered after attention.

RUSSIAN WINS.

A quickly taken reverse double arm lever and shoulder-press gave Zaranoff the lead in round two, but after twice sending the Russian crashing into the corner post, Arroyo equalized in the fourth with a body-slam and press. The minute's interval before the next round proved sufficient for Zaranoff to recover, for in less than a minute of the fifth Zaranoff came charging off the ropes in a flying tackle, landing high on Arroyo's chest and shoulders to flatten him for the winning fall. To wind up the evening Joe Murphy [Dublin] and Cliff Beaumont [Wigan, a real ring craftsman if ever there was one] battled out a 1 – 1 draw.

HALF NELSON.

So even though my match was only supposed to be a preliminary warm up to bigger and better things to come, the local press had given my match and performance 'top billing'. This became a regular occurrence, and of course added a lot of fuel to my arrogance and self confidence, and also a lot of fire to other wrestler's jealousy.

In spite of the fact that I had wrestled with the cream of the lighter weight divisions through September, which included main event contests against both Mick McManus and Jackie Pallo, there was one match which totally eclipsed the rest. It took place on September the 20th against the Bombastic Billy Stock. It was not so much my opponent who was responsible for making this the most exciting, most anticipated, most memorable, and most satisfying match of my career so far, but the venue itself. For years I had dreamed of wrestling in Dumfries Place Drill Hall in

Cardiff. I had long ago lost count of how many times my physical body had sat in the audience of that very arena, enthralled by the spectacle that was unfolding before me. While my spiritual body was right there in the ring with them. Matching them hold for hold, blow for blow and slam for bone jarring slam, until I triumphed and raised my fist in victory to the blast of applause from my own Welsh countrymen. That night my dream came true, Billy was the first to stride to the ring, and I received instant gratification when I heard the loud boos and jeers his entrance evoked. When it was my turn to make my entrance, the feeling I experienced being bombarded by the ear shattering applause of my Welsh fans threatened to surpass what I had felt a few years earlier when I had made my very first entrance into a professional wrestling ring. Dale Martin's Masters of Ceremonies had already given up trying to get their mouths around the pronunciation of my home town, 'Brynmawr' by now, and so the M.C.s would announce me from Cardiff instead.

'Never mind, being introduced from Cardiff, in Cardiff would make my new devoted fans even more enthusiastic,' I thought. I was wearing white trunks, white boots and a white jacket with the Red Welsh Dragon flag on my left breast,

'The colors of the ultimate good guy'. I thought, while my opponent in contrast was appropriately dressed in a black leotard with matching black wrestling boots. The bombastic Londoner, Billy Stock, was 2 or 3 inches shorter than me, but was built like a small tank, and I would soon learn first hand that he possessed all the power that his stocky build suggested. The bell rang and my fantasy match had begun, at first I proved to be too slick and elusive for my very powerful adversary, and outmaneuvering him proved to be a piece of cake. My Welsh audience was thrilled to see their own nimble Welsh hero skillfully run circles around his ponderous opponent. But ponderous or not Billy could explode into short bursts of speed that belied his shape and weight, and halfway through the second round it was such an explosion that was responsible for my head being caught and crushed in a headlock that resembled a steel Bear trap. My clever counter move and subsequent escape evoked much enthusiastic response from the audience. But no sooner had I broken free, than I was once again snatched right back into a cranium crushing headlock that ripped all the enthusiasm right out of the fan's open mouths. Time and again I managed to escape, but each time I would be caught once more in the same brain numbing, skull cracking hold. Bit by bit as the powerful headlock began to wear me down, escape became more difficult and less frequent. By the time the bell rang to end round 3 it was the bell and not my skill that was solely credited as the cause of my release. Saved by the bell, I staggered slowly back to my corner in a very sorry state, and hardly had time to reach out for a little support from the top rope, when the bell sounded to start round 4 and Billy the Bully shot out of his corner like a steel ball out of a cannon. Once again Billy wrapped his huge arm around my head, but with the force of his mad dash across the ring the impetus hurled us both into my corner, and halfway through the ropes. The referee ordered Billy to release the hold, but even though we were both tangled up together in the ropes, my opponent was unwilling to relinquish the advantage. It was only the threat of being disqualified that finally persuaded him to let me go. Immediately he went after my head again, but I managed to evade his initial assault, and ducked and dodged around the ring in an attempt to keep my skull out of his vice like grip. After a few more unsuccessful attempts by Billy to secure a grip on my head, he became impatient and frustrated and barged into me shoulder first catching me under the sternum, and smashing me back into the ropes. Before I could recover he hit me again, and then again. By this time I had collapsed onto the canvas, which gave my opponent the time to take a couple more steps back which gave him even more force behind his next shoulder block the very second I was able to stand up. Crash! Down I went again, and Billy took off across the ring with the idea of bouncing against the ropes and hitting me with the full blast of his whole weight in his rebound and charge. Billy hit the ropes on the opposite side of the ring, and as he hurtled towards me I met him feet first in the middle of the ring with a dropkick that almost decapitated him. It had been a do-or-die effort, and the whole of the Cardiff crowd exploded in a way that was reminiscent of the way that both my boots had exploded into Billy Stock's face. He was sent flying backwards out of the ring which gave me a great knockout victory. I raised my fist in triumph and my Welsh fans cheered with all the magnitude and ferocity that I thought befitted a tribute to the great Celtic Hero I imagined myself to be. Little did I know that this would be the last time that I would ever get applauded so enthusiastically by my own loyal fellow countrymen in this arena.

For the rest of the year my opponents included most of the wrestlers that I had already wrestled with before, plus Peter Szakacs of Hungary, Miguel Santos of Argentina, Tony Cassio an Italian from South Africa, Joachim LaBarba of Mexico, Chic Purvey of Scotland and Eddie Capelli of Italy. The most memorable match during the remainder of 1961 was at The Purley Orchid Ballroom on December the 5th, which was my 21st Birthday. I was wrestling in a match against Bob Archer O'Brien. As Purley was in the London area, and it was my 21st Birthday, I had planed to take Jean to the show with me, and then find a good restaurant afterwards where we could both celebrate the 21st anniversary of my birth together. Instead we had a flaming row about something, and out of spite I decided not to take her with me, but to go off on my own and start my celebrations early – and where better to celebrate than Soho.

There was a club called 'The Golden Guitar' that the wrestlers sometimes used as a meeting place when making their own way to the wrestling shows by car. The club was in Romilly Street and it ran parallel to the back of 'The 2 I's Coffee Bar. When I walked in there that afternoon both Glen the manager and Harry the Barman, better known as Glendora and Harriet were behind the bar serving. Stefan Milla was sitting under a wall light in the corner just in front of the bar. As he recognized me, he called out in a voice which was as equally effeminate as Glendora's and Harriet's,

"OOOOWEEEE! Don't you think this wall light above my head makes my hair look like spun gold?! As the light was making his whole scalp gleam under his thinning blond hair, I replied,

"Yes it does Stephan, but from here it looks like most of it has spun off."

Glendora and Harriet giggled like girls, while Stephan scowled and moved to a different seat, and asked me in a more sober voice,

"Are you wrestling anywhere tonight?"

"Yes," I replied, "at Purley - but I thought I'd start celebrating early as it's my 21st Birthday today."

"OOOH! Let me buy you a Birthday drink," came a voice from the opposite corner of the bar. 'It's not every day a boy becomes a man – unfortunately." It was Daniel Farsen, TV Broadcaster and author who a number of years later, penned 'The Man who wrote Dracula', which was a biography of his own Great-uncle Bram Stocker.

Well we had a few drinks and all sang 'Happy Birthday to me'. Then Daniel was joined by two very large uniformed Guardsmen, and we had a few more drinks and sang Happy Birthday again, while Glendora and Harriet performed some strange snake-dance. 'More to celebrate the arrival of the uniforms.' I thought, than my 21st. Daniel and one of the Guardsmen were becoming very affectionate towards each other, and we drank some more, I remember staring at Stefan, who seemed to be having great difficulty remaining upright on his barstool. He was beginning to look more and more like Dorian Grey, but without his portrait, and I thought it was time to leave. But we drank some more. Then the Guardsman with his arms all around Daniel, for some reason called Daniel 'the ugliest man in the World', which caused Daniel to scream, disengage himself from the Guardsman's embrace and sob,

"How dare you call me the ugliest man in the World, apologize at once or I'll throw my drink in your face!"

I thought it was time to go - but I'd just have one more for the road.

"Okay, I'm sorry," exclaimed the Guardsman, "you're not the ugliest man in the World - I am." Daniel looked as though the retraction had pacified him a little, until the Guardsman added, "But you're definitely the second ugliest man in the World!"

Daniel began to cry, and I thought it was time to leave - after just one more drink. Until I looked at Glendora and Harriet, who were beginning to look quite attractive and then I knew it was time to leave. I felt as though I was on board the Titanic as it was suffering its final death throes before plunging to the bottom of the Atlantic, as I attempted to navigate the badly listing stairway that led from The Golden Guitar to the now darkened Street's of Soho. Although the darkness panicked me, it did nothing to clear my head. 'Shit! What time is it?' I wondered, as I tried to adjust the focus of my eyes on the tiny face of the bracelet watch that Mam had bought me for my 21st Birthday. I knew that I was to wrestle in the opening match and it was very late, but suddenly I was unable to work out how I was supposed to get from Soho to Purley. With a brain that was trying it's best to imitate a pin-ball machine, I made my way to the nearest Underground tube Station, and I staggered in a purple haze down Shaftesbury Avenue towards Piccadilly Circus. Well to cut a long and very fuzzy story short, I got hopelessly and helplessly lost, and finally arrived at my destination with barely enough time to get changed in time to wrestle in the last match. My opponent, Bob Archer O'Brien was furious, as he had made arrangements of his own to take advantage of an early match in a local arena which I had now totally ruined for him. The fact that he also had to wrestle with an opponent who seemed to be making a monumental task out of simply attempting to lace up his wrestling boots, and probably smelled like a Brewer's apron, must have done very little to improve his mood. As drunk as I was, the demeanor of my adversary was not lost on me, and I knew I needed to think fast if I was to survive this upcoming ordeal in one piece. but with a brain who's ingredients seemed to comprise of two parts porridge to one part Frog's spawn, it was no easy task. After staggering from the dressing room and stumbling into the ring, I came to the conclusion that the best method of defense would be to attack. So as soon as the bell sounded to begin the match I took a very swift hop, skip and jump across the ring, launched myself into the air and caught Bob Archer O'Brien with a beautifully performed dropkick which hit him right in the chops. The roar of the crowd was suddenly cut short, as instead of hitting the canvas like a ton of bricks after taking such a tremendous kick, O'Brien began hoping up and down shouting,

"HA-HA, YOU MISSED!" Now it was my turn to be furious, I hadn't missed and everybody knew it, I thought to myself as I put everything into another great dropkick, 'Let's see you hop up and down after this one!' But this time I did miss, in fact Bob didn't only sidestep just in the nick of time, but smartly lifted the top rope so that it would not impede my journey right out of the ring. Instead of connecting with my opponent, I succeeded in dropkicking the timekeeper right out of his chair and into the ringside audience, as I landed on top of his table. I struggled up and jumped off the timekeeper's table and back into the ring bent on vengeance. And, vengeance would have been meted out with extreme prejudice, if I had known which of the three --- or was it four Bob Archer O'Briens that was now hopping up and down in front of me. It was a very unfair match, as I always seemed to be whacking one of the wrong Bob Archer O'Briens, while the right Bob Archer O'Brien was whacking me. Badly outnumbered, I lost my 21st Birthday wrestling match and swore that I would never enter the ring drunk again, it was an oath I almost kept - almost, but not quite.

If you think that it would be impossible to embarrass myself any more while performing at Purley Orchid Ballroom than I managed to do on the night of my 21st Birthday, then you don't know me, and were obviously not in attendance when I next appeared at that venue.

The next time I went to 'The Golden Guitar', Glen and Harry presented me with a belated 21st Birthday gift of a very nice ring jacket. The Jacket was white which matched my trunks and boots, but it had a black collar with matching cuffs, and I wondered if I could find myself a new pair of trunks which combined both those colors. I lucked out when I found a pair of bright white trunks, with jet black Leopard spots on it. The only problem was that my waist was very small while my thighs were proportionally very large. So, while the waist was a great fit, the legs were so tight that they tore both sides the first time I wore them. On that night I had been wrestling against Jackie Pallo, who told me that the trunks didn't suit me as soon as he saw them, and seemed to be very gratified indeed when he saw the damage that just one match had caused them. All wrestlers in those days only wore trunks of one solid color, except Jackie Pallo. After his sudden rise to fame he had begun wearing stripped trunks which became his trademark. I knew full well that the only reason he told me that my trunks didn't suit me, was because until then he was the only wrestler who wasn't wearing one solid color. Realizing that fact, made me even more determined to wear them. So I bought some very wide black elastic, and had Jean sew a triangular strip into each side of the trunks, wide edge at the bottom to make a better fit for my thighs, and going up to a point at the waist. Wrestlers always wore an extra pair of trunks underneath the ones that show, which gives more support and helps to keep everything in place while wrestling. In order to make absolutely certain that my new and repaired trunks would remain intact, I got Jean to sew my new trunks to the ones that I wore underneath them. Their trial run was at my next appearance at Purley Orchid Ballroom, and on that occasion I was wrestling against The 'Gormless Greek' Basil Coloulos. I liked Basil, he was a very tough guy. Outside the ring he could be so funny without even realizing it, and apparently, without even trying. Inside the ring he could be so bloody dangerous, also without even realizing it, or without even trying, and no one, including Basil had the slightest clue what he was doing, or what the Hell he was going to do next. In fairness to dear Basil, I am sure that there must have been a lot of audience speculation, concerning my own performance that night. Considering the fiasco I had been engaged in during my last appearance at that venue. But, I don't think anyone could have foreseen the events that did occur.

During my drunken Birthday contest I had collided with the timekeeper and knocked him out of his seat, and into the ringsiders. In this contest it seemed as though boisterous Basil developed a grudge against the timekeeper, and was using me as a missile to punish him. I lost count of the times that I bounced off the timekeeper's table after being ejected from the ring, being hurled through the ropes, or completely over them by Basil who it seemed, was temporarily incapable of doing anything else. The climax came when I attempted for the umpteenth time to climb back off the table, and into the ring, but not, apparently fast enough for Basil. He reached from the ring over the top rope, grabbed me around the neck with his left arm, and by the leg of my newly repaired trunks with his right hand. Once he had secured me, he then tore me right off the timekeeper's table over the ropes, and back into the ring in his own crazy version of a suplex. There was a tearing sound as I sailed through the air and landed right in the centre of the ring – wearing nothing but my boots!

The crowd roared their appreciation as I leapt to my feet with one hand on my crotch, while I grabbed what was left of my tattered trunks out of Basil's hand with the other, while he stood staring at me with his jaw hanging on his chest. As I attempted, as best I could to hide myself with the remnants of my new ruined trunks, my quick thinking second leapt to my aid by throwing my towel around my waist. The crowd's loud cheering never abated one iota, as I leapt from the ring, rushed to the dressing room, and 2 minutes later reappeared wearing my old white trunks. I Leapt back into the ring to finish my match, 20 minutes later the crowd cheered once again as I raised my hand in victory and I thought, 'Jackie Pallo was quite correct, those trunks didn't suit me.'

I first met Russell Plummer in Kings Lynn on the night that I wrestled there against Bob Anthony the eldest son of Bob Archer O'Brien; Bob junior was a classy Middleweight who put me very much in mind of a younger, and trimmer version of the great heavyweight 'Judo' Al Hayes.

Russell Plummer was a journalist, who, in spite of the fact that he was even younger than I was, had been writing about professional wrestling for about the same length of time that I had been doing it. I was very flattered when he told me that he had journeyed all the way from Brighton to Kings Lynn that day, for the sole purpose of conducting the interview with me. I was thrilled to bits when the article appeared in 'The Wrestler' which was the very best British wrestling magazine that was ever printed. It was not only the first time that I appeared in 'The Wrestler' but was the first time that I had ever appeared in any wrestling magazine; the interview was accompanied by one of my favorite physique shots by Bill Jones, which was also the first time one of Bill's photos had ever appeared in a wrestling magazine. This is the interview, -

Following in the famous footsteps of Welsh Middleweight Tony Charles is a sensational young Welsh Welterweight who is just as slick. His Name is ADRIAN STREET and wrestling expert R. A. Plummer unfurls the story of the

WELSH SENSATION of 1961.

Few newcomers have made a greater impression upon wrestling followers of all ages than a young Welshman by the name of Adrian Street. He has recently been appearing for the first time at halls in Wales, East Anglia, and Southern England.

But believe me, no one has worked harder for success, or can be more deserving of it than this likeable 20-year old. For two and a half years he struggled to break into top-class wrestling and in particular the Welterweights, one of the most fiercely competitive divisions of all. And what a baptism he received when his big break eventually came! Included in his first dozen contests were matches against the Champion of Europe, Alan Colbeck, London's fiery Mick McManus, 'Mr. TV' Pallo and Lightweight Artist, British Champion Melwyn Riss. Against this formidable and experienced cross-section of the hierarchy of lighter weights, the Welsh boy stood his ground well; gaining experience that will be invaluable to him in the months ahead.

Originating from Brynmawr, near Cardiff, Adrian has lived in London for several years. He was an amateur member of the famous Forester's Club before turning pro to wrestle at first outside national control. But after a string of irregular contests against indifferent opposition he is now wrestling in JOINT PROMOTIONS ORGANIZATION. His great Idol is the Mormon Giant Don Leo Jonathan, who may appear in England later this winter. Although he had seen only pictures of the top-ranking American Star, it was as 'Kid Jonathan' that Adrian first took up wrestling professionally. Some of the young men who look upon themselves as aspiring wrestlers could do a lot worse than to have a chat with Adrian Street or one of the other eager members of the Welterweight class. Their illusions about an easy life as an overnight sporting idol would soon be shattered. As Adrian told me: "It is easy throwing your friends about, but try the real thing ---."

He has found a tremendous difference in the standard of wrestling in his new surroundings, but stands ready to pit his skill against the best of Europe's little men.

A keen painter in his spare time, Adrian has also done quite a bit of weight training. He has been in demand as a photographer's model – his picture was on the front cover of a leading Bodybuilding magazine on a couple of occasions.

Turning again to the ring, the going will be hard for Adrian Street in the months ahead. What is more, fans everywhere having seen the courage and ability that can take him to the top are certain to give him the encouragement that he deserves.

- by Russell Plummer.

I was tremendously thrilled with the write up in a real wrestling magazine, the inspiration I derived from it was indescribable. It seemed as though I had been striving to reach this point of my life for an eternity. From the time I lifted buckets of rocks in the garden, then later lifting barbells and dumbbells, wrestling my friends on the Welsh mountains and in grimy gyms. Fighting in the school yard against any bully who dared to challenge me, fighting in pubs, dancehalls, back-alleys and slag heaps around the coal-mines. Then to London, bodybuilding, weightlifting, posing for magazines. Wrestling in gyms, boxing on the Fairground Booth and wrestling pro for small time independent promoters and finally wrestling full time in the big time. The journey had been hard and often frustrating but I had had many great moments, and much encouragement from my photos appearing in bodybuilding magazines. Recognition for my weightlifting accomplishments and being awarded my black Weider T-shirts were like receiving diplomas of achievement. But my write up in the best wrestling magazine in Great Britain meant more to me than just another diploma it was more like a certificate of graduation – I had proved I belonged. Then all the people who had told me I was too small and there was no such thing as a fulltime professional wrestler came to mind. They were all wrong, I had been wrestling now for five months as a fulltime pro, against some of the best wrestlers in the World. Dale Martin's had given me exactly 100 matches in that time, including a dream come true when I wrestled in Cardiff. I had also been told that I had another match there in the beginning of the New Year, which was in a few days time against Leon Fortuna from Tonga, and I was more than ready to go for it big time. It was now New Years Eve, 1961 was fading into history and a new year was dawning. I was revved up, ready to go and determined to begin 1962 with a bang - but it was Jean, not me who dropped the biggest bombshell when she announced,

"I've missed my period!"

1962

On Wednesday the 3rd of January 1962 I once again wrestled in Dumfries' Place Drill Hall in Cardiff against Leon Fortuna, The Friendly-Islander from Tonga, who much to my delight turned out to be one of my old independent promotion's opponents, none other than Young Sullivan, who had also changed his name after graduating to Dales.

If you think that my baptism into the big time was rough, tough and dangerous, just imagine what poor Leon Fortuna had to go through, wrestling against me on my own turf. Especially after the incredible reception I had received the last time I had wrestled in 'MY' arena, in front of 'MY OWN' Welsh fans. I wouldn't have wanted to be in Leon's boots for anything, and I certainly wouldn't have wanted to be in anyone else's boots but my own. I couldn't wait to get into the ring that night and get the fix that I had become addicted to. The cheers, the action, the violence and my ultimate triumph. Leon made his entrance and as I waited impatiently for my turn. I remember being very surprised by the very loud cheer that his first appearance in Cardiff evoked from 'MY' Welsh fans.

'They probably haven't realized who he is going to be wrestling against tonight,' I thought, 'Let's see how much applause he gets after they see it's Adrian Street of Cardiff, Wales here again!' The loud fanfare began as 'The march of the Gladiators' was played at full blast, I burst out of the dressing room and into the spotlight that would highlight my journey into the ring. I braced myself against the deafening roar that my appearance would evoke - 'What a time to go deaf.' I thought. Although, the music was still blasting away and I could hear that okay, but there seemed to be a thunderous silence issuing from an arena crammed with my fellow country folk, that was transforming a heart filled with pride to a gut filled with an iron cannonball.

'What's wrong with them?' I thought, 'they cheered like Hell last time I wrestled here, they can't have forgotten me already.' I leapt into the ring, the Welsh Hero who was ready willing and able to defend 'The Land of his Fathers' against any and every foreign invader. Whether they were from Tonga or Mars. I pointed at the Red Welsh Dragon on the breast of my white jacket before raising my fist and saluting my faithful Welsh fans,

"Cymru am Byth - Wales Forever!" I shouted.

"FUCK YOU!" Was more or less the response I received from my faithful Welsh fans. Bewildered, I looked over at Leon, who was grinning like the Cheshire-Cat in his corner of the ring, he stepped forward raised his fist in salute and the treacherous Welsh crowd erupted like Mount Vesuvius in 79 AD.

'Okay,' I thought as I glared at Leon, 'if you want to play that game, I'll be Mount Vesuvius and you'll be Pompeii!' I felt like blowing my nose on my Red Welsh Dragon to show my contempt for the shabby welcome I had received from my fellow countrymen. But I am too proudly Welsh to want to disfigure the emblem of my country - but, on the other hand I would happily and enthusiastically disfigure my opponent. - Especially under the present circumstances. Introductions were made, the bell sounded and I went for Leon like a fox goes for a chicken,

'Let's see who you support after you see what's going to happen to your friendly foreign hero now'. I thought. I enveloped the unfortunate Leon like an avalanche of agony - SLAM – KICK – STOMP! Within seconds he had been ragged, bagged and shagged. Tattered and bruised, he lay on the canvas and looked up at me with his big dark eyes and must have looked to the audience like a cute little Kitten who was being savagely beaten by a sadist with a baseball bat. My Welsh fans roared their disapproval at me as only the Welsh can, and I responded by meting out my revenge on each and every one of them by using my unfortunate opponent as a proxy.

"Take that you bastards!" I shouted at the crowd as I kicked Leon right between his big appealing Kitten-like eyes. I had so wanted to be the Hero and Champion of my own race, and this was the treatment I was receiving as a result. But if I offer something so precious, only to have it thrown back in my face – just wait and see what I'll offer you next, and the poor Friendly Islander was going to have to bear the full brunt of it. The more I beat on Leon the louder the crowd booed, the more the crowed booed the more I beat on Leon, and I suddenly realized that he was getting far more sympathy from 'MY' Welsh fans, than I had got from them when I wrestled in Cardiff the last time against Billy 'The Bully' Stock. The difference was, I began to appreciate, was that Billy Stock had already become a well established wrestling villain by the time I wrestled him, and most any opponent as a result would have received loud cheers from the audience, more to piss the Villain off than to show their approval of his opponent. Bearing that in mind, I wondered if I could reverse our roles by myself becoming the underdog, and attempt to turn Leon into the Bullying aggressor. I decided to give it a try, I grabbed hold of Leon and as I tore him up off the canvas I growled at him,

"Take over." I didn't have to ask him twice, Leon suddenly turned into a Human threshing machine, while I was transformed into an acre and a half of withered wheat. He turned me upside-down and inside out, he hit me from so many different directions that I thought that the whole of the audience must have joined in. And talking of the audience – did I get any sympathy from them? Like Hell I did, I thought that their cheering would blow the roof right off the Drill hall,

"Kill the Bastard Leon!!!" they screamed.

'Be patient,' I told myself, 'they'll come around in the end.' And did they? – Like Hell they did. The more I got beaten up the more 'MY' Welsh fans cheered for Leon. I began to think that if Leon had pulled a revolver out of his trunks and shot me dead, he would have got the biggest applause of the evening, and a few hundred witnesses out of the audience who would have sworn in court that I'd asked for it - that it had been self defense, or that I'd been the one who had produced the gun and accidentally shot myself while trying to kill Leon. 'Be patient,' I told myself again, 'this might take some time.' And I continued to take a beating like an egg in a blender.

'Well it's now or never.' I thought, I charged Leon like the Light brigade charged the Russian guns at Balaclava, only with a much more triumphant result. Culminating when my devastating patent dropkick sent Leon hurtling through the ropes and onto the heads of his now deflated Welsh supporters. Again I raised my fist in victory,

"Cymru am Byth!" I roared once more, but more as an insult to my disloyal and traitorous Welsh fans than a salute of a victory for Wales. I was booed like never before and I wondered if I would be able to reach the dressing room from the ring without being lynched by my own Welsh Countrymen just for scoring a victory for Wales. It was beyond me why a Welsh Audience would cheer for a foreign looser over a Welsh winner. But I did know that I would not have swapped my bad win, for my opponent's loss, even if the exchange had made me the most popular wrestler ever to have appeared in Cardiff's Dumfries Place Drill Hall.

I had been a member of the Forester's Club for almost 4 years and the Club's 11 and 12 stone Weightlifting Champion for the last two and a half years, but since I had began wrestling full time, and the Foresters was only open in the evenings, my time there was sadly over. I re-joined the YMCA so I could get my workout in before I made my way to Dale Martin's offices in Brixton every day, and enable me to ride their transport to the various venues that I would be wrestling at each night. Another reason that I re-joined the YMCA was due to the fact that my manager Mike Dimitri trained there every day, and I was still determined to get something back from him to warrant the 10 percent of my wrestling wages that I was paying him. That was where and when my shoot and submission wrestling lessons began. By this time Mike had lost more than half of his 10-percenters, mostly victims of an occasional unfortunate ring 'accident' - Yeah, right! – Or blatant excessive violence more like it. He agreed with me when I pointed out to him, that his tuition would help protect his own interest as well as ours. Out of the few wrestlers that Mike had left, there was Ron Wiltshire, who now wrestled as Ray Fury. Ray was born in Turkey, the son of a British Diplomat and a Greek Mother. Then Johnny Apollo who was born in Greece, and so was Miguel Santos before emigrating to Argentina. Mike Dimitri was also a Greek, which left me as the only member of our group without an Aegean flavor. Mike Dimitri had become the European Junior-heavyweight champion in 1939 when he defeated Stanislaus Karolyi, and then 10 years later he defeated 'The Farmer' George Broadfield to become The Junior-World Heavyweight Wrestling

Champion. After the fiasco in The Seymour Hall, Mike had retired from wrestling professionally, and was now refereeing instead. As he seemed to have difficulty in merely standing up, I wondered how capable he would prove to be in his effort to teach a group of eager young thugs the violent Art of Submission Wrestling. At this time Mike had to be in the region of 60 years of age, and the first time I faced him on the wrestling mat in the YMCA he explained that as his hip and shoulder joint had deteriorated so badly he would begin our lessons with him on his hands and knees while he gave me the advantage of starting our match on top. I do remember not being very flattered, that he could ever imagine that he would stand any kind of chance against me, especially after giving me such a tremendous advantage, nevertheless I thought,

'Teacher will just have to learn the hard way not to underestimate my aggression, strength and ability.' But, once again it was I who was the one to learn the hard way. Mike Dimitri may have been an 'old cripple' and I say that without any animosity whatsoever. But the wrestling skill and knowledge of this 'old cripple' was nothing less than amazing. I soon found out that I wrestling against Mike Dimitri was like Brea-Rabbit wrestling with The Boston Tar-Baby. Little by little he would slowly but surely just swallow me up, by slyly and patiently immobilizing one limb after another, until I was completely wrapped up in an agonizing cocoon of my own arms and legs. It got that I began to regard our encounters as a victory on my part, and a defeat for Mike, if I could just manage to escape his clutches and stand up after being subjected to the pretzel like positions he was capable of twisting me into. Mike regarded my escapes in the same way, and proved to be a very sore loser. I was made to pay very dearly, and very painfully for every one of the very rare minor triumphs I managed to score and enjoy. One day after struggling in agony for almost an hour, I managed to untangle myself and break free of the several painful holds that he had been constraining me with, all at one time.

"Okay, come on, let's go again!" demanded Mike aggressively, pissed off as Hell that I had managed to escape.

"Okay, Mike," I replied, I stood with my back to him, while I pretended to stretch and twist my painfully disjointed limbs back into place. "Just give me a second to straighten myself out." I remained standing with my back to him, and just turned my head as though readjusting my neck. I was really looking through the corner of my eye to see exactly where Mike was on the mat. He was on his hands and knees with his face like an angry thundercloud, demanding my immediate return to where he could reach me and finish the job that he had just barely failed to complete. In a flash I spun right around on my left foot and dove right at him. I hit him like a battering-ram, taking his head in a front chancery with my left arm while barring under his left arm with my right. The impetus tore him off the mat before depositing back onto it like a ton of bricks, flat on his back where I pinned his shoulders to the mat and gave him the 3-count 3 times, as loud as I could. Just to leave no doubt in his mind, or in anyone else's, that I had just beaten him - even though it was the cheapest of cheap-shots that won me the one and only victory that I ever scored over Mike Dimitri ex-Junior Heavyweight Wrestling Champion of the World. I was under no illusion that I would pay very dearly for my brief and dubious triumph, and true to his nature he did not disappoint me. Even so, like a self destructive masochist, I never tired of reminding Mike Dimitri of my one brief moment of glory over him, every single time he scored another victory over me.

Often Mike would just watch, as the rest of us paired off, and he would advise and correct our wrestling moves. Showing us a variety of easier or more effective ways of crippling each other. Out of the other three wrestlers in our group I enjoyed wrestling with Ray Fury the most. Although he was barely two inches taller than me Ray weighed a very solid 200 pounds, and as one would expect as an ex resident of Turkey, he already possessed a very solid and extensive shoot background. Ray had begun shoot wrestling in 1948 at the age of 12; his Coach was Yasar Dogu, the 1948 Heavyweight Olympic Gold Medalist. I believe that as Ray and I had become very good friends, he probably held back from showing me his full wrestling potential. I matched his strength even though he outweighed me by 50 pounds of muscle, and I seemed capable of holding my own against him, but with the extra weight combined with his superior wrestling knowledge, I'm sure he would have proved more than I could handle in those days if he had decided to go all out.

Although Miguel was a few inches taller he only outweighed me by about 25 to 30 pounds. I had watched Miguel improve as a professional by leaps and bounds over the last few months, and had complimented him on his progress, as had many other wrestlers. Unfortunately as a result, instead of being encouraged by our compliments and striving to advance even further, he developed a head as big as a watermelon, and overnight convinced himself that he was a big Star and had learned all there was to know about professional wrestling. Even his performances in the ring in my opinion went from extremely promising to total crap; he seemed obsessed with performing huge theatrical gestures of triumph every few minutes, before he had even executed the wrestling moves that would provoke a response from a wrestling audience worthy of such gestures. He had become uncomfortable to watch, embarrassing and painful to wrestle against – and not so much physically as mentally. I knew, but didn't care that he was well aware of my growing contempt for his professional performances, and fully expected him to attempt to domineer and bully me on the mat. Once again I wasn't disappointed - but he was!

His attempted bullying provided me with the excuse I was craving to spitefully beat the living crap out of him, and show him as painfully as possible that he had a very long way to go before he could call himself a real wrestler.

Johnny Apollo was something else entirely – but, please don't ask me what! The first time Mike Dimitri paired us against each other, Johnny shot me a glare of utter loathing before running back and forth on his side of the mat, throwing punches, kicks, chops and forearm-smashes at an imaginary foe. Working himself into a total frenzy in a way that was reminiscent of an ancient Viking Berserker. As I watched Johnny Apollo's performance with a mixture of fascination and apprehension, he suddenly turned to face me and charged with all the speed, grace and savagery of a giant, demented Silverback Gorilla with a bad toothache. As he collided with me, the shear force of his attack jarred every joint in my body, from my shoulders right down to my heels. I managed to stand my ground, but with the impact of his charge both of my opponent's feet shot up into the air and he fell flat on his back, dragging me down on top of him. He struggled and thrashed about all over the mat, but clung to me with such a grip that I couldn't have relinquished my position on top off him even if I'd wanted to. I frantically fought with him in order to force his arm into a double-wristlock, which eventually, after a superhuman effort on my part, I managed to secure and savagely twisted until he screamed out in submission. I released him and helped him back to his feet; he didn't utter one word, but instead went back to his wild and weird pre-fight war dance, and off we went again, with an almost identical result. Wrestling Johnny Apollo was like trying to ride a drunken, three legged Bucking-Bronco, who was on a toxic dose of PCP and roller-skates. As a real submission wrestler Johnny Apollo was worse than pathetic. Once again the words attributed to Napoleon Bonaparte rang true - 'Never interrupt an enemy when he's making a mistake.' I soon found that I didn't need to fight to beat him, all I had to do was to hang on to him and he would beat himself. Nevertheless, I must thank him for teaching me another very valuable lesson, a lesson I called patience. It eventually occurred to me that I could conserve a lot more energy by merely hanging on and waiting for Johnny to position himself for me to take the submission hold I needed to beat him. Rather than thrash about all over the mat with him fighting tooth and nail for something I could take easily if I just waited for him to give it to me. Plus, the longer I hung onto him while he bucked and struggled the more exhausted he became, which would make him easier to control and even fight him for a hold if I needed to as a final resort.

I would always get to the YMCA at least a couple of hours before I began wrestling in order to get a good workout with the weights in first. I was working out one day when a very deep and gravely voice demanded,

"Come 'n' give me a spot on the bench, Mate!" I turned to recognize the granite-like features of 'The Iron-Man' Steve Logan.

"Okay," I replied, "I'll join you if you like." I followed Steve over to the bench and saw to my amusement that he had already loaded the bar so that it weighed a puny 145 pounds. I was already well aware by now of The Iron-Man's very dry, off the wall sense of humor. I just stood there and laughed out loud as he settled himself down comfortably onto the bench as he waited for me to hand him the light barbell. Steve Logan was one of Britain's foremost Light heavyweights; both his arms and legs were proportionately slim compared with his large head, huge Bullfrog face and barrel-sized chest, but I would have expected 'The Iron-Man' to toy with at least twice the amount of weight he had on the bar, and thought that he was merely acting the fool at my expense.

"What's funny Mate?!" The Iron Man inquired.

"That barbell," I giggled, "How much more weight shall I put on it for you?"

"I'm warming up, I don't need any more weight on it!" he replied indignantly.

I roared with laughter, and even though I was still convinced he was messing about I decided to humor him and I handed him the barbell. He pressed it up and down for about 12 reps, and when he indicated he had finished I took it off him and replaced it on the stands. I added 90 pounds for my own first set and matched his 12 reps with it. I wondered how much more weight Steve would add to it for his second set. Instead he took off the weight that I had added, and once again did about 12 reps. Steve did 3 more sets with the same light weight while I increased the poundage steadily each set until I finished off getting a few reps with 345 pounds, which I wasted no time in mentioning to the 'Iron Man'.

"I'm a wrestler, not a fucking weightlifter!" Steve growled, as we concluded our bench-pressing, and he walked away in a huff, but he still asked me for a spot on the bench and still lifted the same poundage every time we trained together in the YMCA.

One morning after I had finished with the weights, I was waiting for the other wrestlers to arrive, when I was approached by Frank Nottingham. I had probably wrestled with Frank more than 100 times over the years. Both in the Forester's and in the YMCA since that enlightening day, when I had wrestled with both him and Alf Jacobs, and they had twisted me up in a way that a Clown twists balloons into toy animals in order to amuse young kids. Frank must have regarded me as one of his favorite opponents, as over time I had improved steadily, and had provided him with stiffer and stiffer competition. But never quite enough to score a victory at his expense. It seemed that in spite of gaining strength, weight and skill, he still had my number, and in the end he always emerged the winner.

"Hi Adrian, would yer like a pull around?" he asked hopefully.

"Sure - why not indeed?" I replied. I felt great that morning, as fit as a Butcher's Dog, as strong as a Lion and as mean as the wages I received from Dale Martin's Wrestling Promotions. As Frank stepped onto the mat I pounced and almost tore him in half, I liked Frank a lot; he really was one of the nicest guys I had met since I had moved to London. But I felt spiteful and was full of beans, although I had never even scored one fall over Frank Nottingham in all the years I had known him and wrestled him. That day I just bounced him from one side of the mat to the other and I pinned him 15 times in less than 10 minutes. Poor Frank was shocked and shattered, while I was exuberant and more than ready to pin him 15 times again, but I had given him such a battering that morning he never ever asked me to wrestle with him again.

"We'll have to go and see the Doctor," Jean announced. We had both waited apprehensively for another month to see what would happen, but still no period, "that's the second one I've missed," she told me, "we can't wait any longer."

I'll always remember the relief I felt, as Jean came out of the Doctor's office with that huge smile on her face after being examined, while I had been sitting in the waiting room on tender hooks, with my fingers, toes and legs crossed. Then my eyes crossed and the relief evaporated as we stepped out of the waiting room, and into the street.

"Well, that's it - I'm pregnant," Jean proclaimed, still grinning unnervingly, "When are we getting Married?!!!

****

Not everyone was enthralled by the huge surge in wrestling's popularity, especially store keepers whose most lucrative time of the week used to be Saturday afternoon. Now almost everyone in the British Isles was glued to the television between 4p.m. and

4.45p.m. every Saturday. It proved to be double jeopardy for the poor store keepers, as now not only were they missing out on their former weekend profits, but they were also missing out on watching the wrestling on tele that everyone else in the country, - except them, were watching and enjoying immensely. And they weren't the only ones affected; I have a personal theory that wrestling's new found super popularity may have had a hand in bringing down the ever growing Empire of the super slum-lord 'Polish' Peter Rachman.

One night when 'Polish' Peter was giving a party in a Soho Club, the festivities were suddenly and very rudely interrupted when the party was crashed by The Kray Twins, who were among the East-ends most violent and vicious Gangsters. Ronnie and Reggie Kray were known for bringing knives to fist-fights, antique sabers to knife fights, as well as guns as a backup. Rachman was threatened by the Krays, and he agreed to pay them protection money. He paid the first installment by check and then did a disappearing act when the check bounced. His disappearance however did not prevent the Krays from retaliating. Rachman's enforcers and rent collectors were savagely beaten and robbed by the Kray gang, and became victims of more violence than they had been used to dishing out, as Reggie observed,

"Rachman's rent collectors were big, but our boys were bigger."

For instance the ex-World Light heavyweight Boxing Champion, Freddie Mills was a well known associate of the Krays. Freddie Mills had always been one of my favorites, as I very much enjoyed his rough, tough all action style. He won the World's title in 1948 from American, Gus Lesnevich and lost it 16 months later to another tough American, Joey Maxim. But as tough as Freddie's opponents were, after his retirement from Boxing he was known to keep far rougher company than he ever kept in the ring. As a result met a very violent and mysterious death in 1965 when he was found shot to death in his car outside the nightclub he owned. Till this day, no one seems to know if Freddie committed suicide as a result of the humiliation he suffered after being arrested in a public toilet, and charged with Homosexual indecency. Or as it was also rumored that he was a suspect in 'The Jack the Stripper Murders'. Between 1959 and 1965 eight Prostitutes were found murdered after being savagely beaten, and one theory had it that Freddie Mills was the serial killer 'Jack the Stripper,' and that he committed suicide when he felt that the net was closing in on him. Another theory was that his suicide was staged by The Chinese Mafia, who murdered him in order to get their hands on his Club.

In hiding or not, Rachman realized he would have to come to terms with Ronnie and Reggie's gang or watch his business disintegrate. But, 'Polish' Peter was very astute and realized that even if he paid the Krays what they demanded initially, they wouldn't be satisfied until they bled him dry. In order to rid himself of their threat once and for all Rachman offered to sell the Krays a 'Golden Goose' in the form of the gambling Club 'Esmeralda's Barn' – a club which incidentally, didn't belong to him. Before the shit hit the fan for the second time 'Polish' Peter very conveniently suffered a heart attack while gambling in a London Casino and 'supposedly' died after being rushed to Edgware General Hospital. Underworld speculation rumored that there had been a body switch, especially when it was reveled that all that remained of Rachman's reputed 25,000,000 pound fortune was about 20,000 pounds that his personal estate was valued at. More rumors soon arose that 'Polish' Peter Rachman had been spotted everywhere from the Continent to the United States, in fact questions concerning the case was even raised in Parliament, but the official Police report maintained that Peter Rachman was dead and is buried in an unmarked grave in a cemetery in Hertfordshire.

Be that as it may, but the remark made by Reggie Kray,

"Rachman's rent collectors were big, but our boys were bigger." Was only made AFTER professional wrestling had exploded and the part time wrestlers who had formerly relied on full time employment from 'Polish' Peter, were now full time professional wrestlers, and no longer employed as enforcers, rent collectors and bodyguards by Rachman. Rachman had also no longer enjoyed the protection afforded him by 'Mad Fred' Rondel, as a result of distancing himself from him after the 'Ear-biting incident. In fact Fred had added considerably to 'Polish' Peter's precarious predicament by phoning him, and threatening both him and Serge Paplinski to reimburse him for time served in prison after the ear munching. The Krays who for years had frequented the same clubs as Rachman, must have been aware of who, and what he was. And let's face it 'Polish' Peter Rachman didn't dress to go un-noticed. But it wasn't until after television had popularized wrestling to such an extent, and had robbed 'Polish' Peter of his roughest, toughest employees that the notorious Kray Twins thought it safe to make their move on him. That's my theory - I rest my case – For now.

Talking of Twins - I was invited by Joe Cornelius and Stefan Milla to accompany them both to 'The United Wrestling Club' where they sometimes worked out. It was there where I first met a pair of identical, 15 year old wrestlers who were built like Whippets and moved just as fast when they went into action on the wrestling mat. In spite of their very tender years, I wrestled them both at the club - or at least I think I did, as it was almost impossible to tell them apart.

It was also at the United, where I first met Pauline, a lady who did the catering for the club, during my first conversation with her, she invited me to have lunch with her at a restaurant in Paddington the very next afternoon. As I was wrestling in London the next night I accepted her invitation. Over lunch she told me that she hoped I had plenty of time and energy to spare before I went off to wrestle, as she had booked a room in a nearby Hotel.

'What a coincidence.' I thought, as I had spent the night in a Paddington Hotel only a few of days earlier. Although it turned out to be a different Hotel, the time I spent there with Pauline did turn out to be just as entertaining. Pauline enjoyed playing 'dress up' and had brought a number of kinky costumes and wigs with her into which she changed before and after each round. Adopting the character that each of her costumes suggested. Pauline did have a very hard act to follow however. At the other hotel, Tony Woods and I had very bravely taken on 4 naughty Ladies, and acquitted ourselves with flying colors, as we did in that particular hotel most Saturday nights. Our Saturday night entertainment was always arranged by a Girl named Carol, who I had met at the wrestling arena in Luton. Tony who still had professional aspirations would often drive us both to my matches on the weekends in his car, and share in the fringe benefits that were always in a very abundant supply at all of the wrestling shows. I had met Carol the first time I wrestled in Luton, which was towards the end of the Summer of 1961 just after I had began wrestling for Dale Martins. On that particular night I had ridden to Luton with Tony in his car, and was wrestling in the first match against Billy Stock. We arrived at the arena car park the same time as Dale Martin's transport van, which was in the process of voiding itself of its occupants as we both walked by and into the arena. As I walked into the dressing room, I had hardly had time to put the case containing my wrestling gear down before I was accosted by my opponent Billy Stock.

"What did you bring that fuckin' idiot with you for?!" he demanded to know.

"Who are you talking about - Tony Woods?" I inquired.

"I don't know his name," he snapped, "that idiot you came in with - why did you bring him?!"

"Well actually I didn't bring him, he brought me," I replied, "and what fucking business is it of yours anyway?" I never did find out what the problem was between Billy and Tony. When I asked Tony about it later, he didn't seem to know either. I was surprised that they even knew each other. Billy had been an amateur wrestler at The Forester's Club for 15 years, he had stopped going to the club when he turned professional which was around about the same time that Tony Woods started going there. I have to admit that Tony did have a very flashy, cocksure way about him, but I thought it came over as amusing more than offensive. Although Billy copped a very aggressive attitude in the dressing room, by the time the match started he seemed to have settled down a tad and things began on a normal and even keel. Things didn't continue in that fashion for long however, the very moment that the audience really started to get excited and involved in our match, Billy caught sight of Tony Woods sitting a few rows back from ringside. He was cheering me on with the best of them, and that's all it seemed to take to send bombastic Billy off the edge, and into a horrible rage. Fortunately for me I caught a hold of the situation a split second before Billy got a hold on me, which saved me from a lot of pain and suffering. Billy bulled into me furiously attempting one throw or trip after another, but to no avail. I am blessed with excellent balance, so in spite of my opponent's 15 years worth of amateur experience, try as he may, he was unable to take me off my feet. His fury turned to frustration, and he eventually resorted to throwing himself down onto his hands and knees, adopting the strong position and challenging me to come down and join him on the mat. I declined Billy's dubious invitation, and instead buried the toe of my boot right up his fat arse; - he leapt to his feet bursting with fury while the audience was bursting with laughter. He bulled into me again, but got no further than he did on his previous attempts, so he once again threw himself onto his hands and knees; he issued the same challenge and got another very stiff kick up the arse, while the fans laughed like Hyenas on dope. Again and again Billy attempted to tempt me into playing his game and again and again he received a good kick up the arse for his trouble. I'd been around long enough to know that you should never play your opponents game - it could get you hurt. Just as you don't box a Boxer, you don't wrestle a Wrestler, and as far as I'm concerned, if I ever have to fight a Shark, I'll fight it on the beach rather than in the ocean, thank you very much. Well it was a very different kind of contest than I'd ever been involved in before, but as the audience found it both amusing and entertaining, and I succeeded in getting my hand raised in victory at the end of it, so I was happy. This was more than I could say for my opponent who got right in my face the moment I reentered the dressing room,

"Why were you showing out all the time to that fuckin' idiot you brought with you for?!" Billy demanded. I hit Billy hard in the chest with the heels of both hands, and as the impact knocked him back a step, I took a step forward and asked him,

"Do you want to fight?" He declined my challenge, and that was the end of that. I never did learn what his nasty tantrum was caused by, but in spite of it, over the next number of years Billy and I gradually became very good friends.

While signing autographs after the match I was accosted by Carol for the very first time and found myself in the saddle on the back seat of Tony's car about 10 minutes later. Carol began attending all the matches I had in that area such as Dunstable, Bedford and St. Albans, as well as Luton. With the enormous amount of venues that Dale Martins were running, my appearance at any of these particular arenas was sporadic to say the very least. It was Carol who came up with the solution and began renting a very large attic room in a Hotel in Paddington most weekends; with the result that Tony and I always had something warm to look forward to on our journeys back to London on Saturday nights. The room sported eight beds, which was just as well, because Carol would bring anywhere from one to four other girls, beside herself with herself and they would all be waiting patiently, and comfortably for Tony and myself to arrive and the action to begin.

All of the wrestling arenas were simply swarming with Women and Girls who seemed to be spellbound by our powerful physical prowess, and super athletic ability in the ring. At least that was what we liked to think was true, but even more especially in our prowess outside the ring when the wrestling was over for the night, which was probably a lot closer to the truth. I should like to stress at this time, that unlike myself and some of the others, not all professional wrestlers were obsessed with the hordes of sex mad Lady fans that infested our battle grounds, and they would never have dreamt of extending the evening's entertainment beyond their performances in the ring. The wrestlers who abstained mostly regarded the wrestlers who took advantage of the situation, as perverted sexual predators who took advantage of star struck Females. In truth most of the 'Lady wrestling fans' were not after autographs, and were far more predatory than we were. And that is saying something, as no sooner had I completed one encounter, than I would be racing back into the arena to pick up another,

"That's no way to treat a Lady!" I often heard said, but the Lady in question would be anything but offended or upset, as she would be too busy running back into the arena herself in search of another wrestler, and would probably claim one 5 minutes before I claimed another Girl - Mind you that's only because a Lady with her skirt up is able to run a lot faster than a man with his pants down.

****

'Tiny' Car, who was one of Dale Martin's referees often sold suit lengths of fabric, and offered the services of a Tailor friend of his who would manufacture a very nicely tailored suit from them. I bought two bolts from 'Tiny', one a light blue, and the other a pale grey with a very narrow pink stripe, and I had them both made up into a couple of very smart three piece suits. I was wearing the pale grey suit for the first time when I entered a restaurant with the other wrestlers while traveling from London to Bath in Dale Martin's transport. After I had sat down and been served my meal, I began to cut into the steak I had ordered. Unfortunately for me it was on a plate that had been placed a little too close to the edge of the table. Either the steak was tough or the knife wasn't sharp enough as my attempt to slice through the steak resulted in my overturning the plate containing my steak, with four eggs, tomatoes and a heap of baked beans right onto my lap. All the other wrestlers exploded with laughter, especially as it had been the first time they had seen me wearing a smart suit. I as a result, and for their benefit had found it impossible to resist strutting in a way that would have made the proudest Peacock resemble a common Sparrow by comparison. The restaurant's proprietor who had also witnessed the incident suggested that I should go into the back room and ask his Wife who was working there, if she could help to clean me up a bit and so I did as he suggested. When I entered the back room I found a very pretty young Lady slicing up potatoes for making chips. After explaining the situation and displaying the damage to her, she put down her knife, dampened a dish cloth and began sponging the front of my trousers. As if that wasn't titillating enough, she then told me it would be better for me to remove my trousers to enable her to do a better job of cleaning off the mess. I did as she bid and stood there looking quite ridiculous wearing a jacket, waistcoat, shirt, tie and a very brief pair of undies, 'courtesy of Lon of London'. When she finished with my trousers she examined the front of my briefs and decided that they also needed a cleanup. We both immediately discovered that Lon of London's line of tiny, flimsy underwear was not built to withstand the kind of reaction that a gentle sponging provokes. Although things began to escalate out of control, it was obvious to both of us that this was neither the time nor the place to continue our little adventure. In the heat of the moment I suggested that we might venture a lot further into the unknown if she came to the show in Bath that evening. But she being a newly married Woman, I was aware that that obviously wasn't going to happen. I thanked her for cleaning my pants, and thanked her even more sincerely for sponging my undies. I then very reluctantly dressed and walked back into the restaurant heralded by more laughter and silly quips from my traveling companions,

"Looks like yer pissed yer bleed'n' trousers!" Observed 'Iron Man' Steve Logan.

"Oh, it doesn't look too bad, it'll be fine when it dries" the proprietor told me, "here you are, I've cooked you another meal, try to put it in your mouth this time instead of all over your pants," He added in a cheerful voice, "It's on the house." He told me, as I attempted to pay him for it. I thanked him for the meal, but felt terrible. All that I could think of was, that while I had wanted to get up to mischief in the back room with his wife, the proprietor had been busy replacing my meal that I had been clumsy enough to end up wearing instead of eating. If he hadn't have been so kind and thoughtful, I probably wouldn't have given it another thought. I had seen him many times before when I'd stopped there to eat, but never said anymore to him than "hello", "goodbye" and "thank you." Apart from telling him what it was that I wanted to eat. His kindness and friendliness bathed him in a new light, and I really regretted the events that had 'almost' taken place in the back room of his restaurant. If that made me feel guilty, you can't imagine how I felt later that evening when one of the wrestlers came into the dressing room and told me there was someone outside who wanted to see me. I stepped out of the dressing room and was appalled when I came face to face with the proprietor's Wife, and horrified when I saw that she was in possession of two large suitcases.

"I'm coming to live in London with you." She informed me, with a smile.

"Oh, no you're not!" I informed her right back – but without the smile.

"Why not?!" she wanted to know.

"Three good reasons," I replied, "number one, you're married, number two, I'm getting married in a few weeks time – and number three, you weren't invited. You had better go back home before your Husband notices you're not there." I added.

"I can't," she agued stubbornly, "I've left him a note informing him that I'm leaving him and going to live with you!" she told me that in such a way that she thought would end our disagreement, broach no argument and force me to concede to her wishes.

"Go home." I told her with a note of total finality in my voice, and returned to the dressing room to finish getting changed, leaving her to her own devices. I did sympathize with her, but couldn't believe that she could be so gullible. I couldn't put all the blame on her either, under the circumstances. But I decided there and then, especially as I was soon getting Married, that it was time to grow up, give up all my promiscuous Womanizing ways for good and settle down.

True to my decision, the next time I spent an afternoon with Pauline, who was dressed on this occasion like Marie Antoinette during the period when the Queen of France still enjoyed having a good head on her shoulders. I explained to her that this would be our final encounter and after I got Married any other Women would be strictly in my past. Pauline countered by offering me a job.

"How much money do you earn a week from wrestling?" she inquired.

"About 50 pounds." I lied, the truth was, that even if I wrestled 7 days a week I would be lucky if I cleared 30 pounds, and I still had to pay 10 percent of that total to Mike Dimitri.

"I'll pay you 60," She told me, "plus, all the food you can eat." She added.

"For doing what?" I wanted to know.

"I'm opening my own restaurant," she informed me, "and I want someone to keep order and just to be there when I need them." I must admit that Pauline's offer made my head whirl, I had never been offered that much money before in my life for doing anything - plus all the food I could eat, WOW! With an appetite like I had, that was some offer – and, what she had meant by 'just to be there when she needed them' wasn't lost on me either - BUT – I had come to London to become a full time pro wrestler, that is what I had become and I would not give up that dream for any amount of money, or anything else that

Pauline had to offer. I liked Pauline, but I loved Jean and intended marrying her and that meant saying goodbye Pauline. The same weekend I told Carol the same thing; this would be the last time that I would spend with her, her playful friends and Tony Woods at the Paddington Hotel. She and Tony agreed to continue seeing each other, but for me it was goodbye Carol and friends, I was getting married the very next weekend.

It turned out that the former Ladies in my life weren't the only ones who were not exactly over the Moon at the prospect of my upcoming Marriage. When I told Jack Dale that I would not be available to wrestle on the 10th of March and explained the reason why, instead of congratulating me as I had expected him to, he responded with,

"What time is the Wedding?"

"Early afternoon." I replied.

"Oh, that's no problem then," he responded happily as he looked through his ledger, "I've got you booked in Southall, so you'll have plenty of time to get there after the ceremony – you'll be wrestling Len Wilding."

"JACK!!!" I shouted, "I'm getting married, and the only wrestling I'm going to be doing next weekend will be with my Wife!" 'It was Jack's own fault,' I thought, that he had riled me up, and wanting to get back at him I brought up the one subject I knew for sure would piss him off.

"Jack," I told him, "now that I'm going to become a married Man with a Baby on the way, I think its time I got a raise in wages."

"Oh yes," he replied, "and how much more do you think you're going to get?"

"Obviously not as much as I want," I told him, "but I'll settle for 6 pounds a match for preliminaries, and a couple more for main events – FOR NOW!"

"Sorry," he told me, while looking anything but, "we've got a lot of wrestlers coming in from overseas, their fares are killing us."

"Okay, 5 pounds!" I insisted, but I ended up accepting a compromise of 4 pounds 10 shillings for preliminaries, and 6 pounds for main events. I attempted to convince myself that getting my first raise in wages from Dale Martins was a good omen, but couldn't shake off the feeling that an extra 10 shillings a match was too little, too late. Especially as I would soon have 3 mouths to feed, when on the amount of money I earned as a full time professional wrestler, I could scarcely afford to feed my own.

On the Monday before my marriage I was wrestling in Aylesbury against Miguel Santos, who by now seemed to imagine he was the 'Larry Olivia' of grappling, I was convinced that the 'Larry Olivia' of acting would probably have made a better wrestler than Miguel. It wasn't only Santos' attitude that had deteriorated, even his actual wrestling skills seemed to have receded even more dramatically than his performances. He seemed to be jointed like a Teddy-bear; if you pulled one of his arms up, the other seemed to automatically do likewise in a mirror image. Unfortunately for me his legs appeared to be jointed the same way. I caught him in a sweeping leg-dive and tore his left leg completely from under him, but his right leg mimicked the one I had whipped away, with the result that the sharp edge of his heavy right wrestling boot clipped my left ear with such force I thought he had kicked it completely off. The pain took my breath away, but not my instinct for immediate revenge. Leaping upright onto my feet I pretended that the blow to my ear had dazed and disoriented me. I pirouetted, staggered backwards, surrendered to gravity and dropped like a bomb - arse first right on top of Miguel's upturned face. What could have been described as a Flying Butt-Butt. The force of my full weight mashed both his nose and his mouth, while smashing the back of his head deep into the lightly padded ring boards. I was gratified when I stood up again to see his lips torn and blood gushing from both barrels of his snout, as my left ear still felt as though it had just been stung by the largest Wasp from Gulliver's Island of Giants. A little later, after examining my ear in the dressing room mirror, I was surprised to see no more damage than what looked like a small round blister; nevertheless the pain seemed to be out of all proportion to the actual injury.

After wrestling in various venues all week, I was asked by one of the other wrestlers as I was going to get married the next afternoon, what plans had I made for celebrating my final day of freedom?'

"This may have been my last night of freedom," I told him, "but tomorrow will definitely be a day to remember." – And what an understatement that turned out to be!

****

'What a great omen.' I thought, 'not only am I getting married today, but the wrestling photos that I had sent off to the States for had arrived bright and early by the very first post.' There were 5 glossy, black and white 8x10s of two of my American Wrestling Idols, Antonino Rocca in action against Dick 'The Bruiser.' My favorite photo out of the 5 pictures I received that morning was the one where 'The Bruiser' had made a successful grab for Rocca's wrist, but got countered by a large barefoot planted smack in his gob from one of Antonino's patented high kicks. They were great, I was so impressed by them that I took them with me, as I couldn't bear the thought of leaving them at home while I went out to complete the first quest of the day. I phoned the Tailor who was making my new suit to find out if it would be ready in plenty of time for the wedding. The great omen seemed to be fulfilling its promise, not only would my suit be ready in time, I was told, but it was ready and waiting for me right now. All I had to do was go over to Harlesden, pay the balance that I owed on it and pick it up. Unfortunately there was one small problem, although I had already paid a deposit for my new suit, I was pretty sure that I still owed more money on it than I presently possessed. 'No problem,' I thought, 'I'll pay them most of what I'd got, which was barely any more than the wages I'd earned the night before in Ipswich, and pay the final balance some time next week after I earned some more money.'

That was about the time the 'great omen' began to turn sour. It had started to drizzle just before I reached the phone box that I'd been calling the Tailor from, but now it was pissing down. Oh well, rain or no rain I had to leave the shelter of the phone box to get my new suit. I was soaked to the skin before I had even walked to the bus stop, and after waiting almost half an hour for a bus, I had perfected my performance of the breaststroke, the backstroke and the doggy paddle. At last the bus arrived, I boarded it, paid my fare, then sat and squelched until I reached my destination. I alighted from the bus into an almost solid sheet of ice cold pouring rain. By the time I got to the Tailor's shop I had began to think I had rediscovered 'The Lost City of Atlantis' rather than Harlesden. The icy cold rain made my injured ear sting as though it had been impaled by a poisoned arrow. I staggered with relief into the shelter of the Taylor's shop and imagined that my immediate problems were over, not so, after inquiring how much I still owed on my suit I found that it was roughly twice as much as I had in my pocket. I explained the situation to the Tailor, who listened patiently but unsympathetically. He then informed me, that there was no way that they would allow me walk out of their shop with my new suit until I had paid the full amount that was still outstanding.

"If I haven't got enough money I can't give it to you can I?" I asked reasonably, "I am supposed to be wearing the suit to get married in today, if I can't have the suit today, I won't want it at all now will I, and then you'll be left with a suit that nobody wants won't you?" I pointed out these facts hoping that he would reconsider, but, no dice. No money – no suit. Disappointed, I walked back out of the shop; the worst of the rain had stopped, just to be replaced by a light but constant, penetrating drizzle.

'Where was I going to get the money?' I wondered. 'It was strange,' I thought, 'the last time I had bought a suit from this very same tailor I had wondered how I was going the be able to pay the balance, but I had won a substantial amount of money betting on the Greyhounds at White City Dog-track which had taken care of that problem for me. But what the Hell was I going to do now?!'

As if things weren't bad enough, I suddenly realized that I was no longer carrying the envelope containing the American wrestling photos I had received that morning. They had been too precious to me to leave at home where they would have been safe. I spun around and galloped back to the Tailor's, but even before I arrived I realized that I must have left them in the phone box while calling the Tailor earlier. After riding the bus back and then zooming to the phone box as fast as I could zoom in my squelching, waterlogged boots. I found, as I expected, no sign of the photos that I had sent off to America for, and then waited weeks for, just to look at once, and have in my possession for about a half an hour before I lost them forever - I was gutted.

'Well no use worrying about them now,' I thought, 'I've got bigger problems to worry about, I have to get a new suit from somewhere, and I'm fast running out of time.'

I remembered seeing a second hand store a couple of miles away on the Harrow Road that sold just about everything, including clothes - it was a long shot, but I just couldn't think of anything else. The shop was just opening as I got there, but that's where my luck seemed to end. After browsing and re-browsing there was nothing suitable - no pun intended. 'In fact,' I thought, 'any one of the 3 suits that I already owned would have been a much better choice than anything this second hand store had to offer. But then my eye caught sight of a sign that said, 'Bought & Sold.' I wondered if I could sell them anything to make up the difference between the money I had, and what I needed to finally purchase my wedding suit. I rushed home, grabbed my 3 suits and all their accessories then I rushed back to the store and EURIKA! They bought almost all the clothes I owned for a price that not only covered the balance, but left me with a few shillings over. I would need that for fare to get to Epsom Baths Hall, where I would be wrestling the following Monday night. After returning to the Tailor's shop in Harlesden, and at last purchasing my new suit, I rushed home and barely had the time to shave and take a hot bath, before donning my new, dark midnight blue, 3 piece wedding suit. Then run a mile and a half down the road to the Church on the corner of Harrow Road, where I was to be married in about another 20 time. As I approached the corner I spotted my Brother Terence, who was to be my Best Man,

"Where have you been?!" he asked belligerently, "we've been looking everywhere for you!"

"I'll tell you all about it the next time I have about a month to spare." I promised.

While I had been having my problems it seemed that my family had been having there's, Terence and Cousin Raymond, I learned later had also been celebrating my Stag night in 'The Drum and Monkey' Pub, the night before. And much to my Mam's chagrin they had staggered home together as pickled as a pair of Newts. she told them both that under no circumstances were they to be late for the train the next morning, or they would probably miss my wedding. That morning as Mam, Dad, Pam and Cousin Mary arrived at the Railway Station, they all stepped onto the platform just in time to watch their train leaving without them. Both Terence and Raymond laughed while they waved goodbye to them through the window of their carriage compartment. Mam, Dad, Pam and Mary had to catch the next train, and fortunately made good time because as coincidence would have it, it would be the second wedding of the day they would attend. My Cousin Joan had married her fiancé Fred Furness, in the very same Church, that very same morning. Another coincidence was, that it had been my Father's 52nd Birthday the day before.

Most of the other Guests were from Jean's side of the family. The only others invited by myself in addition to my family, were my very good friends, Tom McBride and of course Tony Woods. Ter and I walked into the Church and we stood in our allotted places in front of the priest who would be conducting the ceremony, and I began to unwind for the first time that day. I remember feeling a little tingle of excitement in anticipation of Jean's reaction when she saw me standing there waiting for her wearing my very smart, brand new suit that would be a surprise that she would not be expecting.

'A surprise that almost didn't happen.' I thought. The strains of 'The Wedding March' erupted, I turned my head in order to watch Jean's grand entrance, and my jaw must have dropped a foot - she looked absolutely gorgeous, a surreal vision in white, flanked by Jean's Sister Shirley and my Sister Pamela who were her Bridesmaids.

"I like your new suit." Jean told me smiling shyly, as she mounted the steps and stood beside me. The sight of her had caused the 'infamous suit that almost didn't happen,' to evaporate right out of my mind, and I had to shake my head in an effort to refocus it. I couldn't wait to get the ceremony, the reception, the wedding cake and everything else that I'd have to endure out of the way and over with, before whisking Jean away to our flat where I could have her all for myself. The reception was held in an upstairs room in a Pub on the corner of Middle Row just across the road from The Forester's Wrestling Club. I couldn't take my eyes off Jean; she looked so lovely in her white wedding gown, that I would have happily and very enthusiastically forgone the ceremony, the reception with the cake cutting and all the trimmings just to be alone with her. But, the reception dragged on and on, we cut the cake, we ate some food, we drank some alcohol. People made speeches, while my fantasies concerning my new Bride seemed to take me to the very brink of spontaneous combustion. The only incident that succeeded in penetrating my private reverie was being told that a fight was brewing in the main barroom downstairs. I had to go down and force my body between a couple of local thugs and my Brother a split second before his fists began to fly. Ter, true to form after a couple of drinks, was ready to defend the honor of all Welshman as a result of overhearing a reference about 'Mountain Goats' after his accent had been detected.

"Please don't spoil my day." I told him, as I turned him towards the stairs and began to coax him away from the violence he'd been so anxious to dish out. I cast a look back at the two thugs and was thankful that Brother Ter couldn't see the smug looks of triumph on their faces as they watched the aggressive Welshman being lead away. If he had have seen them, it would have taken more than me to prevent him from spreading them both all over the bar. Raymond came to my assistance, but being the worse for wear himself all he managed to do was drape himself around my neck. He almost stubbed out a lighted cigar that was hanging out of one side of his mouth, into my injured ear hole as I struggled to guide my staggering Brother up stairs. When I once again entered the sanctuary of the upstairs room with my belligerent Brother in tow, all it took was one smile from Jean to melt away all the tension that the incident in the bar had evoked. Every glance or smile from her held a promise of things to come, and my desire to whisk her away immediately returned tenfold. That was when Cousin Raymond slid off my neck and landed with a resounding thud flat on his face, smashing his lighted cigar all over his chops. I had to hang on to Terence with all my strength as he began laughing so hard he almost fell on top of Raymond. 'Well at least it's brightened up my Brother's mood.' I thought. With my Brother's help we managed to hoist Raymond off the floor and lay him along a row of chairs to sleep it off. A girlfriend of Jean's came over with a paper towel and wiped the remnants of his smashed cigar off Raymond's face.

"I'll look after him." She offered kindly, as she sat down and gently lifted Raymond's head onto her lap. She then began stroking his hair, probably thinking that this was her big chance to land a handsome Welshman as her friend Jean had done. That's when Raymond moaned, turned towards her and threw up all over her lap.

'There endeth another prospective romance.' We all thought.

At last the ordeal was over and we arrived at our flat. It certainly wasn't the romantic setting that I would have liked, in fact it was a dingy two roomed flat with a shared bathroom. Both my wrestling commitments and the money situation had disqualified the option of a proper Honeymoon, but we had a bed and I had the most beautiful and desirable Bride I had ever seen. So what more could I want?

The moment we entered our bedroom, I unfastened my tie, threw it on the back of a chair, with my jacket following in quick succession. I started to unbutton my waistcoat and Jean began to remove her beautiful white Wedding gown, so I said to her,

"Don't take your dress off yet." From the first moment I saw her enter the Church I had anticipated this moment, she had looked so beautiful and desirable that I just wanted to savor the vision for as long as possible and allow my fantasy to play itself out.

"Why not?!" she snapped, looking at me suspiciously.

"Just leave it on for a while." I replied suggestively as I continued to undress, while flashing her my most lecherous and sexy smile.

"Nah!" She replied, "Yer ain't gonna mess my dress up!"

"I won't mess it up," I promised, "just leave it on for a little while."

"Nah!" she insisted, "It'll get messed up!"

"Well you're not planning on wearing it again are you?!" I asked her a little testily, while I felt the mood that had been growing rapidly all day begin to slide away.

"Nah, I ain't leavin' it on," she repeated, "it'll just get messed up." And with that she took it off. I was so disappointed, not just being deprived of the fantasy that had completely consumed me from the first time I had seen her enter the Church, but with her surly and uncooperative attitude. I could feel a libido that could have stood unchallenged for ever and a day in 'The Guinness Book of World Records' evaporate like a tear on a hotplate. Disgusted I turned away from her, finished getting undressed and got into bed. I found it strangely easy to deprive her of my usual undivided attention as she finished undressing. As she got into bed beside me, I turned over on my right side with my back to her. I really couldn't say for sure if Jean could have coaxed me out of my filthy mood or not, if she had really made the effort. It turned out to be a question of conjecture for within 5 minutes of her head hitting the pillow she was snoring like a Sow, while I was seething with the fury of a category ten Hurricane.

'What a thoroughly crappy end to a thoroughly crappy day,' I thought, 'and this is supposed to be the happiest day of my life.' I didn't sleep a wink that night, and all night long, my heart pounded, my head throbbed in rhythm, and then my injured ear decided to join in the chorus, as all the mean things that Jean had ever done, or said to me kept playing over and over in my head.

For me the biggest sexual turn-on could be easily described with one word and that word is 'enthusiasm'. I had had many friends who were Prostitutes, but the very fact that they charged money for their services to my way of thinking robbed them of their enthusiasm for sex, and suggested that they merely endured sex for a living rather than for mutual enjoyment. Even the way a Woman dresses would suggest to me enthusiasm or the lack thereof, Jeans, trousers, unenthusiastic - dresses, skirts enthusiastic.

Jeans and trousers, the ultimate turn-off. They delay action, make their wearer less accessible and look too masculine. Skirts and dresses suggest Femininity, accessibility and self inflicted vulnerability. Not to mention the fact that they are the only thing besides flying a kite that are capable of making a very windy day extremely enjoyable. Dressing-up in order to stimulate one's partner as Pauline liked to do was definitely a sign of enthusiasm. She had played 'Cleopatra', the 'Queen of Sheba' an 'Hawaiian Hula-Hula Girl', a 'Turkish Belly-Dancer' the 'Naughty Nurse', the 'French Maid', ooo-la-la, the 'Shy School Girl', the Sexy Girl-Scout' and the 'Cheerful Cheer-Leader', Rah-Rah-Rah!

But to me, Jean could have blown away Pauline and every

one of her many sexy characters, plus Carol and every one of her playful pals combined, into insignificant smithereens if she had simply, but enthusiastically just played the Beautiful Bride.

'I should have gone to Southall and wrestled Len Wilding instead I thought, I probably would have received a more friendly reception from him, and got paid for it in the bargain!' As dawn broke I leapt out of bed just as I had the morning before – and just like the morning before I had a quest to perform. After a quick wash and shave I got dressed and left the flat while my new Wife still slept the sleep of the just – and just thirty minutes later I was knocking on Tony Woods' front door. At the wedding reception the day before, after making a ribald remark or two to Tony concerning my intended upcoming weekend activities, Tony assured me that he would be likewise engaged,

"Mum and Dad are away for the weekend," he had told me, "Carol is coming up with her mates tomorrow to spend the whole day with me."

Tony opened the front door and invited me in, and was already cooking our breakfasts when Carol arrived with two friends, she was not only surprised to see me, but delighted to find that competition was going to be much stiffer than expected.

It was late evening by the time I made my way back from Tony's house to our dingy two roomed flat in Fermoy Road,

"Where have you been all day?" Jean wanted to know, as I entered the kitchen/dinning/sitting room.

"Out." I replied. 'In and out would have been closer to the truth.' I thought.

'It was just as well,' I mused, 'that I had spent the Day with Carol and Tony, at least there had been plenty to eat between rounds,' as back at our flat the only food we had was a few slices of wedding cake and a loaf of sliced white bread that I had scavenged the day before from the wedding reception.

As I was wrestling in Epsom Baths Hall the next evening and Jean would be in work all day, rather than stay at home on my own, I had intended to go to the YMCA for a workout in the morning. But I now wondered if the few shillings I had left after purchasing my suit would be sufficient to pay my bus fare to the YMCA and still have enough left afterwards for my fare to Epsom. Plus, I was always hungry, especially after a good hard workout, and I would need at least a couple of good nourishing meals to carry me through the rest of the day, and a hard fought wrestling contest later that evening.

"How much money have you got?" I asked Jean, hoping that if she would lend me a couple of pounds. It would take care of all my immediate traveling and eating problems. "I ain't got nuffink." She replied. I wondered what the Hell she did with her money. I was about to ask her, when it occurred to me that she, like me, may have spent the last of her rubles on her wedding ensemble, and just one word mentioned about that fucking dress would have been more than enough to – well I think you get the message!

'Oh well,' I thought, 'I'll have to get up early in the morning and walk to the YMCA, so that I can save the little money I had for the transport fare from the YMCA to Epsom.' With that in mind, I asked Jean,

"What time do you have to get up for work in the morning?"

"I ain't goin' to work anymore," she told me, "I've quit."

"Why did you quit work?!" I asked her, completely bewildered.

"Well I'm married now, ain't I?!" She stated, as though that would make any sense to me.

"Yes," I conceded, "– but what difference does that make?!"

"Well I ain't carryin' on workin' now that I'm married, am I?" She asked condescendingly, as though I was a stupid child.

"Why the fuck not?!" I wanted to know.

"Well most of the girls where I used to work 'ave given up workin' when they got married." Jean explained.

"And what do you plan on doing all day instead of working?" I asked.

"I can come wiv you, or go 'round an' see Mum." She replied.

"You can't come with me tomorrow for three reasons," I told her, "reason number one, I haven't got enough money for your bus fare, reason number two, they don't allow Women in the YMCA and reason number three, you'll be too bloody busy looking for a fucking job!" Before I began my trek to the YMCA the next morning, I made myself eight pieces of dry toast from the bread I had stolen from our own wedding reception. Four pieces to take with me to eat after I had worked out, and four to eat for breakfast before I left. I could have murdered a hot cup of Coffee with a nice slice of wedding cake, but no money, no coffee. When I arrived at the YMCA I worked out as usual with the weights until Mike Dimitri arrived and we began our session on the mat. By this time I was the only 10-percenter who still trained regularly with Mike. Well, at least as regularly as my very heavy professional wrestling schedule would allow. Ray Fury, who I mentioned before had enjoyed a very extensive wrestling background from his native Turkey, and seemed to consider he had enough skill and ability to survive any persecution from the 10-percenter haters. Both Miguel Santos and Johnny Apollo, on the other hand, could have really used as much tuition as they could possibly get, but the very fact that the smallest, cockiest member of our group would effortlessly but very enthusiastically beat the living crap out of them was far more than their bloated but fragile egos could stand. So they simply stopped training with us. I had improved dramatically as a result of Mike's tuition, there were many positions that he had easily tricked or maneuvered me into when I had first began my training with him, that I had since learned to avoid. But it seemed that for every one of his maneuvers that I succeeded in nullifying, he had two more up his sleeve to confound me with. Never mind how much I improved I was still like a novice chess player battling against The Grand Master. Even so, he did make a very serious mistake that morning as he stepped onto the mat to begin our morning combat when he asked me in the way of a greeting,

"How's married life treating you?" Even the worst positions that Mike managed to secure and punish me with that day I burst out of like an enraged Rhino escaping from a cobweb, just by thinking about the last question he had asked me before we began wrestling. We wrestled for over an hour, and in that time Mike never secured a single submission on me that I failed to break free of. And even though I knew that that was capable of really pissing him off, he now seemed to regard me with a new found respect. Mike may have suffered a psychological defeat that morning, but he had really ground and battered my injured ear with every brutal headlock or nelson he had subjected me to. My energetic, forceful and explosive escapes hadn't helped much either. My whole ear had now swollen to twice its normal size.

"It's becoming cauliflowered," Mike told me, "but if you get it drained now, you may be able to prevent it." On our way to the shower Mike complimented me on my improvement. I responded by explaining that it was his very mention of married life that had caused the surge of super strength and aggression that had made me unbeatable that morning, and went on to explain the whole frustrating story to him. Relating all my weekend mishaps to Mike didn't only make him laugh, but really seemed to have a very therapeutic effect on me, and I began to feel better as a result. I felt better still, when after explaining that due to the present lack of cash I had walked all the way from my flat to the YMCA and Mike said,

"Let me lend you a couple of pounds - you can pay me back at the end of the month when you pay me my 10-percent." I accepted his offer gratefully,

"Thanks Mike," I replied, "I appreciate it, lets go over to 'The Acapulco' and I'll treat us both to a sandwich and coffee." We were sitting comfortably in 'The Acapulco' enjoying our food, and in-between mouthfuls of my delightful and unexpected treat, I was expanding on last weekend's misadventures. I became aware that I seemed to be talking to myself. Mike was sitting opposite me at our table, and seemed to be doing some strange things with his face whilst looking at an angle over my left shoulder. At first I panicked thinking that my newly cauliflowered ear may have burst. But the little involuntary, but subtle smile that began to play around his lips seemed to be at odds with that particular scenario. Mike had told me that although he regarded himself as a descendant of the Ancient Spartans, his family had emigrated from Greece to Montreal, Canada, when Mike was just a young child. His Father opened the very first movie Theatre in Montreal, and eventually ran 14 of them in and around that City. As a result Mike soon became addicted to movies, and became the greatest fan of his undisputed 'Idol' The Latin Heartthrob Rudolf Valentino. Sitting in 'The Acapulco' mesmerized by Mike Dmitri's fluttering eyelids and quivering lips, I turned and looked in the direction of his shy, sly, subtle sidelong glances, and saw the object of his distraction in a pretty young Lady who was sitting drinking coffee at a nearby table. I couldn't help thinking to myself that his impersonation of 'The World's Greatest Lover' left a lot to be desired, and to me he looked a lot more like Oliver Hardy than Rudolf Valentino. I must admit that Mike's method of courtship may have been deemed as more romantic than mine, but I still found that my own method of,

"Hey Nellie, would you like a fuck?!" much more effective.

When I left Mike I walked all the way to the 'Out Patients' in Praed Street Hospital in order to get my ear drained, hoping to prevent it becoming cauliflowered, but after I'd had it examined I was told that draining it would be a painful waste of time, unless I was prepared to take an extended leave from wrestling.

"It will swell back up the moment you get a blow or the slightest amount of pressure applied to it," the Doctor explained, "unless you give up wrestling for at least a couple of months, and even then there is no guarantee that it won't reoccur if you carry on wrestling." He advised me to wear protective headgear, apply lots of ice, 'Lead Lotion' and 'Witch Hazel,' and at least cut down on wrestling, even if I was not prepared to give it up. Not only was I not prepared to cut down, or give up wrestling out of choice, but the financial position I now found myself in made it totally impossible to even contemplate.

After entering the dressing room in Epsom Baths Hall later that evening I was delighted to see another of my old independent promotion's opponents, 'The Irish Whip' Peter Kelly, and even more delighted when I learned that he was to be my opponent that night. Within two minutes Peter had me laughing so hard that all my recent troubles and frustrations all but disappeared, even my throbbing ear seemed to throb a little more quietly and a little less vividly. But suddenly half way through his umpteenth joke, Peter stopped and exclaimed,

"Hey Mate, I didn't know you had a Cauli'!"

"I didn't until last week." I told him, as I turned my head and let him examine it.

"Fuckin' Mary!" he declared, "that's a bleed'n' beauty, but don't worry, I'll look after it." Not really being sure what he meant by 'I'll look after it.' I gave him 'that look'.

"I'm serious Mate," he assured me, "You know you can trust me, I won't even touch it." As it happened Peter Kelly was one of the very few wrestlers that I did trust in those days. But even if he didn't purposely go after my injured ear I knew that he wouldn't be capable of completely avoiding it. Considering that we would shortly be in the ring smashing each other from pillar to ring-post for at least 30 to 40 action packed minutes. Well it turned out that the 'Irish Whip' was true to his word. It was towards the end of the final round, after we had both scored a fall each in the earlier rounds, and so far my ear had remained comparatively untouched. I was to take the winning pin-fall this round, and in order to add a little drama to the action I allowed Peter to subject me to a series of near pin-falls from which I would barely escape. That was designed to give the impression that he was about to win the match just before I managed to snatch a victory out of the very jaws of defeat. Things were going great right up until Peter's last near fall. I was on my back and Peter was covering me, when referee Tony Lawrence leapt down to count the fall, which would begin as soon as he checked to make sure that both my shoulders were in contact with the mat. He did that by sliding his hands along the canvas to ensure that there was no space between skin and mat before he began the 3 count.

"ONE – TWO –!" The referee chanted, and as he did so, he slid his hand with all the force he could muster right into my injured ear. Poor Peter somersaulted through the air like a badly aimed boomerang, as I exploded to my feet in one movement, and grabbed the ref by the throat as my fist recoiled poised to deliver a death blow. It was only his strangled squawk that managed to gargle,

"I'LL DISQUALIFY YOU!!!" that arrested my fist mid flight, before it would have transformed his full Moon face into a concaved crescent. My fury was transferred against my unfortunate opponent, whose body shook the building after I slammed it full force into the mat before covering it for the victory, while my boring eyes never left the face of that clumsy oaf of a referee as he delivered the 3 count.

"You can't disqualify me now can you?!!!" I roared at Tony Lawrence as I burst back into the dressing room and into his face.

"I'M SORRY!!!" He screamed, which was the only thing that he could have said to me, that prevented me from busting his face. I accepted his apology, even though I doubted its sincerity, as he had been the foremost amongst the dressing room's occupants to derive so much amusement from my Cauliflowered ear when I'd first arrived at that night's venue. However I was very sincere when I apologized to Peter Kelly for slamming him so violently, which I realized was a very shabby reward to offer him after he had so gently nursed my ear through 40 minutes of nonstop action.

The next morning with the remnants of my 4 pounds 10 shillings wrestling wages in my pocket, Jean and I went shopping. We bought a cup each, a couple of plates, a pair of knives, forks, spoons and a medium sized saucepan that would have to triple up as a frying pan and a kettle until we could afford to buy those utensils individually.

"Well we have most of our eating irons now," I told Jean, "maybe tomorrow we'll be able to afford some food to go with them, after I get some more wages for wrestling tonight. That night I was wrestling in Hove Town Hall against Tony Scarlo. I breathed a sigh of relief, as I knew that Tony would also try his best not to damage my ear, and the fact that Captain John Harris, who was one of the best referees in the business, was refereeing our match was definitely an added bonus. I wasn't wrestling the next day, so that morning Jean and I went out shopping again. This time for food, Lead Lotion, Witch Hazel and ice. As I didn't want a cauliflower ear to mar my natural beauty.

As I was wrestling in Bristol the next day I decided to make myself a meal to take with me rather than eat with the other wrestlers at their regular watering hole. This decision was made, not so much as an effort to save money, but more to avoid the embarrassment that a confrontation between the restaurant's proprietor, his wayward Wife and I may have caused. My effort proved to be superfluous, as when we arrived at the restaurant it was closed. The wrestlers were quite bewildered, as they had never ever known the restaurant to be closed before, and in all the years that they had frequented it, the premises had always been open from the very early hours of the morning till very late at night. With much grumbling and swearing from the others we pressed on, and found an alternative in a filthy, greasy-spoon dive that caused me very much personal rejoicing in the very fact that I had brought my own grub with me. Just looking at the dump fractured my appetite so badly that I decided to walk on down the road in the direction we would be heading and let the others pick me up after they had finished their meal.

'That way,' I thought, 'the exercise would do me good and restore my appetite.'

"Who gave you a lift?!" they all wanted to know, as I stepped back into the van when at last the other wrestlers caught up to me. Of course my ego soared as a result of the fact that not one of the wrestlers on board could be convinced that I could have covered that much distance without help in the time it had taken them to devour their meals, and then catch me up. Add to that, the fresh air rather than continually breathing the other wrestler's second hand tobacco smoke. The exhilaration from the exercise, my renewed appetite, and the appreciation of the beautiful English countryside viewed from a different perspective. It all succeeded in braking up the endless monotony of traveling in Dale Martin's van and got me totally hooked. From that time on, the only thing that would prevent me from walking while the other wrestlers ate, was in the event of very bad weather. Even then I would still consume my own specially prepared healthy food rather than eat in a greasy-spoon café. That night in Bristol I found myself pitted against the bombastic bully, Billy Stock. Billy no longer seemed to harbor any undue animosity resulting from his humiliating defeat in Luton, but it was impossible for me to wrestle against an opponent whose major offensive consisted of headlock, after headlock, after headlock, without my suffering major pain and major damage to my already painfully damaged ear. Looking in the bathroom mirror after my post contest shower, I saw that my left ear was swollen larger than ever, and was sticking out at right angles to my head like a car with one door wide open. On the way back home after the matches the wrestler's worst fears were realized when they found that the restaurant was still closed. They weren't able to find an alternative eatery that was still open at that late hour until we were on the very outskirts of London. I was to learn that for the next few weeks the restaurant was open for the wrestlers, both to and from the venues that they were appearing at when they wrestled in that direction – 'but', only if I was wrestling in a different area on the same day. The next time I was wrestling in

Bath, once again we found that the restaurant was mysteriously closed when we arrived there. None of the wrestlers could understand why; - but I began to have a suspicion. Eventually, my suspicion was confirmed. It turned out that I was the Jonah, the proprietor refused to elaborate, but told the other wrestlers not to expect his restaurant to be open when he knew that I would be appearing at any of the venues that would bring them past his premises. Naturally, this situation made me a tad unpopular with all the other wrestlers whenever we wrestled in that neck of the woods,

"Oh, fuck it - look who's with us today - now where are we going to eat?!" I heard that almost every time we traveled in that direction. I told them to tell the disgruntled proprietor that I had no intention of ever invading his restaurant again. I now regularly brought my own food, and enjoyed walking while the other wrestlers ate. It wasn't that I wasn't man enough to apologize to the restaurant's proprietor for my totally inexcusable behavior, it was just that I didn't know how to. Especially as I didn't know what excuses his Wife had made to him, or even if they were still together as a result of that very unfortunate incident. Eventually the restaurant's proprietor must have got the message, and he remained open for the wrestlers whether I was with them or not. But I would still always walk while the others ate, and then eat healthy after they caught me up, and as I promised I never ever set foot in that restaurant again.

But, gossip travels very fast in the wrestling business, especially in the direction of Dale Martin's offices, and one night, just a little while later when I was wrestling in Acton, and as I was approaching the venue I spotted that night's wrestling posters plastered all over the front of the building. I looked to see that I would be wrestling against Stefan Milla - then I did a double take, as I saw that I had been billed as 'Nature-Boy,' Adrian Street.

'THE NATURE-BOY'

I couldn't wait to get my hands on that night's wrestling program in order to see whether I would be described as 'The Nature-Boy' Adrian Street in that too - I was – and not only that, the program also contained an article written by Charles Mascall, explaining the reason why I had been honored with such an illustrious title. To most people in Britain at that time the title of 'Nature-Boy,' probably wouldn't have meant very much. But to me it couldn't have meant more, even if I had been billed as 'World Champion' Adrian Street. The reason given in the program's article it seemed, had simply been inspired by my new method of training. It went on to describe my running, jogging and fast walking, followed by a healthy meal consisting of meat, or fowl, or fish with salad and fruit, which was all washed down with large quantities of either milk, fruit juice or Adam's Ale.

There may have been 'Nature-Boys' before him, and I have lost count of how many there have been in the World of Wrestling since. But to me, then, as now, there was only one 'Nature-Boy,' and that was the one and only 'Nature-Boy' Buddy Rogers. To use his own words 'Often imitated – never duplicated.' I agree that he never was, and he never will be. Buddy began his professional career in the early 40's as Dutch Rhodes; he even wrestled against the horrific 'French Angel' Maurice Tillet in 1945 before changing his name to Buddy Rogers, and later adopting the 'Nature-Boy' nickname. I had grown up as a 'Nature-Boy' Buddy Rogers fan; he was one of the first wrestlers who had really caught my attention soon after I had been introduced to American Professional Wrestling by my best friend, Peter 'The Strangler' Inge. Even though all but the most avid and voracious of wrestling fans in Europe in those days would have been totally ignorant of who the great 'Nature-Boy' Buddy Rogers was, I still thought that it was a very heavy crown to bare upon my brow, and I immediately decided that I needed to take some very serious action in an effort to live up to such an illustrious title. The very fact that I had been dubbed 'The

Nature-Boy' by none other than the great wrestling authority and Worldwide wrestling journalist, Charles Mascall gave that title a very distinct air of legitimacy. Charles Mascall had been a professional wrestler going back to the early 1930's in his native Canada, when he had been known then as 'Spider' Mascall. He had since made his way to Europe and had been employed for many years as editor for Dale Martins Promotion's magazines etc. Charles occupied one of Dale Martin's offices, but he also wrote for most of the foremost 'combat' magazines in the World. Including all of my favorite American magazines, and as a result he would have been well aware of every professional wrestler of note on the Planet. And was obviously very much aware of 'Nature-Boy' Buddy Rogers and what he meant to wrestling. 'Nature-Boy' Buddy Rogers had always been one of my two favorite wrestlers. The other one being Don Leo Jonathan. Dale Martins hadn't allowed me to use the name Kid 'Tarzan' Jonathan, which I would have regarded as my way of paying a tribute to one of my favorites. But now out of the blue I was handed the mantle that would allow me the privilege of paying tribute to my other most favorite. The effect that that very illustrious title had on me was IMMEDIATE! In all of the matches in which I had wrestled against Stefan Milla so far, I had virtually been taught by Stefan to follow his lead and had more or less spent the whole match setting myself up for Stefan's very clever counter moves. The result would mostly be a comparatively easy contest where I would apply hold after hold on my opponent, who would appear to almost effortlessly turn every one of my attacks around to his own advantage. Outsmarting me at every step and giving the 'new kid' a thoroughly good wrestling lesson. After this type of contest I would usually receive the lukewarm applause given most generously and condescendingly to a game but frustrated underdog. While Stefan would bask in the uproar reserved for the valiant victor, who had displayed a clever answer to every one of his less skilled opponent's offensives. More often than not I would lose my matches against Stefan with an occasional contest that ended in a draw, at which times I noticed that Stefan would be inclined to be a little more greedy. He would also make sure that he was always very much on the offensive as the match ended, giving the impression that if the match had gone just a few minutes longer he would have once again emerged as the victor. But, tonight was going to be different, tonight Stefan Milla wasn't going to be wrestling against Adrian Street. He was going to be wrestling against 'Nature-Boy' Adrian Street, and even though I agreed that Buddy Rogers couldn't be duplicated, I made my mind up there and then to give it a bloody good try.

"What happened to our good, easy little match tonight?!" Stefan wanted to know when we both returned to the dressing room after our contest had concluded.

"I got bored with it," I told him bluntly, "I thought it was time for a change."

The look on Stefan's face registered total bewilderment - 'who did this little whippersnapper think he was, who had the audacity and effrontery to alter the format that Stefan had so carefully tailored to meet his own ends?!' he must have been thinking.

"What the fuck do you mean, you got bored with it?" he demanded to know, "and who the fuck gave you the right to change the rules?!" In my opinion, I thought we'd had a much better match than normal, for me anyway! Throughout the match I had skillfully countered his best countermoves and threw a few more in of my own that 'Grandmaster Stefan' had no answers to at all. It also brought out the very best in Stefan who now had to fight for anything he could get instead of me handing them to him. Then at the conclusion of the contest I made certain that it was me, me and me again, who was giving and not receiving the punishment. It was also a much more exciting match from the audience's point of view, and they all rewarded me with a collective WOW!, at the end of the match which confirmed it.

"What rules are you talking about Stefan?" I inquired, "Oh yes, I forgot, your rules, the rules that makes you the wrestling Master and me the slow learning, dim witted pupil," I added sarcastically, "well it my come as a shock to you, but I didn't work my bollocks off all these years just to be any other wrestler's stooge. From now on I won't be in the ring with you for the sole purpose of handing you your props, I'll be in there wrestling to the very best of my ability, and I advise you to do the same. I didn't become a wrestler for you, I became a wrestler for me!" Stefan turned to the rest of the wrestlers in the dressing room rolling up his eyes, while turning up the palms of his hands in a silent gesture of helpless frustration, in an effort to elicit their sympathy. The dressing room had become uncharacteristically quiet as a result of our argument, and as I glanced at the others, I was met with a myriad of expressions ranging from the highly amused, to the highly speculative, to the downright hostile. I then realized that I had thrown down a gauntlet, as I met their collective gaze I willed my own expression to register one of total indifference. While I thought of the words attributed to my favorite singing Minstrel,

"You ain't seen nothin' yet!"

****

As I suspected, Jean found it almost impossible to find work in job starved London, but finally as a last resort she had managed to get her old sewing job back. That proved to be a waste of effort, as by now she was starting to show some signs of being seriously pregnant. That didn't only put pay to her sewing career, and the meager wages it generated. It also put pay to being able to remain any longer in our dingy little flat in Fermoy Road. As soon as our Greek Landlady noticed Jean's large round tummy, she explained to us that her Brother and his family were in the process of immigrating to Britain from Greece. As a result she would need our space for them to live in after they arrived. Both Jean and I suspected that it was just an excuse to get us out of their property before she gave birth, but we didn't really care as it was quite a horrible flat and we both wanted to move out anyway. That proved to be much easier said than done, as things in the flat finding business hadn't changed much. We were now hampered by the same apartment adverts that had really shocked me when I had first come to live in London - 'Whites Only need apply' - 'No Blacks' - No Irish or Children'. Well we weren't Black or Irish, but Jean was getting mighty round. At first Jean would always accompany me when we went out searching for a new place to live, as she obviously wanted a say in our choice of habitat. But as soon as Jean's condition was detected it was,

"No, I'm sorry we let the flat yesterday, and I haven't had

time yet to go and take our advert out of the shop." Or the more honest of them would blatantly point an accusing finger at Jean's belly and say,

"Didn't you read our advert properly, - it said, No Blacks, No Irish and definitely no kids!" I had always sympathized with both Black and Irish people in this regard, but now we were getting first hand experience of how it felt to be regarded as 'undesirable.'

"You're just going to have to trust me to get the best place I can get," I told Jean at last, "we're never going to get anything if you come with me when we go searching for somewhere to live." I had decided that I would prefer to live much closer to Dale Martin's offices. Most nights after returning from a show in their transport I would have to walk all the way from their office to Fermoy Road after I had been dropped off at all hours of the early morning. That meant that sometimes I'd get home with just about enough time to grab some breakfast and pack a lunch before running out to catch public transport all the way back to Dale Martin's offices again. I began leaving for Dale Martins much earlier to give myself time to explore the surrounding area. After a very prolonged and aggravating search I finally lucked out when I made contact with yet another Polish Landlord, Mr. Sikorski, who owned a number of properties in Streatham, which was my area of choice. One of the first things Mr. Sikorski asked me was, did my Wife and I have any pets or Children. I told him no on both counts, but somehow I completely forgot to mention we did have a Child on the way. Amongst the flats he had available there was one on the ground floor with French Windows leading out to a small, but pretty little back garden, very quiet and completely enclosed. I loved it, and couldn't wait to show it to Jean. I could just imagine sitting in that garden with Jean on a nice sunny day, and watching our new Baby as over time it learned to crawl, walk, run and play happily in the garden's safe and quiet confines. That dream evaporated the second I introduced Mr. Sikorski to Jean.

"You didn't tell me your Wife was expecting a Baby." He accused bluntly.

"You didn't ask." I replied innocently. Mr. Sikorski told us that as a result of Jean being Pregnant we couldn't rent the flat. I told him that we had to have it, as we had already given up our previous flat, and the Landlady's family was waiting to move into it the second we moved out. We argued and finally reached a compromise. He was adamant that we couldn't have the little flat with the garden that I had fallen in love with, but he would rent us a flat in another part of Streatham. It wasn't nearly as nice as the one with the garden, but was an awful lot nicer than the one in Fermoy Road and a lot closer to Dale Martins. A week later we moved ourselves, and our scant belongings into number 4 Brancaster Road, Streatham. We still only had a kitchen, bedroom and a shared bathroom, but they were much larger and brighter than Fermoy Road. The bedroom was very large, so large in fact that it also served as our dining room and lounge. As we settled into our new abode, Jean seemed to be more content and a lot less confrontational. I was still quizzed and cross-examined about 'other girls', but not so often or so intensely as in the past, this in turn made me less aggressive and rebellious. I fully appreciated the fact that it had taken a combined effort for Jean to attain the condition that she now found herself in, and my heart would melt when I saw her ever swelling tummy as she tottered about on her long slim legs. That mental picture began to haunt me and smother me with guilt whenever I was approached by 'other girls' at the arenas, and though I can't truthfully claim that they were easy to resist, I did manage to succeed in a very successful attempt at total celibacy during that entire period when I was away from home. Unfortunately, my newly found fidelity came at a cost. Tony Woods often used to drive me to my matches on the weekends, but as I no longer took advantage of the 'fringe benefits' that was always so abundant, it now meant that Tony would miss out too. Add to that the fact that I now lived on the other side of the Thames in South-West London, instead of a mile or so away from Tony's home in North-West London and Tony gradually but completely faded right away. I was by now far too busy to worry about it, but I was surprised as Tony had also wanted to turn professional and was on the very brink of realizing his aspirations. I had put a number of words in for him to Jack Dale, which had resulted in a promise that he would soon be given his big chance. Tony had even hinted that he had a professional name and image in mind, and had already designed and ordered an appropriate ring outfit to compliment that image, so as to ensure that he would begin his pro wrestling career with a bang.

Tom McBride would come to many of my London matches in my early months with Dale Martins, but as we both became increasingly busy with our respective careers he too slowly melted into my past. It seemed that my very best, and oldest friend Peter Inge was the only true friend I had left. The last time I had seen him had been the last Christmas time, when Jean and I had been in Brynmawr for a few days holiday with my family. Peter had assured me then that it was still only a matter of time before he at last joined me in London where we would both pursue our dreams of wrestling stardom together. We had still intended to get a place where we would share the rent, then train, wrestle and travel together; Peter told me that he was going to buy a motorbike that we would be able to ride to all our matches on. I must admit that that idea didn't appeal to me at all. I have never liked motorbikes and I suggested that his hard earned money could be put to much better use, like getting to London as soon as possible for instance.

I obviously didn't know at that time, that within the next few months I would become a married man with my first Child on the way. That in itself would have put pay to our years old plan, but future events were destined to put a stake in the very heart of our plans forever.

I was wrestling in Dumfries Place, Drill Hall in Cardiff again on the 13th of June 1962 against Len Wilding, and Peter had got word to me a couple of days earlier, that if he could get his motorbike in time, he would use it to ride down to Cardiff to watch me wrestling. Although Len Wilding was an excellent wrestler, and a good opponent for me he was a 'Blue-Eyes', which was what wrestlers called the 'good guy' wrestlers. As Peter was going to be there to watch, I would have preferred to wrestle against a bad guy wrestler. The 'bad-guys' were called 'Villains' in Britain, in the States the good guys were called 'Baby-Faces' and the bad guys were called 'Heels'. It was only on account of Peter coming to the matches that night that had caused me to have preferred to wrestle a villain rather than a Blue-eye. As far as the Cardiff fans were concerned, I couldn't have cared less. I would get lukewarm applause if I wrestled a villain, and booed if I wrestled a Blue-eye. As a result I had completely lost faith in them, I felt they had betrayed me and I am not a very forgiving person. I left word at the box-office that evening that I was expecting a guest named Peter Inge, and requested that he be allowed in free of charge. But I still paced back and forth from the dressing room to the box-office, in order to see whether he had arrived yet, right up until I had to enter the ring for my contest. All through my match I scoured the audience hoping to see Peter's face. Then when the contest ended, instead of returning to the dressing-room, I walked straight from the ring to the box-office to inquire if my guest had arrived at last. He hadn't, and he didn't make it there at all that night and I wondered what excuse he had this time, last time poor Peter had polio, - 'now what?' I wondered.

It was the 12th of June 1962; the day before Peter was going to come to Cardiff and see me wrestle, he had bought his motorbike that same day, and as Deakin's Fair was in Brynmawr he decided to ride down there to show off his new acquisition to some of his friends who he thought would most probably be there. They were and were all suitably impressed with his new toy, but during their conversation one of his friends mentioned that he had seen a Girl that Peter was very keen on, a little earlier in Marie's café in the Market Square. Peter sped there at once and arrived at the café just as the young Lady in question was leaving there with a girlfriend, Peter had hoped to impress her with his motor bike, but she wasn't impressed.

"Would you like a ride on my new bike?" Peter asked her.

"No," she replied, "I don't like motorbikes." Naturally he was very disappointed, but the Lady's girlfriend, who obviously must have taken a fancy to him, chirped,

"Oh, I like motorbikes; I'll come for a ride!" So off they sped together, they were rounding a corner near Beaufort Ballroom when Peter lost control of his bike, they hit a telegraph pole and were both killed, Peter died aged 20 years old.

The very next night, still unaware of this tragic and deadly accident, I wrestled just 30 miles away from where my best friend Peter and his unfortunate passenger took their very last breath. My friend had been dead about 27 hours as I stepped into the ring once more in Dumfries Place, Drill Hall, in Cardiff to wrestle against Len Wilding, serenaded as usual by the jeers and boos of my fellow countrymen.

I can not even begin to describe how upset I was when I received the terrible and unbelievable news; Peter had been my best friend for almost both of our lives. It was Peter who had first introduced me to professional wrestling, it was Peter who first introduced me to what became one of my favorite offensive weapons, namely his own version of the dreaded 'Guillotine, and it was Peter who I have to thank, for not only giving me a career, but a purpose and direction for my entire life, a career, a purpose and direction that we had always imagined we would share.

It was probably about that time that my already fragile religious beliefs really began to corrode; I had prayed my heart out just a few years earlier for my best friend's recovery when he had been stricken down with polio. It had seemed that in answer to my prayers, Peter had made a full recovery – and now this.

'If there is such an entity as God,' I thought, 'he must have a worse sense of humor than the most spiteful wrestler I had yet encountered - and that's really saying something!' That may have been the beginning of my disbelief in an Almighty being, but it would still be many more years before the first time I uttered,

"Thank God I'm an Atheist!"

****

By now all of Dale Martin's wrestlers were aware of my unique training schedule, and the great shape and conditioning that I had attained as a result. After our move to Streatham I found that we now lived about a mile from 'The Dazzler' Joe Cornelius and his family. Joe without a doubt was one of the best and most charismatic heavyweight wrestlers that Britain ever produced. What a presence The Dazzler made when he entered the ring, extremely handsome, with jet black wavy hair and eyebrows to match, dazzling smile, and personality as big as the Royal Albert Hall, and a ring savvy second to none, Damn, he had it all. He was like a puppet master with strings fastened to the hearts of every member of the audience. If he laughed, they laughed, if he cried, they cried, if he grew angry, so did they, if he suffered, they suffered, but when he finally triumphed - Whoops! There goes another arena roof! I remember being so flattered one day when in answer to a knock on my front door I opened it and found 'The Dazzler' himself on my doorstep. Just a few nights before, after my match, Joe had asked me all about my training methods which had made me feel very important, and he had suggested that we should begin training together.

"Fancy going for a run?" he asked me, as I stood with the door and my mouth hanging open.

"Certainly," I replied, "where shall we go?" Not that that would have made any difference to me, I was so much in awe of 'The Dazzler' I would have accompanied him on a marathon across the surface of the Sun if he'd asked me to.

"What about Battersea Park?" he suggested.

'Even better,' I thought, - and a lot cooler.'

"Great," I answered, "come in and I'll get changed into my workout gear."

That was the start of my training sessions with Joe Cornelius, when ever our wrestling commitments, and weather allowed, Joe would come and pick me up from home in his little dark green Volkswagen, and we'd spend an hour or more running around Battersea Park. I am sure that our training sessions benefited 'The Dazzler' and helped to keep him in tip-top shape. But our sessions benefited me even more, as with so much sage advice from one of the World's best performers, and biggest wrestling names in Britain, I began to learn details about my chosen profession that had never before even crossed my mind. If Joe's ears hadn't already been cauliflowered I'm sure that they would have been in great danger of getting that way by my constant yapping, he must have had the patience of a Chinese Jobe,

"Hey Joe," I'd tell him as we ran along the Park's lovely flowered pathways,

"I learned three new wrestling moves last week, there can't be very many more that I don't already know." Joe's eyes twinkled he'd flash me a dazzling smile and reply,

"Yes Ada, I remember being like you myself - Until the penny dropped!!!!." He went on to explain that in his early days, just like me, he had measured his wrestling progress by the number of new holds and throws he was able to demonstrate during each contest, and felt he was improving by cramming more and more of them into each match. Until 'the penny dropped' as he had put it, and he realized that a wrestling match could be so much more entertaining performed as a story, rather than just displaying a series of disjointed [no pun intended] wrestling maneuvers.

"During my first two years in this business," he told me, "in every match, I tried to inject more and more different holds, more and more different throws, until the penny dropped and I realized that just as a great book doesn't need every word in the dictionary to be a best seller, and a great painting doesn't have to contain every color in the spectrum to be considered a masterpiece. A wrestling match doesn't have to have every wrestling move ever devised in the History of the sport to make it into a great contest. After that it seemed I did less and less of a variety of holds every match instead of more and more. Any move that didn't add something to the overall story was regarded as superfluous, and was simply dropped out of the contest." Many of the things that Joe told me may not have made a great deal of sense to me to begin with, but I began watching the Dazzler and many of the other masters of our sport from a slightly different perspective. I started analyzing what I saw, it slowly began to dawn on me and eventually the penny did drop, but only with time and only after Joe had explained to me what to look for.

I asked The Dazzler how he got started in the wrestling business and it seemed that Joe's Baptism was even more reckless than mine had been. To begin with Joe was a huge fan of professional wrestling, just as were the majority of all of us who entered our sport. What made Joe unique was the way he went about it. Sitting in a ringside seat at Blackfriar's Arena one night, Joe became so incensed at the blatant brutality displayed by one of the Main Event contestants that he leapt out of his seat, dove right into the ring and challenged the perpetrator on the spot. If you don't think that in itself was reckless enough, just wait until I tell you who that the brutal, main event wrestler was. Yup, you've got it, none other than 'The Baron of Brutality' himself, Bert Assirati.

In an uncharacteristic display of mercy, Bert grabbed hold of Joe and hurled him head first over the top rope and back onto the ringside seat that Joe had just vacated. If that doesn't sound too merciful to you, just imagine what Bert could have done as an alternative. Joe did eventually wrestle against Bert on a number of occasions – and thanks him very much for both his cauliflower ears.

I had first heard of Joe Cornelius as the result of a far worse injury than the cauliflower ears he had got off Bert. During a match against an ex-bodybuilder from France, 'Mr. Europe' Robert Durant, it looked as though Joe was well on his way to yet another great victory. When 'Mr. Europe' took a one-legged Boston-Crab on 'The Dazzler' and almost tore Joe's kneecap off. The vicious hold gave 'Mr. Europe' a victory over 'The Dazzler' and 'The Dazzler' an injury that plagued him for the remainder of his wrestling career. I was also surprised to learn from Joe that the wrestling groupies who preyed so voraciously upon us poor defenseless wrestlers, were anything but a new phenomenon in the sport. He told me that Joan Collins and her Sister Jackie had been amongst the wrestling fans who attended Bermondsey Baths every week, and were regarded as the most predatory Females to haunt that arena when they were both just young teenagers. Then I was amazed one afternoon when I asked Joe where he was wrestling that Saturday night.

"I don't wrestle weekends." He replied.

"What do you mean, you don't wrestle weekends?!" I wanted to know.

Joe went on to explain that after investing some of his hard earned savings in a Hair Dressing Salon which his Wife ran, he didn't need to wrestle every night any more.

"Dale Martin's keep asking me to wrestle more often," he told me, "but I will only wrestle 4 times a week. No Saturdays, no Sundays, and I take one day off during the week, so I get 3 whole days to myself. There's more to life than wrestling he added, "I get 12 pounds a match, plus the money my Wife earns at the Salon, so why should I want to wrestle any more than that?" The very thought of earning as much as 12 pounds a match completely boggled my brain.

'12 pounds a match,' I thought, 'that would be 84 pounds a week if he'd wrestle every night - my God! I would have signed a contract to span the rest of my wrestling career for 12 pounds a match!' As you can see, I knew nothing about inflation in those days. Joe also told me that he could earn more than that if he wrestled up North for the other promoters in Joint Promotions, but he wouldn't do that either.

"I'll only wrestle in the South, so that I can be home in my own bed every night and I'll only wrestle 4 times a week, there's more to life than wrestling." Said Joe again, adamantly. I couldn't understand why anyone would refuse matches, especially for that kind of money – and if there was more to life than wrestling – I really couldn't begin to imagine what that could possibly be?!

From the time I was a very young Child, I had always thought that I was special and very important - unfortunately for me no one else seemed to be aware of it. But with the new friendship and attention I received from Joe, I had never felt so special and important before in my life. Or at least not since that man in the black uniform had knocked on the front door of number 8 Queen Street, during the second World War and had handed me a Pink Gas Mask when I was just a 3 year old kid.

Joe told me that he was going to be wrestling against 'Dropkick' Johnny Peters in an upcoming show that Johnny was promoting in a home for the Handicapped at Newhaven, a town close to where he lived in Hove. He explained that it wasn't a regular show, but a charity show - and not a show to raise money for any charitable cause, but to entertain the actual inmates of the home itself.

"There will just be two matches," Joe said, "I'm going to be wrestling against Johnny, but we need another wrestler to wrestle Stefan Milla in a preliminary match."

"Count me in." I offered without a second's hesitation.

"There'll be no wages." Joe warned me.

"Count me in." I repeated. On the day of the show, Joe drove both Stefan and me from London down to Johnny Peters' home in Hove, where we all enjoyed a lunch which consisted of Smoked Salmon in Poppy-seed encrusted rolls, before Johnny drove all 4 of us to the home in Newhaven in his car. This would only be the second time I had ever eaten Smoked Salmon. The first time being at the home of Michael the photographer and his pretty Wife, Monica. Over lunch at Johnny Peters' home, Johnny thanked me for volunteering my services free of charge, and then told me that it seemed that it would be me, rather than Joe Cornelius and himself who would be the 'Star' of the show at the home for the handicapped. At first I thought that I was being made sport of, especially when Stefan and Joe began to laugh, and I remember thinking that making fun of me was a very poor way of expressing gratitude. My resentment evaporated after he explained that upon hearing that I was to be one of the contestants, one of the patients at the home claimed to be an old friend of mine. He had become a Star attraction there himself, after recounting countless tales of our adventures together in years past. I asked Johnny if he knew the name of this person, as I couldn't imagine for the life of me who it could possibly be. I suspected that it was most likely some poor handicapped inmate who suffered with delusions. Johnny didn't know and I began to feel a little apprehensive, as I wondered if I would need to pretend to know who this person was when I met him, rather than burst his bubble and embarrass him in front of all the other inmates of the home.

When we arrived at the home we were greeted by a short, plump Lady, with graying hair and a cheerful smile, she introduced herself as the Governess and shook hands with all of us. As she shook mine she asked me if I was Adrian Street, and after admitting that I was, she said,

"Oh, Raymond will be so excited to see you again; - you're all he's talked about ever since he heard you were going to be here today."

"Raymond?" I inquired, arching my eyebrows to their extreme in order to emphasize my puzzlement.

"Yes, Raymond Bailey," she replied, "he told us you were friends, and both grew up together in the same town in Wales." She looked as relieved as I felt, when I told her,

"Oh, yes I know Raymond very well; we even attended the same schools since we were both infants!" We all followed her through a small hall where the wrestling ring was already set up, and into an adjoining communal lounge where all the residents and staff had gathered, while patiently awaiting our arrival. In spite of the fact that I had consciously steeled myself against any display of negativity when I first came face to face with a large room full of handicapped children and young adults, the sight that awaited me was still a shock. Many of the room's occupants were terribly deformed, some only had stumps instead of arms or legs, and there was a little Girl without any arms at all, whose tiny hands were attached to her shoulders. Joe, Johnny, Stefan and I were introduced to everyone in the room, and we shook hands and stumps or patted anyone who didn't have anything to shake. There was a huge Boy with an enormous head, who had eyes the size of golf balls, that protruded from their sockets like those of a Chameleon. He had a small mouth, completely off centre that twisted up one side of his cheek as he attempted to smile. When I shook his hand, I discovered that it was more like a bunch of sweet potatoes than the hand of a Human being. I felt as though I was holding myself together fairly well until I heard the Governess say to another of the inmates,

"Well here he is Raymond; - Adrian is here to see you at last." And as I turned to greet my old friend I all but lost it. After our epic schoolyard brawl, Raymond and I had gradually become very good friends, and we had enjoyed many Boyhood adventures together. But the image that greeted me that day was one that I would have never recognized as my old friend if it hadn't been for the Governess' introduction. Raymond had been the strongest, and one of the most powerfully built Boys that I had ever met in my life, in spite of his ever deteriorating lower limbs. He was like Hercules compared to the rest of our gang. Now as I looked down at him lying in a wheelchair, instead of the 'Incredible Hulk' that I had expected to see, I found myself gazing at something that bore more resemblance to a ventriloquist's Dummy. My friend's huge muscular physique had completely shrunk away as though he had been cursed by a macabre spell of some Ancient Evil Sorcerer. Raymond beamed a smile at me that threatened to split his face in two, while my reaction to what had become of him threatened to split my heart in two. I seemed to require all the power of the Incredible Hulk himself, to prevent myself from crying my eyes out in front of everyone. One of the staff Ladies inadvertently came to my rescue, when she offered us all some light refreshment, and in the time it took us to accept her offer, also gave me the opportunity I needed to compose myself.

Everyone gathered around us, and we all chatted away as we nibbled fruit cake and sipped coffee. At first sight I would have imagined that attempting to converse with many of these inmates would be like trying to communicate with aliens from outer space, but I could not have been more mistaken. In spite of their appearance they were as sharp as razor blades. Also, looking around at the deformities and disfigurements borne by these poor, unfortunate people, I would have thought that this or any home for the handicapped would be one of the most miserable places on Earth. Once again, I could not have been more mistaken. It seemed that in less than half of the time it usually takes to break the ice in a roomful of strangers, here everyone was laughing, joking, even at one another's expense, in a way that initially made me cringe. But I soon warmed to their brand of humor, as no one appeared to take the slightest offense, and even seemed to revel in the attention that a barbed, but amusing quip afforded them, that caused them to laugh at themselves as loud as anyone else. The Boy with the eyes and the enormous head was hilarious, and almost every time anyone said anything about anything, he would cap it off with a one-liner that had us all in stitches, and then chuckled in a way that made us laugh even more. It suddenly crossed my mind that we wrestlers had come here to entertain these 'handicapped' people. Who were now not only entertaining us instead, but were going to be a hard act for us to follow. There was a small kid there, who was almost sitting on Raymond's lap in order to get right into the centre of our powwow. As my old friend and I recounted our past adventures. Apart from looking a little fragile and pale he appeared to be perfectly normal, and I imagined that he was probably the Son of one of the staff members. When I asked him what he was doing at the home, he told us that he had some condition that caused his bones to be extremely fragile,

"I'm breakin' me arms an' legs all the time," he stated, "I'm in plaster-of-Paris more often than not." Unfortunately for him, he was afflicted with three problems, which proved to be a very bad combination indeed. Firstly there was his chronically fragile bones, he was also frantically hyperactive, which was only exceeded by his extreme clumsiness. He didn't seem to be able to walk anywhere, and he would suddenly rush off while possessing the uncanny knack of bumping into everything remotely in his path like a missile in a pinball machine.

"He's a real rascal," the Governess assured us with a twinkle in her eye, "always falling down and always up to mischief, even on crutches and encased in plaster."

When I asked him his age, I was amazed to find out that he was only a little younger than I was, as I imagined that he was only about 12 or 13 years old.

"Bleed'n Doctors don't know nuffink," he stated with authority, "wiv' wot I got, I was supposed to be dead before I was 18, but I'll be 21 next Birfday, so that'll show them, won' it?!" We all agreed that it would, while marveling at this little guy's spirit, attitude and fortitude.

As we made our way to get changed into our ring gear, Johnny Peters suggested that as I had been such a big hit with everyone in the lounge, that Stefan and I should wrestle each other in the Main Event, while he and Joe would begin the show as the preliminary match. Johnny and Joe wrestled each other to a draw, while I squeezed out a close fought victory over Stefan. It may have been the smallest amount of people that I had ever wrestled in front of. But it may also have been the most enthusiastic, and we all enjoyed tremendous reaction from some of the most incredible people that I had ever met. After the matches, and before we left the home we all returned to the lounge to say our goodbyes. I had brought a stack of photos with me which I autographed for all who wanted one, the stack diminished so rapidly that Raymond almost panicked in fear that they would all be gone before he got one. I saved the last one for my old friend and I signed it 'To my friend Raymond, the only Welshman to beat me wrestling!'

I handed it to him, he read it and held his arms open as an invitation for a farewell hug, and as I complied I automatically braced myself against the power that I remembered my friend possessing. There was nothing there, that huge, brawny body had been transformed into a little bag of bones. I could have easily picked him up and walked away with him tucked under one arm, as he could have easily done to me less than a decade earlier. As I disengaged myself and waved goodbye, the tears streamed down Raymond's face like a mountain brook of our homeland, while I tried to swallow the lump in my throat that seemed to be impersonating a hard-boiled Ostrich egg.

We rode in silence back to Johnny's house to pick up Joe's car in order to continue our journey to London. Johnny thanked us again and wished us a safe trip. We were almost approaching the outskirts of London before anyone else uttered a syllable and then we all seemed to begin talking at the same time. To strike one wrestler dumb for more than two minutes is an accomplishment - three, during an entire trip is a miracle. But we all agreed, when we at last found our tongues, that in volunteering our services free of charge we had all got much more out of the bargain than we had delivered. In spite of the fact that we were all at the very peak of physical power and fitness we still found it so easy from time to time to moan and grizzle about any miniscule discomfort, inconvenience or mishap that may befall us. In contrast, our audience that afternoon who suffered every minute of their lives, with afflictions that would make a strong man cringe in their boots with horror. They accepted their lot and lived their lives with the courage, dignity, fortitude and a cheerful attitude, that was to us, both humbling and inspiring.

A quote by Ralph Waldo Emerson, had never before made more sense to me -

'It is one of the most beautiful compensations of this life, that no man can sincerely try to help another without helping himself.'

****

Stefan Milla may have been the first to experience my attitude adjustment after my being dubbed the 'Nature-Boy', but he was by no means the last. From that time on I began to tailor my response to my opponents styles and offensives more and more to my own advantage. For instance in the match that I had had with Tony Scarlo in Sheerness a few years earlier where I had been throwing Tony off the ropes with a series of monkey-flips – a throw that is performed by jumping off the mat at one's opponent and in one movement grabbing him behind his neck with both hands, while you place both feet into the front of his hip-joints. Then as you fall backwards onto the mat, you straighten out your legs as forcefully as possible in order to throw your opponent into a somersault right across the ring. I had been successful in launching Tony off the ropes in this manner for a number of consecutive throws, when at last he countered by grabbing both my ankles as I leapt on him, leaning back against the ropes, and then throwing my feet back over his head. This turned me upside-down into a somersault over Tony and the top rope and out into the audience. I remember landing arse first onto the heads of some of the spectators a number of rows back from ringside. As the chairs were fastened together I took out a couple of rows of chairs and their occupants before struggling over their bodies and seat wreckage in order to clamber back into the ring just in time to miss the ten-count. It was a scenario I had put in the back of my mind and had since been using it to my own advantage a lot after I had begun wrestling for Dale Martins. It may sound strange to think that I could take advantage, or make use of such a dangerous, but spectacular method of losing a wrestling match, so let me explain my psychology. The build up to that finish was the Monkey-flips. The more I did, and the more aggressively I did them, the more surprising and spectacular the finish would look. That would make it necessary for my opponent to take an almighty battering before he managed to pitch me over the ropes in a last, do or die effort. Although the result would see me flying upside-down though the air yards above the heads of the ringside spectators, and crash right into them several rows back with the impact that would cripple Sampson. I would then shock them all by bouncing right back up, and taking just enough time to struggle through the mêlée of chaos I had created with just enough time to miss the 10-count. Then I would leap aggressively back into the ring ready to wreck vengeance on my opponent. He in the meantime would barely manage to scrape himself off the canvas in time to beat the count after the terrible beating he had received at my hands right up until the second he had been 'lucky' enough to escape defeat with his very last ounce of strength. So imagine how good I would look, if I had just wrestled with say, someone like Alan Colbeck. At the end of the contest, even though my opponent would be getting his hand raised in victory, I would hit the ring rearing to carry the fight on, while the European Champion was fighting to remain standing after taking the amount of punishment that I had administered. It would make the spectators think that 'if' I had managed to get back into the ring just 2 seconds earlier, I would have been more than capable of dispatching my illustrious adversary with little trouble. This would raise my status to the level, if not beyond that of the European Champion. It would also make me appear to be the toughest of the tough, to be able to get up and back into the ring after taking such a devastating tumble, and still look to be in better fettle than my 'victorious' opponent. So spectacular was that finish in those days, that all the other wrestlers would come out of the dressing room to watch its execution, and speculate how many rows back from ringside I would make my crash landing. Now that may have been a great way to lose a match if I was wrestling someone like Alan Colbeck, Mick McManus, Jackie Pallo, and any of the other Main event wrestlers in my weight class. But, one night after a lackluster main event contest had concluded, Jack Dale came up to my opponent and I in the dressing room, and in an attempt to try to make it up to the fans with some extra last match action, he said to me,

"Adrian, do your 'over the top rope finish', it'll be a great way to end the night's wrestling." I would have been happy and flattered to comply - 'IF' I had been wrestling any of the top names in a main event contest. BUT, I was to wrestle another preliminary wrestler in a preliminary match. It would have suited Jack Dale's purpose to send the fans home more satisfied with a very spectacular finish, but I decided that it was time to kiss that spectacular finish goodbye for good as it no longer suited my purpose. My motives were purely selfish, as that night I was wrestling in the last match against Tony Costos from Cyprus. Tony was an excellent wrestler, exactly my weight and height, an amateur Champion of his own country, but had a lot less professional experience than I. Up until now I had never been told to lose a match to him, and I didn't intend losing to him tonight, or any time in the future. So when I replied to Jack Dale, I simply lied and said,

"I wish I could do it tonight Jack, but I hurt my back performing it a couple of nights ago and I don't think I'll be able to do it again until my back gets better. But it is a great move, so maybe Tony could do it instead?" Tony was standing facing me when I made the suggestion, and it amused me to see the cloud pass over his formally exuberant expression. I knew full well that I had just placed him in the lose – lose position. If Tony claimed that he wasn't able to emulate my move, he would be admitting that he lacked my skill and agility, so therefore shouldn't win a match against me anyway. If he claimed he could emulate my move he would have to lose the match in order to prove it. Before he was given time to think, Jack turned to Tony and enthusiastically asked him,

"Can you do it as good as Adrian does, Tony?"

"Yes, I think so," replied Tony - but without the enthusiasm. Jack seemed very pleased with the solution, but as he left the dressing room, Tony asked me to explain to him how I performed the move and I was happy to comply. Poor Tony wasn't happy at all, he was almost shitting himself with fright at the very thought of somersaulting headfirst out of the ring and flying upside down into the audience. After describing to my opponent what was involved, Tony became less and less enthused and came up with a compromise that he hoped I would approve of. He suggested that we could perform the very same lead up to the finish, but then execute the actual finale in the centre of the ring, instead of against the ropes where he would end up flying into the fans.

"I'll take a great bump," he promised, "but right in the middle of the ring."

"If we do it that way, I will have to pin you after you take the bump, in order to win the match." I told him, pretending to appear not too pleased with his compromise.

"That's okay with me," he assured me, and added, "I hope you don't mind?"

With the sigh of a martyr, I agreed that if he felt unsafe going over the top rope, we could do it the less spectacular way in the middle of the ring as he suggested. Although I feigned disappointment, I was secretly ecstatic, as I realized that Tony had missed the whole point behind the risky finish. It was a very dangerous move, but I had been more than willing to take the risk, as even when I lost a match with it, the way I did it made me look more like the winner than the winner. Even if he'd been regarded as the best wrestler in the World. It was designed to make the spectators think that 'if' I had managed to get back into the ring just seconds earlier, it would be me who would have had their hand raised in victory. The way Tony wanted to do it would make me look like Superman at the end of the match rather than a victor who was hardly capable of raising his hand in victory after the beating he had taken. Plus, there is no excuse for losing when you get pinned right in the middle of the ring, other than the fact that you have been beaten by a superior wrestler. When we came towards the conclusion of our match, I purposely allowed Tony to beat the living crap out of me. Then when we went into the Monkey-flip routine I was hurled all over the ring in somersault after somersault. Just when it looked as though I couldn't possibly survive another one, I grabbed him bodily as he leapt at me and flung him backwards over my head behind me. Then while Tony was still in en-route towards the canvas, I launched myself into a backward twisting dive. For one long second we both hovered in mid air before Tony crashed onto his back on the mat and I simultaneously crashed down on top of him to score the winning pin-fall. The crowd reaction was tremendous, 'more than enough to satisfy them and Jack Dale, with plenty left over for me.' I thought. Back in the dressing room after the match, Tony was delighted by the enormous amount of crowed response he had generated during the severe beating he had administered against me leading up to my victory. I in turn was delighted that now instead of affording me a spectacular loss, the finish now afforded me a very spectacular victory. I was even more delighted, when Tony, who seemed to be under the impression that I had just done him a favor, suggested hopefully that we might use that finish whenever we wrestled against each other in the future. With the air of 'okay Tony, but you owe me one' I kindly granted his wish.

Peter Szakacs may have been considered the less accomplished of the two brothers from Transylvania, who later moved to Hungary, but was, nevertheless a very skilled wrestler in his own right, and was a former Amateur title holder of his adopted country. His big brother Tibor was in the Heavyweight division, and as well as winning a silver medal at the 1954 World Games was the possessor of a very unique style of wrestling. Some of his methods of escaping from seemingly unbreakable submission holds had to be seen to be believed. Although they were both refugees, it was Peter who was reputed to have been a very brave and aggressive member of his country's Freedom Fighters during the Hungarian Revolution. A revolution that left 250,000 of Hungary's populace dead, and an estimated 200,000 refugees who fled their country in order to avoid torture, imprisonment or execution. Before he became a refugee himself, Peter was involved in street battles throughout the city of Budapest, fighting against Pro-Soviet Communists, State Security Police and Soviet Troops. Firing through the windows of houses, speeding cars and hurling Molotov Cocktails at Soviet Tanks.

In my earlier matches against Peter Szakacs he would always emerge the winner, but lately much to Peter's chagrin I had been awarded an occasional draw. True to many competitors tradition in those days, I found that he would be much more generous with the amount that I got out of a match on the occasions when he was the eventual winner than the odd occasion when I was lucky enough to score a draw. In a normal match Peter was energetic, enthusiastic and gave good value for money, but if the match was a draw he would become very greedy, or lethargic and lackadaisical. His obvious lack of interest in the match was very contagious, and would soon be echoed by the audience. Add to that the revolting and monotonous grunting and scraping his throat noise that he made all through his contests, whether he won, lost or drew and it was easy to discover the reason why Peter Szakacs was not at the top of my favorite opponent list. I was half way through a contest with him in Cheltenham one night, and due to the fact that Peter had been told to win, we had been enjoying a comparatively good match. I was laying on the mat attempting to wrestle my way out of the hold I was in when all of a sudden I became aware that he became more domineering and much stiffer to wrestle against. I also noticed that his grunting and scraping noise had been replaced by a chucking, panting sound. Like the sound I would imagine a Dog would make, if Dogs were capable of laughing. I had tried a number of methods of escape, and then of reversing the hold I was in, but Peter forcefully blocked each attempt, chuckling more and more as each of my escapes or counters failed. By now I had managed to maneuver myself into a sitting position while Peter was kneeling behind me, with one of my arms and my head secured in a very uncomfortable version of a Chicken-wing. Even though I was in a position that hampered my vision as well as my movement, as I twisted around in order to attempt another counter I realized that my opponent was directing all his attention to the corner of the arena closest to the dressing room. I managed to focus into the corner that Peter seemed to be playing to, and as I recognized the occupants of the corner, this whole scenario became infuriatingly clear. Amongst the group of wrestlers watching our match were 3 very prominent members of Billy Riley's famous Wigan Gym. Cliff Beaumont, Jimmy Hart and Jack Dempsey. The 3 denizens of the 'Snake-pit' were enjoying my frustration and discomfort immensely, as Szakacs enthusiastically displayed his extensive knowledge of shoot wrestling, using me as a demonstration dummy, as he attempted to slide me from one painful position into a tighter one yet. I didn't like the little game he was playing at my expense one little bit, and felt as though he had been showing off and I had been on the receiving end of the action long enough. But as I attempted to gently ease myself out of the hold and counter him just one more time, with a loud throaty chuckle he again very forcefully blocked my escape. THAT WAS IT!!! If these Lancashire wrestlers want to be entertained, so be it, for their benefit as well as my own, I used the move that Jack Dale had told me was called a Lancashire-turn. I exploded out of Peter Szakacs' grasp, I spun around behind him and as he was still in a kneeling position I used the full impetus of my spin as I smashed my right knee hard into Szakacs' back. The air hissed out of his body, making a more disconcerting sound than he usually made, as the powerful blow pitched my opponent face first into the mat where he remained as the referee tolled the count of 10 to end the match in my favor. As Peter Szakacs was being carried back to the dressing room I saw the 3 Wiganers splitting their sides with glee, but this time it was at my opponents expense not mine.

The heavy blow to Szakacs' back, cracked and separated some of his ribs. Although this painful injury kept my opponent out of the ring for more than a couple of weeks, he didn't complain until after I had struck out again. The second incident was a complete accident, due partially to Peter's posture. He always seemed to have his neck parallel to the ground with his head and face stuck out a neck's length in front of his body when he was on his feet and ready to wrestle. Szakacs was also a notorious spoiler in the ring and seemed to derive much satisfaction in ruining his opponent's best moves. In order to stop him spinning away from a second dropkick I threw at him - as he had the first one that I had attempted to deliver, I first grabbed one of his wrists to anchor him in place. This maneuver prevented his fast escape, but also gave me much less space in which to bring up both my feet for the kick that I intended aiming high on Peter's chest. But with his face thrust forward, thanks to his bad posture the bottom of my boots smashed into Szakacs' nose breaking it amidst a fountain of blood. This gave me yet another unscheduled victory over an opponent I was meant to lose to, again Peter didn't complain that night. The next night Peter Szakacs was wrestling in a different town against another opponent, but within a couple of minutes of the very first round, without it even being touched Peter's nose began to bleed like a tap pouring water. The next night the same thing happened, then the night after that. Once again Szakacs had to take time off from wrestling in order to heal, which obviously cost him a lot of money. The night he made his return to the ring his nose bled again, but eventually it healed up and things got back to normal for him. During this period our paths hadn't crossed, but the word got back to me that Peter Szakacs had been threatening severe revenge. It was at that time that I first learned of Peter's violent reputation during The Hungarian Revolution, from wrestlers who wanted to add as much spice to the relish of their warning to me of our pending confrontation. The next occasion that I came face to face with Szakacs couldn't have come at a worse time.

Dad had come to London to visit Jean and me and he was present when Szakacs and I met. There was not enough room at our flat in Streatham, for Dad to be able to stay with us. So I had arranged for him to stay at a house that the French wrestler, Jean Morandi and his Wife kept for Jack Dale on Brixton Hill, in which foreign wrestlers were boarded when in Britain wrestling for Dale Martins. No one outside the wrestling business were normally allowed to stay at the house, or to travel in Dale Martin's vans. But when Jean Morandi learned that his new visitor was my Dad, as a special favor he arranged with the office for Dad to accompany the wrestlers, including myself to an afternoon show which was held in a Football Stadium in a town near Reading. Dad and I were sitting in the van as it stood in the car park in front of the office waiting to leave. I had already introduced him to all the other wrestlers by the time the driver had started up the van to begin our journey. That was when Peter Szakacs, who was also on the card entered the van just as it was about to leave.

"Hey Peter," I called to him, "this is my Father – and this is Peter Szakacs." I told Dad in way of introduction. Ignoring both Dad and the introduction, Szakacs glared at me with all the hostility his face could muster,

"Today I break your nose and your arms and your leg!" he snarled.

"Why would you want to do that?" I asked him, as I attempted to subdue the angry and startled expression that I could feel beginning to transform my face into a mirror image of my oppressor's.

"You break my nose and I lose a lot of money - every time I try to wrestle my nose bleed everywhere, now I break your nose – and your leg!" He added.

"That was an accident Peter." I told him, but he just gave me a last grimace of shear loathing before he sat down. Strangely enough, he never mentioned the time when I had cracked his ribs and put him out of wrestling for a period, and that had been done on purpose. It would have been impossible to argue my point with Szakacs while Dad was present without compromising the very essence of our profession. Plus the mood he was in, was completely incompatible with a parley anyway, instead and in order to completely change the subject and the atmosphere, I said to Dad,

"I'll bet you remember this one." And much to Dad's delight, I began singing hymn after hymn that I had learned from the time I had began attending the much dreaded 'Tabernacle'. All the wrestlers except Szakacs, seemed both surprised and amused by the attitude I had adopted, and I smiled as angelically as I could at Szakacs when he occasionally attempted to bore a hole through me with the hot hatred in his eyes. He refused to acknowledge my existence as I directed the verse from 'To be a Pilgrim' especially to him in a very loud strong voice that goes,

"He who would valiant be against all disaster,
Let him in constancy follow the Master.
There's no discouragement, that makes him once relent,
Theirs is a vow intent, to be a Pilgrim.
Those who beset him down with dismal stories,
Do but themselves confound his strength the more is.
No foe could stay his might, Though he with giants fight,
He will make good his right, To be a Pilgrim."

My singing seemed to have the desired effect on everyone, Dad, the other wrestlers, myself and most of all Peter Szakacs. Both Szakacs and I had been under the impression that we were wrestling each other that afternoon, but when we arrived at the Football Stadium we found that Szakacs was wrestling against 'Iron Jaw' Joe Murphy, and I was wrestling against Len Wilding. So the big buildup that had occurred since we left London turned out to be a chronic anticlimax. I can't say that under the circumstances I was disappointed that our pending confrontation had been put on hold. Normally I prefer to clear the air one way or another immediately, but with Dad in tow I was glad of the temporary postponement. Once again Peter Szakacs and I went through a period of a couple of months with no contact between us at all. I didn't see him again until we were scheduled to wrestle against each other in the seaside town of Bognor Regis. As I walked into the dressing room, the first eye contact I made with anyone was with Szakacs himself, and was disconcerted by the fact that he had managed to perfectly preserve the exact hot and hateful expression he had worn when he had threatened me in Dale's van. It was as though he had been keeping it in the oven for this occasion. I forbade my own expression to betray any emotion at all, and without acknowledging him in any way, I chose a seat as far away from him as possible on which to sit while I got changed into my ring wear. I was still lacing my boots when that night's M C entered the dressing room to tell all the contestants which match they would be wrestling in, and the results of each match. Szakacs and I would be wrestling each other to a draw in the last match we were told. Szakacs allowed everyone to witness an expression of displeasure at the news, and then totally ignored me for the rest of the night. Normally before their match, two opposing wrestlers will discuss a few details, such as what rounds they will take their falls or submissions in, and what pin-fall or submission they will use. Szakacs' continued silence spoke volumes and his indifference to my very existence spoke more concisely of his future intentions than any threats he may have issued. The time dragged on as the clock ticked away the seconds slower and slower. By the time the main event match was underway all the other wrestlers were either out in the arena watching the wrestling, or had left and gone home. That left just Szakacs and myself in the dressing room, still he seemed to pretend that I was completely invisible. At last it was our time to enter the ring and settle things once and for all; as yet I hadn't formed any plan of attack or defense, and decided to play it by ear. I reminded myself of my own motto - never box a boxer and never wrestle a wrestler, various scenarios were revolving through my head. Although I knew that my own wrestling skills had improved by leaps and bounds, especially as a result of the time I had spent training with Mile Dimitri. But I still didn't know how they would stack up against a National Champion of Hungary, a country that was World renowned for the great skill and ability of its wrestlers. Well, as I have already stated, if I have to fight a Shark I'll fight it on the beach rather than in the ocean. I believed that Szakacs' only chance of breaking my nose, arms and legs, as he had threatened to do, was if I was dumb enough to play his game. The only way I had continued to survive when I boxed against a superior Boxer when I fought on the Fairground Boxing Booth, was by fighting in the most unorthodox manner that I was capable of employing. That was exactly what I was going to have to do tonight. I made my mind up there and then to defend myself in any way I could, whether it could be deemed as wrestling or not. Even if I got disqualified for my efforts, as long as it got me out of the ring and back to the dressing room in one piece, that would be all that really mattered. I also knew full well that if I did get out of the ring comparatively unscathed, that Szakacs would be furious. - Furious enough, I hoped to either attack me in the dressing room, or better still agree to finish our disagreement in some nearby back alley, which had always been one of my own favorite playgrounds.

After I entered our battleground I looked across the ring at my opponent, who it seemed in order to display his utter distain for his opponent stood in his corner with his back to me. He only turned to wave to the audience when introduced, and then once again turned to face his own corner with both his hands resting on the top rope.

'Well this is it.' I thought, as the bell sounded to begin the match, and I shot straight out of my corner, leapt high into the air, and as Szakacs turned around both my feet smashed right into his face. In an atom of a second the very air between my face and the glaring ring lights was clouded by a pink mist, as the blood exploded out of Szakacs' face and liberally be-speckled me, the wrestling mat and the ringside spectators. My adversary crumpled back into his corner like a broken rag doll. I scrambled back up to my feet in a flash waiting for Szakacs' reaction to my audacious attack, but there was no reaction whatsoever. Nor would there be, the only movement coming from my downed opponent was in the torrents of blood cascading down his chest after gushing out of his re-broken and mangled nose. The match was over within seconds of the first round, and there was not a single ounce of fight left in my would-be bully of an opponent at all. I described my attack as audacious, and it was, as anyone who fights or has wrestled in a 'straight' match will tell you that the chances of actually delivering a successful dropkick during a real fight is extremely unlikely. Due to his latest injury, and another spell out of wrestling as a result, it was a long time before Szakacs' and my paths crossed again. When next we did meet, in complete contrast to what I expected, there were no threats, or displays of hostility from him whatsoever. In fact I could never, ever remember Szakacs being so amiable towards me before. In spite of the fact that I was awarded my very first official victory over Szakacs, outside the ring he became quite friendly. Inside the ring he was still the same old stiff, awkward spoiler that he ever was, more so in fact, as now if we didn't wrestle to a drawn decision, it was me rather than Szakacs who usually won the match. I was happy that the hostility between us had at last seemed to resolve itself, and that we were now on a much friendlier footing than ever before. Did I ever come to trust Peter Szakacs in the ring as a result – What! Are you nuts?!

Son of veteran wrestler Vic Hessel and younger Brother to Bert Royal, Vic Faulkner must have been a firm believer in the saying that attack was the best method of defense. Whenever the opening bell sounded in a contest in which he was engaged, he would explode out of his corner and across the ring like a rocket on pep-pills. His first move was to slam his opponent into the ropes, and add the resulting bounce to the impetus needed to hurl his unlucky adversary into a spectacular somersault which would land him flat on his back right across the ring. Then before his shaken foe had hardly regained his feet, here comes the flashing Faulkner hurtling towards him to repeat that maneuver again, then again and again, then yet again. In fact he would have been very happy to spend the whole of the first round, and probably the second round too bouncing his hapless opponent off the ropes to slam him each time with a bone jarring crash landing. During the action all the wrestling fans would be cheering Vic like crazy, and only reach a crescendo when his opponent was hanging on the ropes exhausted. In my early matches against Vic Faulkner in spite of the fact that I seemed to be blessed with boundless energy, by the time the match concluded I would hardly have enough strength left to stagger groggily back to the dressing room. It was Stefan Milla, who not only gave me the remedy on how best to combat that particular problem; it also gave me a formula that began to transform my wrestling style, and eventually my very wrestling image. Stressing extreme fatigue one night as I flopped down into a chair in the dressing room after a particularly hectic bout with Vic, Stefan casually past off my complaint when he suggested,

"Why don't you do a roll up now and again instead of taking all those frightful bumps?" – AND THAT WAS IT! From that time on whenever I wrestled against Vic, every time he hurled me off the ropes, which he would do without fail a dozen times or more to begin our match. Instead of flying in a somersault and land in a heap with a resounding crash right across the other side of the ring. Which made Vic look good, I would use the impetus of his throw while I dived into a spectacular roll-up that would bring me gracefully and effortlessly right back up to my feet, which made me look good. Not only was that strategy much less damaging and exhausting, it was now me instead of Vic who received all the cheers from the audience in appreciation of such a clever counter-move. Plus, this way it probably took more effort for him to throw me off the ropes than it cost me to roll up from his throw. In fact, I would now have to wait a split second standing up against the ropes for Vic to charge over and throw me again.

That simple strategy made all the difference, now instead of dreading my increasingly frequent matches against Vic Faulkner, I looked forward to them. Now there was now no way on earth, that even a human dynamo like Vic could exhaust me. I explored more and more ways of turning Vic Faulkner's very extensive arsenal to my own advantage. Very soon I found ways of using my roll-ups in order to counter many other throws from many other angles from many other wrestlers. Head-mares, flying-mares, arm-drags. I even began learning to land on my feet whilst taking a back-drop, or a monkey-flip, which resulted in much less wear and tear on the body and much more appreciation for my new found skills from the wrestling fans. From that time on I began to explore methods from which I could exploit the other wrestler's tactics to my own advantage. A prime example was during my matches with another great Hungarian wrestler, Kalman Gaston. Even as a young schoolboy he was regarded as an exceptional wrestler, winning the Budapest Junior Championship on three occasions. He joined the famous Honved Wrestling Club where he learned Greco-Roman style, and then went on to become National Middleweight Champion and a member of the Hungarian team who wrestled in Moscow in 1955. Kalman was regarded by Dale Martins to possess 'Superstar' potential from the first time Jack Dale watched his performance in the ring. Standing 6 feet tall, he was extremely handsome, bearing a very strong resemblance to Roger Moore, who at that time was enjoying great success and fame playing the title roll in the TV series 'The Saint'. Dale Martins exploited Kalman's look-alike to Roger Moore's Saint for all they were worth. They even put halos above his head in all the publicity photographs that appeared on their posters and programs. His fine physique and movie star good looks acted as a very powerful magnet to droves of young Ladies who would help to swell the audience to full arena capacity wherever he appeared. Add to that Kalman's wrestling pedigree, including the fact that he was an-ex amateur champion, a status which Jack Dale set huge store by, and wrestling's answer to Roger Moore was on the fast track to wrestling superstardom. In order to achieve their objective, it was crucial that Kalman was portrayed as a winner. And so armed with the invincible 'office hold' he cut a swath through all competition, using the Greco-Roman Belly-to-belly suplex followed by a body-press pin-fall as his devastating patent finish. When I first met Kalman we instantly became friends and spent much of our training periods together. At that time he was living in a one roomed flat overlooking the market in Brixton. He would often visit our flat in Streatham for a meal before we went off to the gym or to the office in order to catch their transport to the various wrestling venues. We were at the YMCA one morning, and after an hour or so lifting weights I was attracted down to the wrestling mats by the sight of a wrestler who I had never seen before. What had initially caught my attention was the Herculean shape this guy was in. He couldn't have been any more than a couple of inches taller than me, but I had never before seen so much muscle packed onto a man of that height. As I approached him I recognized an Aussie accent when he asked,

"D'ya wanna wrestle mate?!"

"Certainly mate." I replied, and we both stepped onto the mat and got stuck right into one brutal confrontation, a confrontation which I believe surprised both of us. Although this massive Australian must have outweighed me by at least 50 pounds I was still amazed by his strength. Usually, even when pitted against larger opponents I could shock them severely with my superior strength, and whenever I won a contest against a more skillful adversary, it was my superior strength that I had to thank for my victory. On this occasion the shoe was on the other foot. I, it seemed was a much more technically skillful wrestler, and my opponent was as strong as a Bull on steroids. The result was that struggle as we may, neither of us could do anything with the other. I was too smart for him, and though I was loathe to admit it, he was too strong for me. We tore and ripped at each other for what seemed hours with neither of us gaining any advantage, or even to be capable of taking one another off our feet. This description of our battle probably makes the contest sound much more exciting than it was, as Kalman, who by now was standing by the edge of the mat watching our struggle, seemed to be bored out of his skull.

"C'mon Ade," he yawned, "how much longer are you going to be?"

"As long as it takes." I told him irritably, as I tried for the umpteenth time, and failed yet again to take this Aussie powerhouse off his feet. Even above the heavy breathing, and guttural grunts of exertion issued from the lungs and throats of my adversary and myself I could hear Kalman's loud, exaggerated sighs of impatience. That coupled with my frustration was really beginning to piss me off. Kalman had claimed he was hungry and wanted to go and eat, but I already had my teeth fastened into something that was proving too hard to chew, but I wouldn't let it go, never mind how long it took. I was too skillful, my opponent was too strong, this was a brand new experience for me and I wanted to see it through to the very end. Like a Dog with a bone I refused to let it go, so we battled on and on and on. At last it seemed Kalman could stand no more of it, he strode onto the mat, pushed me aside and exclaimed,

"Here, let me show you how it's done!" I was appalled by his audacity, and the only reason I relinquished my unbeatable opponent to Kalman was to watch my brash Hungarian friend being taken down a peg or two.

'If this Aussie powerhouse is too strong for me, cocky Kalman is really about to get his comeuppance in spades.' I thought. If I hadn't seen what happened next with my own eyes I would not have believed it. In fact, in spite of seeing it with my own eyes, I still couldn't believe it! Bulling straight into the muscle-bound Australian, Kalman ripped him off the mat with the ease it would have taken to snatch a Baby out of its crib. He deposited him right off the mat onto the unyielding hardwood floor. Without a split seconds hesitation he dived after him and hurled him off the floor back onto the mat with a repeat of his vicious suplex. As he landed on the back of his head Kalman was there again, and again he sent the battered mountain of muscle back into orbit. This maneuver was repeated over and over, the

Australian wasn't even given the opportunity to stand up or draw a breath. Kalman would grab him right off the mat and smash him right back into it, by hurling himself backwards and using his opponent to break his fall, as he used his opponents head to bruise the canvas. To say I was impressed was the understatement of the decade. I was awestruck. Instead of the attitude adjustment that I thought Kalman would receive, and justly deserved, he did more to the other wrestler in two or three minutes than I came within a mile of accomplishing in an hour or more of grueling, gut wrenching grappling. Where neither I, or my opponent had given or gained the slightest quarter. I looked down on the crumpled figure of my former adversary laying helplessly on the mat, and felt as though I owed him an apology for inadvertently causing the state in which he now found himself. But I don't think he would have heard me if I had, as he now seemed to be completely out of it. I couldn't tell who sustained the most damage, my battered and bruised former opponent, or my bruised and battered ego.

Another example of Kalman's fighting prowess occurred one time after the show in The Colston Hall had concluded for the night, and all the other wrestlers were sitting in the van waiting impatiently to leave. However, there was no sign of the Hungarian Heartthrob whose only major weakness was the weaker-sex, and true to form he was once again missing-in-action.

Sometimes when there was a shortage of van drivers available one of the wrestlers on the card would be asked to drive the van instead. It was a coveted job, owing to the fact that the driver would be paid an extra 2 pounds wages. On this occasion one of Kalman's fellow countrymen, Peter Szakacs was the designated driver, and like all wrestlers, when the wrestling was over, Peter was anxious to go home. So, after waiting for a considerable period for Kalman, who was still a no show, Szakacs decided to leave him in Bristol and drive back to London without him. An hour and a half later all the wrestlers were lining up at the counter of a late night café waiting to order their meals, when Kalman who had managed to thumb a lift to the café burst in. He said something that sounded extremely unpleasant in Hungarian, before he went ape-shit on poor Peter Szakacs, and beat him into a heap of insensibility within about 5 minutes. By the time Kalman had finished with Peter, he was in such a sorry state that Kalman had to drive the van the rest of the way to London. Kalman was a very good friend, as well as an extremely proficient wrestler. But I still resented having to sacrifice my own wrestling ambitions by losing to a less experienced professional in order to make him appear to be a wrestling superstar. I also hated the method Kalman used to score his victories. I had witnessed first hand what a devastating weapon the suplex is in the hands of an expert like Kalman, on the day he hurled the Australian juggernaut around the mat at the YMCA as though he were a soft toy. The first time I experienced it myself, I was torn off the mat and sent flying over Kalman's body as he dropped back into a wrestler's bridge, with such velocity that I felt as though all the blood in my body had been left where I had been standing in the ring a micro-second before when Kalman had grabbed hold of me. Then he would land lightly on top of his head, and use the impetus, while still holding onto his opponent who had broken Kalman's fall, with what ever part of his body hit the mat first. He would then slide over on top of him to score his victory pin fall. I think I may have been on the receiving end of Kalman's super-suplex victories about 2 or 3 times before. When one night we were wrestling each other, and had all too soon reached the spot where once again I would be sent flying helplessly upside-down into orbit. I was facing Kalman when he grabbed both of my arms under both his armpits, and prepared for takeoff, when a vivid picture of the Big Aussie's head bouncing off the wrestling mat flashed through my mind. Instinctively I searched for a way to protect my own head during my flight, and more especially during my landing. As Kalman was 5 inches taller than me, I found it easy to place the top off my head under Kalman's chin within a split second of blast-off. The result was, that as Kalman landed back on his head in a wrestler's bridge, the top of my head slammed into the underneath of Kalman's jaw and he went out like a light. I scrambled back to my feet out of the corner of the ring, where I had landed like a sack of shit, and was ready to commence battle. But looking down at my opponent I immediately realized that there was not going to be any commencing.

"Get down and cuddle him." Growled Lou Marco, who was the self anointed Dale Martin's premier referee. When the referee told me to get down and cuddle my opponent, he didn't mean that literally. What he wanted me to do was to dive down onto Kalman and take a hold on him, which incidentally is illegal in Europe after one opponent has actually broken contact with the other. The fact that I would be taking an illegal hold, would give the referee an excuse to order me to relinquish it at once, and let my opponent go. Of course to aid the referee's scheme I would act reluctant to comply, which would cause an argument between us. That would give an unconscious adversary more time to recover. On this occasion I chose to go deaf, but instead of counting over my fallen opponent as he was supposed to do, Lou Marco chased after me and repeated, "Get down and cuddle him!"

"What – and take another bloody suplex – fuck that!!!" I replied.

As I refused to comply, Lou Marco had no alternative but to count Kalman out, which gave me an unscheduled knockout victory, instead of a loss as another victim of Kalman's patent suplex. After both Kalman and I had returned to the dressing-room, and he had recovered consciousness, I had fully expected him to be very upset by the method I had utilized to reverse the final verdict of our contest in my favor. But much to my delight he didn't have a clue what had happened to him. In fact it had happened so quickly that even Lou Marco was unaware of what had actually caused the knockout. He thought that Kalman had knocked himself out by bridging back too violently onto his head as he attempted to perform his big finish. I knew exactly what happened, but decided to keep it as my own little secret, and I wondered if I could pull it off again. I tried and it worked, which gave me a lot of much needed glory by continually beating a wrestler who was being groomed by Dale Martins to beat almost everyone else in the middleweight division. That was the good news - the bad news was that a secret in the wrestling business is at the highest pinnacle on the endangered species list, and doesn't last. All the other wrestlers wanted to know how I was achieving my victories, and all they had to do was watch our match to discover the secret. They were far too smart for me to be able to fool them too. Very soon others were not only utilizing my discovery to achieve the same result, but had also discovered another method of exploiting Kalman's Achilles' heel. Kalman was so highly skilled in the Greco-Roman style of wrestling, where holds are only allowed above the waist, that making use of the much dreaded suplex as the most spectacular mainstay of that sport is mandatory. In order to excel in its execution a wrestler has to learn to bridge – bridge – bridge. In fact Kalman had become so good at his chosen sport that bridging was second nature to him, - a habit. But, in pro Freestyle wrestling his inborn instinct to bridge turned out to be a very bad habit indeed. Most all pro wrestlers used the wrestler's bridge as a neck strengthening exercise, as well as a method of keeping both shoulders off the mat, to avoid being pinned. But, Kalman's style was so finely tuned that he instinctively attempted to land in a bridge position even when he was hurled upside-down across the ring after taking a beal off the ropes. With the result he would dive about 6 feet in the air and land right on top of his head in the middle of the ring knocking himself out in the process. It did not take very long for every wrestler who resented loosing to Kalman, to take advantage and exploit this glaring flaw in the handsome Hungarian's arsenal for all they were worth. The result was that in spite of being a very fine wrestler indeed, Kalman was never destined to become the sensational new superstar that Dale Martins had intended him to be.

There were also many wrestlers who I seemed to be wrestling on a regular basis whose style was almost impossible to exploit to my own advantage. Pasquale Salvo was a rough, tough, Anglo-Italian ex-boxer from Bermondsey; he was extremely stiff and awkward to wrestle with. 'Stiff' was how wrestlers were described who were either unwilling or unable to relax in the ring. They seemed incapable of applying a hold or delivering a kick or a blow, at anything less than full force, and Salvo was definitely one of them. Although his wrestling skills were very basic, relying wholly on roughhouse tactics, he usually emerged as the winner of a contest, unless he was matched against one of Dale's main draws; this was due to the fact that he promoted Bermondsey Baths Hall for Dale Martins. So Salvo would mostly be awarded the 'office hold' which in his case was a devastating overhand forearm smash, which he would hurl from the backyard and all but knock his opponent's head right off his shoulders. Most of the matches I had against Pasquale Salvo at that time would end with the same result. I would score a pin-fall on him in one of the earlier rounds, and then he would knock me out at the finish with his horrible face mashing forearm smash. Every time he ever hit me with his very painful, patent forearm smash, the point of his elbow would strike the left side of my jaw with such force that it would all but dislocate it, and I would experience an excruciating pain in my left ear. It felt as though a red-hot poker had been violently thrust into it with all the force of a battering-ram. The impact would almost turn me upside down as I'd crash down onto the canvas, and I would lay in agony where I would only be able to listen with my right ear to the referee, as he doled out the dreaded 10 count. I went through a period where I seemed to be wrestling against Pasquale every Wednesday night. The continual blows I received on my jaw made the inside of my left ear ache so badly when I chewed my food, that it would still be impossible for me to eat my favorite meal. Which consisted of meat – meat and meat for my next Sunday dinner without suffering the initial agony all over again. It would mostly take until the middle of the next week for the pain to begin to subside, then here we go again. Its Wednesday night and Pasquale is there to knock it back out again. As I have already explained, if any wrestler causes me any injury or excessive pain, I believe in returning it with interest. But the very fact that the injury and pain I was receiving on a too regular basis from Salvo, marked the end of the match, there was no opportunity to repay the debt on the same night. I had noticed that as Pasquale threw his forearm smash, he made a very loud roar and closed his eyes just before impact. Other wrestlers had also noticed this trait, and joked that it was last second compassion on Pasquale's part, as he couldn't bear to see the terrified horror of anticipation etched on his opponent's face, as his steel hard elbow hurtled towards them. And that was a joke, as Pasquale at the best of times was about as compassionate as Genghis Khan with a bad toothache.

Another wrestler who was wrestling against Salvo regularly, and suffering in exactly the same way, was young Mick McMichael from Doncaster. Mick who was also aware that Salvo closed his eyes as he threw the elbow, came up with a game plan designed to protect his jaw. The plan simply comprised of him throwing his own left forearm up vertically to block the blow in a split second before impact. He would then take a big bump back onto the mat, and take the 10 count, while Pasquale, whose eyes had been closed as the elbow struck would be unaware that it had been Mick's forearm and not his jaw that had taken the impact. Well, that had been Mick McMichael's clever little plan. Unfortunately for him, Pasquale's forearm smash was delivered with such force that Mick's own forearm crashed back into his face and broke his nose. Although I must admit that Mick McMichael's little game plan left a lot to be desired, it gave me food for thought and I came up with what I thought would be a much better idea.

The very next time I wrestled against Pasquale, at the crucial moment as he let out his big roar, and threw his devastating forearm I leapt high into the air, with the idea that instead of his forearm smashing my jaw it would strike me high on my chest. The force I knew would be more than sufficient to knock me right back across the ring. I would land flat on my back in a cosmetically spectacular and convincing fashion, where I would lay comfortably until the referee tolled the 10 count and everyone – including me for a change would be happy. BUT – unfortunately for me I didn't jump quite high enough, quite quick enough, and instead of hitting me high on the chest as I had planned, his elbow exploded right into my throat. I thought that I had completely swallowed my Adam's Apple as I landed on the mat with a thud on the back of my head. At first I thought I was dead, and then as I realized that I wasn't that lucky. I wondered if I would die before or after the referee finished his count. Even in my dazed and fuddled brain I knew I had to go back to the drawing board. My usual reaction to any excessive pain suffered at the hands of my opponent was immediate retaliation, designed to let him know that it would be painful for him next, if he hurt me first. My dilemma with Salvo was, that I couldn't retaliate after he'd smashed my jaw, as that was what ended the match. I decided that I would have to do something while I still had teeth and a whole lower jaw to house them in. The plan that I finally decided to adopt was anything but perfect, but it was the best I could come up with under those circumstances. There was a move that I often used to soften up an opponent before I pinned or submitted him that went like this. First I would either grab his left wrist with my right hand, or link the fingers of my right hand with the fingers of my opponent's left hand in order to anchor him where he was standing. Then as I was facing him I would crouch slightly and with my right hand pull my opponent into a likewise position. That would make it very easy to step over his secured left arm with my left foot which would turn my back towards him, and in the same movement I would lash out backwards so that the flat sole of my right boot would land high on my opponent's chest sending him crashing to the canvas. Then as my opponent staggered back to his feet I would be there ready to pounce on him and take my pin-fall or submission. I did have a slight modification if my opponent had done anything to piss me off prior to the kick, I would aim for his face with my foot instead of his chest. As I said, my plan wasn't perfect, as I would have to wait until my next match with Salvo in order to retaliate rather than scoring instant revenge. It also meant that Pasquale would often hit me even harder – if that was possible, in retaliation to the hard kick that I had just administered to his chops. This scenario really did present me with a dilemma, but I was determined to get revenge for my pain, even if I had to wait for another match to get it. I was also determined that I would not be the first one to complain to the other concerning the extra injury and pain we were inflicting on each other. I did eventually get satisfaction of sorts, one night after a particularly brutal match where I had almost kicked Pasquale's head out of the arena, and then he had hit my jaw so hard with his elbow that my head must have spun around faster and more times than Linda Blair's did in 'The Exorcist.'

As soon as we both re-entered the dressing room Salvo said,

"Hey Street, that fuckin' back kick of yours almost knocked all my fuckin' teeth out, - come here, let my show you how to do it properly!" I walked over to him and as he took my arm he went through the motions and explained how to modify the movement to a much less damaging version. "There you are," he explained, "if you kick back it'll be a lot better if you aim for my upper chest."

"Good idea," I replied, "maybe you could throw your fucking big elbow the same way."

"Don't be fuckin' stupid," he retorted, "that's my fuckin' big finish."

"And very painful it is too," I told him, "maybe we could both use a bit of modification."

"You're fuckin' nuts!" he told me as he walked off. In this story, I have been attempting to tell how I gradually progressed and came to grips with various problems as they presented themselves. This problem with Salvo unfortunately did not dissolve overnight, he would hit me just as hard, then I would attempt to kick him even harder. Even though I would often have to wait a week or two to do it, and the only satisfaction that I derived from the whole episode was, that I had succeeded in making Pasquale complain about it before I did.

As I said there were many wrestlers whose styles were very difficult to exploit, the most glaring example of these was Cliff Beaumont, who also wrestled sometimes under the name of Cliff Belshaw. Whether it was Beaumont, or Belshaw, he was better known to all the wrestlers who ever entered the ring against him as "Stiff Cliff".

Cliff was one of 3 brothers who unsurprisingly all hailed from Billy Riley's notorious 'Snake-Pit' in Wigan, and were also coached by shoot legend 'Pop' Saxton. Typical of all graduates of Billy Riley's Mecca of Pain, the Beaumonts, Jack, Arthur and Cliff were all fantastic submission wrestlers. One thing that wasn't typical about the Beaumonts was that unlike the majority of Wigan wrestlers, who were ex-miners, the Beaumont family business was manufacturing coffins and all 3 brothers were reputed to be even much stiffer than their clients.

I used to be very surprised by the many wrestlers who claimed that they actually liked wrestling against Cliff, especially when they were in earshot of Jack Dale. Until I realized that they were probably using the same reverse psychology that I used to employ when I was in earshot of Giles the foreman when I worked for The Water board digging holes in the road. All I had to do was to say I wanted to do one thing, and Giles would order me to do another, and I became certain that the wrestlers were employing the very same tactics with Jack Dale. I became so sick of hearing this claim that in an even louder voice I would respond with,

"Oh yeah, well you show me a man who says he really likes wrestling with Cliff Beaumont and I'll show you a bloody liar!" I knew how unpopular I was making myself but I can't stand hypocrites. I hated wrestling Cliff Beaumont even more, and I didn't care who knew it. Stefan Milla was one who always professed that he liked wrestling Cliff, and one night when he was, we were all in the dressing room when one of the other wrestlers asked Stefan about a match he'd had a few nights earlier when Stefan had accidentally knocked his opponent's front teeth out. Stefan did have a very funny sense of humor, and his description of what had occurred at the climax of that contest had everyone in stitches, he capped off his story with,

"From now on I won't be introduced in the ring just as Stefan Milla from Denmark, but as Stefan Milla – The Demon Dentist from Denmark." Everyone laughed including Cliff - then everyone except Stefan laughed again, when both Cliff and Stefan walked back into the dressing room after their match, and we saw that Cliff had 'accidentally' kicked all of Stefan's front teeth out.

"Hey Stefan, do you still like wrestling Cliff?" I asked innocently. For once in his life Stefan didn't come back with a funny response – but I suppose that missing front teeth can have that effect on some people. Thankfully, Cliff was the only Beaumont in my weight division, but for me that was one too many Beaumonts. I didn't know how old Cliff was; only that his hair was grey, and that he had been wrestling professionally since about the same time that I had been born. He stood about 5 feet 10 inches tall and weighed around 170 pounds. There was not a fraction of an ounce fat on his physique, he was nothing but muscle and bone, his body was just like a steel spring. He was capable of doing things with his body and with the bodies of anyone unfortunate enough to be sharing the ring with him that defied description. Without breaking a sweat or breathing any harder than a normal person would, while sitting in a comfortable chair reading a good book. He was capable of moving in a blur of speed, he only had to touch an opponent to send him spinning in any direction he chose. He could take an opponent apart in mid air and put him back together again by the time he hit the canvas, and before the poor unfortunate could draw a breath or blink an eye he'd find himself airborne again. I am certain that he could have juggled with a half a dozen normal wrestlers in the ring at the same time if given the opportunity as 'Stiff Cliff' was anything but normal. I was convinced he was from another planet. Cliff's eating habits were also not normal, if not unique amongst Wiganers, and were anything but healthy for anyone, let alone a professional athlete. He was one of the many Northern wrestlers who would bring enough jam sandwiches – or 'jam butties' as the Wiganers called them, to last him the week when he came down South to Wrestle for Dale Martins. He was also, not only a smoker, but a chain smoker of Woodbine cigarettes, the cheapest, nastiest cigarettes it was possible to buy. Taking into account Cliff's eating and smoking habits, he should have been a physical wreck, but instead he was a wrestling superman. Bearing all these facts in mind one would imagine that Cliff Beaumont would be the most sensational and exciting wrestler in the World from the spectator's point of view. But the fact that everything that he did in the ring, he did so very effortlessly and with a totally deadpan face, completely robbed his performance of most of the drama one associated with professional wrestling. If Cliff was applying a vicious hold on his opponent, his opponents face may have been etched with pain, but Cliff's features instead of registering force and viciousness would be expressionless, even bored. If an opponent was applying a vicious hold on Cliff, instead of appearing to be in agony, once again his deadpan expression would be at odds with the situation in which he found himself. He would look as equally bored receiving punishment as he did dishing it out. Noise was also something a pair of wrestlers made while engaging in their violent profession, it wasn't called the 'Grunt and Groan Game' for nothing, but here again there was a definite deficit in any audio emissions coming from 'Stiff Cliff'. To watch him wrestle was often like watching a silent Charley Chaplin movie – but, without the comedy.

Obviously I was always thrilled to receive a television bout amongst the list of matches I was sent every month. Even more so if the match was held anywhere in the London area, where the show would be over by five pm, and I would be free to either go home early, or more likely to wrestle in another local arena the same night. Where once again I would not be very far from home. Even more to the point every TV contestant would be paid a hefty 40 pounds in wages, which would double my wages for that week. Plus every TV appearance was watched by millions and did wonders for a wrestler's publicity. On this occasion I was wrestling on television in Beckenham Baths Hall, a London suburb, and was very happy about it until I arrived and found out who was going to be my TV opponent that afternoon. Yep! You've got it in one - 'Stiff Cliff' Beaumont. I had never liked wrestling against Cliff, even in a small arena where there may have been only a few hundred fans to witness my embarrassment and total humiliation. BUT on TV with millions of Britain's most avid wrestling fans glued to the box, watching every single move - ok, this doesn't happen very often, but I'm speechless! Ok, I'm recovered – But, let me ask you a question - would you be happy if someone kicked you in the mouth so hard that all your front bottom teeth came right through the flesh under your bottom lip? – No? Ok, do you know anyone else who would be happy? – Well, you do now, - ME!

Cliff and I were the first match on TV that afternoon and we were going to be wrestling each other in an 8 x 5 minute round contest. We were told that Cliff was going to win the match in the seventh round, that was going to spell a hefty 35 minutes of pain, humiliation and embarrassment for one of the contestants, and I'll only give you one guess as to which one of us that was going to be?! The match began and for 2 minutes I was bounced around the ring like a missile in a pinball machine. In pure desperation I made a grab for Cliff's left arm and secured a very snug submission hold on it. Which triggered an immediate response from Cliff as he dived up into the air, and attempted to counter with a flying head scissors. His execution was very clumsy, with the result that one of his big bony knees smashed into my face and split a gash bellow my bottom lip as wide as my very ample mouth. Blood squirted everywhere, including all over the referee Stan Stone, who immediately stopped the match. In the early days of TV wrestling, too much blood on the tube was strictly taboo, and in my match there was definitely too much blood - for

TV maybe, but not for me. Under the circumstances I couldn't have been happier. At least this way it seemed that it was just unfortunate for me that I had to retire early because of a very bad cut, and it was therefore left to the fans imagination that if it hadn't happened, it would only have been a matter of time before I may have been throwing Cliff Beaumont around the ring in the same manner that I had been thrown around it for the first 2 and only minutes that the whole contest lasted.

I may have bore an ugly scar under my bottom lip, but that for me was much easier to bear than the gross humiliation I would have experienced if the match had lasted for the designated duration. I consoled myself with the fact that I was paid 40 pounds for 2 minutes work - WOW! That was more money than I used to earn digging holes in the roads of London for a whole month!

I had wrestled with Cliff many times before, and was destined to wrestle with him many more times to come, but this was the first of the 3 most memorable matches I had against 'Stiff' Cliff Beaumont, - I'll tell you all about the other 2 later.

Some of the older wrestler's styles were also very difficult to exploit. They were far too crafty, clever and experienced for that. Bob Archer O'Brian would purposely run his much younger opponents around the ring until they were breathing through every orifice it was possible to gasp air through. Then take a hold on them that entailed them being folded in such a way that their legs would be pressed onto their chests with Bob's full weight bearing down heavily on them, which would make it extremely difficult to draw any oxygen into their already depleted and deflated lungs. While his opponent would be fighting for air, Bob would be virtually taking a break, and only expending as much energy as it took to keep his adversary in place and out of air. Then and only when he was well rested, would he drag his opponent back to his feet run him around the ring again before once more taking him back down to the canvas and again cutting off his oxygen supply. This strategy would be repeated throughout the match. With the result that at the end of the contest Bob would do a sprightly hop out of the ring and stride jauntily back to the dressing room while his exhausted, much younger opponent would stagger in his wake looking more like an out of condition 90-year old.

Ex British and European Welterweight Champion, Ken Joyce had these same tactics down to a very fine art. Ken would wrestle occasionally for other promoters in Joint's organization, but mostly he would wrestle for Devereaux promotions which he ran entirely himself for Mrs. Devereaux, the widow of the promotions founder, the late Charles Devereaux. The matchmaker for Dale Martins was Mick McManus, he would decide who would wrestle who on a card for them and who would win and lose. For Devereaux Promotions Ken Joyce was head cook and bottle-washer, and made every decision himself. In his own matches he would invariably emerge the winner, but not until he had fought a very long and very hard contest. Ken at this time was hovering somewhere his late 40s and unlike many other wrestlers of a similar age he looked every second of it. Although he was an avid believer in keeping fit, Ken Joyce would never lift weights, but relied solely on cardio, which for him didn't entail running, jogging or skipping rope, but in the ring wrestling. If you wrestled with Ken, you were always in the ring for at least 35 to 40 minutes, and that would be his daily workout. He would invariably attempt to blow his opponent up, who Ken seemed to regard as his exercise equipment, especially if his opponent was much younger than he was. The worst thing that could happen for one of Ken's opponents was for someone in the audience to shout out to Ken something like,

"Come on Granddad!!!" that would be sufficient to cause Ken to accelerate into top gear and employ every evil little stunt in his encyclopedia sized book of tricks in order to run his opponent right into the ground. Of course other wrestlers on the card, being the pranksters they were would often be the instigators. As there was very little they enjoyed more than someone else's embarrassment, discomfort or distress. They would creep out of the dressing room after the match was underway, and either get someone in the audience to begin the 'come on Granddad' chant, or blatantly start it themselves. Then soon all the fans would be chanting, and the other wrestlers would be chuckling away while they watched Ken Joyce speed up and begin to methodically and systematically run his luckless opponent several miles past complete and total exhaustion. I had watched him when he wrestled with other ring veterans, and found his style very deliberate and businesslike. But Ken was very touchy about his age, which was the sole cause of his alternate ring tactics when wrestling with the youngsters of the sport. Being a youngster of the sport myself I was subjected to the most extreme treatment that Ken was capable of dishing out when I wrestled him, but was more fortunate in a number of ways than most of my young peers. Even though most all young wrestlers were very fit and energetic, there were none more so than myself. I also had a very small waist which only measured about 27 to 28 inches. So even if it was possible to hyperventilate me in the first place, folding me up and putting his full weight on me, would not cut off my air as much as it would to another wrestler who may have had a much larger waistline. I fully appreciated what he was trying to achieve, and I simply refused to play his game. The best weapon in my own defensive arsenal was not only my super strength, fitness or my tiny waistline, but the fact that nothing makes me more contrary than when I am threatened with any form of aggression, and to my way of thinking attempting to fuck me up in the ring in order to fan one's own ego is an act of aggression. Most wrestlers, out of politeness to their opponents, would grab each other fairly firmly, but lightly when they first came to grips at the beginning of a contest. But some, Ken included would make themselves as heavy as they could and make their opponent bear all their weight. Those kinds of tactics where you'd find yourself having to drag a very heavy opponent around the ring all night, combined with the hypoventilation routine would spell exhaustion for the fittest of the fit. In my early days I had been undeterred by any opponent who wanted to do the very heavy thing, as it gave me the opportunity to display my superior strength. But I had gradually began to realize that I was being suckered into playing my opponents game so I stopped playing it. After the opening bell sounded, most wrestling matches would begin with both contestants circling each other around the ring as though looking for an opening while they sized each other up. Building up anticipation in the process. Then they would make contact by linking up with 'the collar and elbow hold' or, what was sometimes called the 'referee's hold'. Then they may push each other away, circle some more, before coming back at each other and linking up again. This procedure would usually be repeated until one of the wrestlers took a hold, or threw his opponent to the mat and then the match would begin in earnest. In order to counter Ken Joyce's, or any of the other wrestlers who practiced linking up with a slam by throwing all their weight into it, and then making themselves as heavy as they could to begin the wearing out process. I did the very last thing they expected me to do. Instead of bracing myself against the extremely forceful initial impact, I would drop like a stone on impact. But hook an arm as I did so, and by adding my own weight to my opponent's onslaught rather than resisting it, it would absorb the shock of the attack, and his own impetus would cost him his balance. This maneuver would not only eliminate all the heavy pushing and pulling in one foul swoop, but would also take the audience by surprise, as much as it had my opponent. The fans who were used to seeing the usual pre-action ritual would be shocked to see two wrestlers come together, and for one to appear to rip the other right off his feet and straight into a strong hold on the mat. This would not only prevent my heavy-handed opponent from making me unduly tired, it would now be he, and not me, who had to expend strength and energy. Trying to either get out of the hold, or fight his way back to his feet while I, made myself sticky and heavy. My answer to Ken's crisscross routine was just as simple. I realized that it would cost Ken just as much effort to run back and forth across the ring as it did myself, and therefore would not tire me anymore than it did him. So I was perfectly happy matching him stride for stride. It was after Ken had taken his hold on his wheezing opponent, and squeezed all the air out of him so that he had to fight for all he was worth just to try to draw each tiny whiff of oxygen. That the distress would really set in, and while this was taking place Ken would be making himself very, very heavy while taking a rest. All I did to counter this was instead of trying in vain to fight my way out of the position that Ken held me in, was to relax myself and try as he may, thanks mainly to my very small waist and very strong Welsh mountain trained lungs he was unable to cut off my wind. Ken would be furious,

"FIGHT!!!" He'd demand as he squeezed harder and harder and made himself heavier and heavier.

"Nah, I don't think so," I'd reply, "if your taking a break so will I." Back in the dressing room after the match was concluded, I'd have to endure a huge piece of Ken's verbal abuse,

"Hey Street!" He'd roar, "If I tell you to fight out of a hold, you fight your way out of it!"

"Not if you hold me that tight and make yourself that heavy," I'd answer, "I wrestle a lot better when I'm not tired or gasping for air."

"If you want to continue wrestling for Devereaux Promotions, you'll do as I tell you!" he insisted. We both knew he couldn't intimidate me with that threat, even if I didn't wrestle for Devereaux I would be wrestling for another member of Joint's promotions. I would be wrestling every night of the week whether it was for them or not. I was too good, and even more to the point where Joint promotions were concerned, too cheap, for them to ever think of leaving me at home on a night that it was possible to include me on one of their cards. I was determined to be completely uncompromising, as I also held a grudge against Ken Joyce. After hearing him on so many occasions claim that after wrestling everyone of note in his native Canada and also the breadth and width of Europe, that The World's Lightweight Wrestling Champion, George Kidd was his hardest, toughest and best opponent. I hadn't seen George Kidd for over 2 years but I still detested the very thought of him, and anyone who was a friend of George Kidd was definitely no friend of mine. The war of wills between Ken Joyce and myself continued, and reminded me of the times when I refused to bend over and get my arse canned by my school Headmasters, Birchmore and Crewe. I was just as determined to win this war as I had been to win those. But Ken continued to try to dominate me until one night after he had me neatly folded and ordered me to try to fight my way out, instead of complying, I wriggled myself into a more comfortable position and began to snore as though I had gone to sleep, Ken was livid. Back in the dressing room after the match he got right into my face and demanded an explanation.

"Well, you had me in a cradle-hold, so I was just making it look as effective as I could by pretending to be asleep." I told him.

"I've told you before Street – and I don't want to have to tell you again, when you wrestle for Devereaux Promotions you do exactly what I tell you to do, and when I tell you to fight out of a hold, you fight your way out of a hold!" He roared.

"If you really want me to fight my way out of a hold, why do you try to make it so difficult to accomplish?" I asked him.

"Because it looks more real that way!" he informed me.

"It looks more real because it is!" I informed him back, then added, "Look Ken, I know exactly what you're trying to do to me, and I know exactly why you're trying to do it, and because of that I'm not going to let you. If you want me to appear to be knackered at the end of our match to appeal to your ego, I'll do it, but don't ever try to do it for real because then I won't do it, and there's nothing you can say or do that will make me!" I can't say in all honesty that he never ever tried again, it was probably part of his nature, just as it was part of mine to resist, but I did notice that his efforts gradually became much less intensive than before and I could live with that.

'Iron Jaw' Joe Murphy, was also as purposely as 'Stiff', and about as thick as two very short planks. But for an entirely different reason, and that reason was in an attempt to build or enhance a hard, tough guy reputation to intimidate his opponents and impress the promoters at the same time. Everything he did in the ring was stiff, awkward and full force, when he hurled himself into the referee's hold, he would raise himself right up onto the very tips of his toes and slam himself down on his opponent, slapping the backs of their necks and upper arms so hard it would take their breath away. Then all the holds and throws he'd apply would be as tight, and as painful as he could make them. When his opponent retaliated with forearm smashes, chops or even dropkicks, instead of taking a good bump to make them look effective, and his opponent look strong he would just stand there, shake his fat head and tell them,

"Harder! – go on, hit me harder!" His opponent would be happy to comply, but his efforts would be in vain, as 'Iron Jaw' Murphy would not go down.

"It's my gimmick." He would explain if his opponent complained to him. It may have been, but there was more to that than met the eye. As I say, it may have been his gimmick. But just standing in front of an opponent getting whacked from all angles and just shaking his head as his only response, takes an awful lot less energy than taking a big bump right across the ring to make the whacking look good. True, spectators were very impressed with his apparent toughness, but fooling the fans into thinking he was as hard as coffin nails was only part of it. The main reason was, that he imagined that the promoters would be fooled too, and there was only one thing that 'Iron Jaw' Joe Murphy liked better than his opponent to complain about his rough, heavy handed performance, and that was for him to complain in earshot of Jack Dale. If Jack Dale was in the dressing room after his match, and his opponent didn't look as though he was going to complain about the rough treatment he had received, Murphy would sidle up to Jack and call out to his opponent,

"Hey, was I loose enough for you tonight?!" Or something along those lines, in order to provoke the complaint he was craving Jack Dale to overhear. When his opponent obliged and gave him a piece of their minds, telling him that he was as stiff as Lazarus was before the miracle, he would chuckle gleefully, look at Jack and roll his eyes almost apologetically as though to say,

'What can you do Jack, when you're so hard, rough and tough and your opponent is not tough enough to stand up to you?' At first, I had also put up with his bullshit, although I knew better than to complain about anything that most stiff or clumsy wrestlers did. As I found that being a little stiffer and a little clumsier than they were was by far the best antidote. But one night after a week of very long, hard trips, and equally long, hard matches, I was wrestling against 'Iron Jaw'. As we came together to link up, my mind and body just revolted against that inevitable crash and resounding, brain numbing slap that had become Murphy's signature start to each of his contests. As the rotund little ogre took in a huge breath, raised himself to the very tips of his toes before unleashing his avalanche force crash into my body, I allowed instinct to rule. Just a split second before he made contact, I suddenly cried,

"Oh no!" in a shrill effeminate shriek, as I threw up my hands and leapt out of range in a way that must have resembled Little Miss Muffet recoiling from the Spider. With the Result 'Iron Jaw' missed me altogether and fell flat on his face in the middle of the ring. The audience exploded with laughter, I had to laugh myself, and from that time on that was the way I wrestled against 'Iron Jaw'. It amazed me that he was unable to do something to counteract missing and falling flat on his face. But it seemed that habit, and the fact that what he hoped to achieve, worked against everyone else prevented him finding a cure when he wrestled me. Mind you, it could have been that he was a very slow learner. He came up short in the dressing room too, when he attempted to provoke any complaints I might want to share with our promoter on his behalf.

He called out in a very loud, 'Jack Dale attracting voice',

"Hey Street, was I loose enough for you tonight?!!!" I would respond with,

"A little too loose for me sweetie - my, you are such a tender petal, so gentle I could hardly feel you in there - Oh dear, I do hope you haven't been unwell, you seemed so very weak and fragile!" His fat face would drop a foot, and Jack Dale would laugh his balls off. But, did it cure Murphy? – Nope! Like I said, he was a very slow learner, although I did once teach him a lesson he never forgot.

One morning after leaving Dale Martin's office in the transport van, we stopped a little way down Brixton Road to pick up a few more wrestlers who were staying at Martini's café. The driver got out of the van and entered the café to let the wrestlers know we were outside and ready to go to that evening's venue. It seemed they could not have been ready as the minutes ticked by and no one came out. Eventually Joe Murphy, who had been sitting next to the door, sighed a huge sigh of impatience, got out of the van and began shading his eyes against the light as he attempted to look through one of the café windows. Wrestlers were always playing rough or spiteful pranks on each other, and as Joe was standing outside the van with his back to me, I took the opportunity to play one on him. 'Poetic justice.' I thought, as I leapt high into the air out of the van, and as I landed on Joe I slammed both my hands down hard onto the backs of both of his shoulders, reminiscent of the way he attacked his foes in the ring. 'Iron-Jaw' almost went head first right through the window into the café and it wasn't just with the force I hit him with but fright. I began to laugh, but not for long, as the poison Leprechaun was not amused, and he came back at me like an enraged Rhino. He stuck his face so far into mine that I went cross-eyed trying to focus on it, as he snarled venomously,

"Fook yer, Yer ever do that agi'n an' I'll break yer in half!" I slammed him back in a way that 'Iron-Jaw' Joe Murphy wishes he could slam, and knocked him so far back that his fat arse almost went through the café window instead of his head. I took two fast steps forward, stuck my face into Murphy's and snarled right back,

"YOU'LL DO WHAT, YOU FAT IRISH FUCK?! IF YOU THINK I'M FRIGHTENED OF YOU, YOU'RE MORE STUPID THAN I'VE GIVEN YOU CREDIT FOR AND THAT'S SAYING A LOT!!!" His eyes and mouth went as wide as the hole I was ready to punch in his fat face, but he answered me timidly,

"I know you're not Ada - nobody's frightened of me." He had suddenly become so subdued that I almost felt sorry for him, but I still added for good measure,

"You ever threaten me again and I'll make you back it up whether you want to or not." He never did.

KING OF THE GYPSIES

I had began to think that I was doing okay, and that my career was on course and going as well as could be expected, although I had always been very impatient. I now felt that I had started to carve a niche for myself, and in retrospect I believe that complacency was beginning to set in. Then an incident occurred that changed my whole perspective on the subject. One Sunday morning one of the downstairs tenants called to me, and told Jean and I that there were two men at the front door asking for me. I imagined that they would be either family or wrestlers, as they would be the only people who would know where we lived. So before I even knew who was inquiring after me, I called them both up to our flat. I didn't recognize either of them as they entered so I introduced myself to them, and then felt the hair on the back of my neck prickle as I recognized their very course Pikey accents when they introduced themselves to me. Immediately a picture appeared in my mind's eye of 'Airy the Gypo, in the crimson splattered, white tiled cinema toilet. Lying in a pool of his own blood and piss. I wondered if he and his grotesque elephantine Mother had since acquired a TV for the dirty tarpaulin tent they called home. Had maybe seen me wrestling on it, and had put two and two together, and worked out that I had been the lethal avalanche, that had engulfed him mid piss. And that these two Gypsy detectives had at last tracked me down on his behalf. As if to confirm my worst fears, one of my Gypsy visitors came straight to the point when I asked him the reason for their visit.

"We want to arrange a fight between a wrestler and our own Gypsy Champion." He told me.

"How much will I get paid, and who do I have to fight?" I asked, believing that I already knew who my opponent would turn out to be.

"Oh no, its not you, who we want to fight our Man," he replied with a smile, "its Mike Marino, we want him to fight against Uriah Burton 'King of the Gypsies,' bare-knuckle, all-in

Champion."

"Why are you asking me?" I inquired, "I'm not Mike Marino's bloody manager."

"We went to Dale Martin's wrestling promotions, but they wouldn't tell us how we could get in touch with him," The other Gypsy explained, "so we came to see if you could ask Mike Marino for us instead?"

"Tell him that if he accepts the challenge we'll pay him 1,000 pounds for an all in, no holds barred fight against our champion." The first Gypsy declared.

Now they had my full and undivided attention!

"Never mind about Mike Marino," I blurted, "I'll fight your King of the Gypsies and the fucking Queen of them too for 1,000 pounds!!!"

The Gypsies both smiled at that, but the first Gypsy replied,

"Mike Marino is the British, European and World Mid-heavyweight wrestling Champion," he told me, "a lot of people would bet a lot of money on him to win if he fought against our champion."

"Well why don't you let me fight him then?" I insisted, "Then, maybe you'll get more people betting on the King of the Gypsies instead."

"That's our point," he explained, "if we're going to make our money back we need people to bet on Mike Marino."

"How do you know your champion will Win?" I asked.

"Uriah is the dirtiest fighter in the World, and he WON'T BE BEATEN." He assured me.

"He'd rather die before he'd lose a fight." The other Gypsy agreed.

"Well if he's that good, and you really want to make some money, let me fight Uriah Burton and bet all your money on me instead of him." I suggested. I had never seen 1,000 pounds in one piece in my entire life, and if there was even a fraction of a fraction of a chance of me laying my greedy little hands on it, I wanted more than anything else that I could think of, to do just that.

"That wouldn't be a good bet!" the second Gypsy informed me.

"There is nothing that Uriah Burton won't do to win a fight," the first Gypsy explained, "he'll head-butt, gouge your eyes, he'll rip your testicles off." Here he gave Jean an apologetic glance before continuing, "his favorite move is to bite though your chest muscle just under your armpit, and that will make you lose the use of your arms."

"Thanks for telling me about The King of the Gypsies favorite moves." I told him, "now I'll be the only one bringing any surprises to the fight - if I were you, I'd bet on me, because there's nothing I won't do – to win 1,000 pounds." I told them that as though we already had a deal.

"He's twice your size and as hard as iron," they assured me, "he's never been beaten, and you wouldn't stand a snowball's chance in Hell."

"THAT'S FOR YOU TO PROVE!" I told him, getting angry, "TELL BURTON THAT I EAT HEDGEHOGS RAW WITH THEIR SPINES ON – AND IF HE'S NEVER BEEN BEATEN YET, ITS BECAUSE HE'S NEVER FOUGHT ME!"

"And he never will," they stated, "he's only interested in the World Champion."

We must have agued back and forth for another hour or more, but they wouldn't budge, their hearts were set on Mike Marino, and so with my heart now weighing about a ton, I finally agreed to approach Mike Marino on their behalf. I had been surprised that they had not taken offense, as I had thought they might, when I had mentioned eating Hedgehogs. I had known to my horror and disgust from the time I was a very young child, that one of my favorite pets were also a favorite meal for the Gypos. We were also told that when the Gypsies prepared a meal of Hedgehog, they would counter the Hedgehog's natural defense of rolling themselves into a ball of very sharp spines, by simply rolling them in clay and baking them whole on an open fire. Then just cracking open the container of hot, hardened clay which enabled them to peel off the spines in order to get at the meat, after the poor Hedgehog was cooked. I don't know if that story is entirely accurate or not, but it was a tale that we were told, that was designed to be derogatory. As most tales we were told about Gypos when we were kids usually were. We were brought up to believe that all Gypsies were villains, and would steal anything that wasn't nailed down including children. That's what we were told, but personally I have never heard of a single incident, and believe me if you had been brought up in South Wales as I had been, you would be no stranger to Gypsies, or them to you. Most Gypsies that I have had contact with were illiterate, and couldn't even read their own names. But, if they couldn't read, they could certainly count, most especially where money was concerned, and they knew as well as anyone, and better than most, very many ways to accumulate the stuff. I learned at an early age, not to confuse illiteracy with stupidity. These people were ultimate opportunists, incredibly smart, and could see opportunities where many others couldn't. They could see a profit where others could only see a heap of rags or a pile of scrap metal, Their women would make money selling baskets they'd woven, wooden clothes pegs they'd carved, wild flowers they'd picked in the woods, or 'lucky heather' they'd gathered from the mountains that surrounded our town. Even though anyone could go and pick as much heather as they could ever use themselves, it would be a very brave soul indeed who would turn away a Gypsy Lady who was selling the 'lucky heather' they had picked and therefore risk the infamous 'Gypsy Curse' that would be administered freely amongst anyone who chose not to buy the stuff that was blessed by the Gypsies. In fact the curse was also extended to anyone who chose not to buy their baskets or wooden clothes pegs.

I remember Paul Lincoln telling me that after he and Big Ray Hunter had bought the coffee bar they had named 'Coffeeville', that they asked Gypsy referee, Billy Barber if he could come up with anything out of his yard that would give Coffeeville that old western theme that its new title suggested. Before the week was out Billy turned up in Old Compton Street outside the café with his ancient van full to the brim with Wagon Wheels, Cowboy Saddles, Chaps, Stetsons, Bullwhips, Antlers and even Buffalo skins. Billy spat on his own hand before he shook Paul's and said,

"Give us 50 quid for the lot Governor!"

Gypsies could also see a potential meal where others would not, as well as the Hedgehogs that I have already mentioned; they would eat wild bird's eggs, probably the wild birds too. Fruit and vegetables would be gathered at night from any farmer's field that was in the vicinity of where these travelers were camping.

They were very skilled hunters and would hunt Rabbits, Hares, Pheasants, Ducks, Swans and even Badgers. When I accompanied Uncle Fred and his cronies, out of London where they would take his Greyhound to race in unlicensed Dog racing events. Very many of the other Greyhound owners and gamblers at these meets were Gypsies. As well as Greyhounds, the Gypsies would be surrounded by other Dogs they used for hunting like Lurchers and Jack Russell Terriers, also with Ferrets in cages or carried on their person. These were the very people who I was meant to protect Uncle Fred and his pals against, if they thought that Uncle Fred and company might be attempting to pull a fast one, a tall order indeed. Although judging by the amount of money they were willing to wager, they didn't look like easy marks to me, and they would brandish wads of banknotes that could have choked a Hippopotamus. Both Gypsies agreed to meet me again the first Sunday of the next month, as I told them that I would most likely bump into Mike Marino some time during that period. Then I could arrange a meeting between the two parties concerned, who could then make whatever arrangements they thought necessary. Now that I had eventually came to terms that it would be Mike Marino and not myself who would be fighting against The King of the Gypsies, I couldn't wait to tell Mike the fantastic news. I even wondered if I could use the fact that I was now privy to some of Uriah Burton's most lethal and dastardly tactics, that I might be able to row myself in as Mike Marino's second. That way even if I couldn't be one of the main players and the hero representing the pro wrestlers, I could console myself by playing the faithful sidekick.

Mike wasn't on the same card as me the next day, neither was I lucky enough to bump into him at the office, as I waited to leave Dale Martin's in the van to that night's venue. All wrestlers love to have stories to tell each other, and there was nothing any of us liked better than to be the first to impart gossip or to break news. But I knew that if I told the others of yesterday's visit from the two Gypsies, that it would definitely be one of them, rather than me who would end up telling Mike Marino of this very potentially lucrative windfall. There was a saying in our business that went something like this - 'If you want news to travel fast, there's television – telegram – telephone, or if you want it to travel really fast – tell a wrestler! In my opinion there was an even faster method of getting the story to encircle the entire globe in an instant - first you swear a wrestler to secrecy and then tell him the story! All day long I was fizzing with anticipation, with no chance of relief, as I knew my path would not cross with my quarry's. The response that was awarded to the other wrestler's jokes and stories as the miles melted behind us made my knowledge pure torture. I had to steel myself over and over again, against the temptation to just go ahead and spill the beans. Thank goodness that the very next day Mike Marino and I were both wrestling on the same card. When he stepped into the van where I was already waiting impatiently for his arrival, I felt the same pang of excitement and anticipation that I had felt about 6 years earlier when I was waiting to confront him as he made his way to the dressing room in Cardiff. When I first spoke to, and had asked the advice of my favorite British wrestler.

When ever Mike traveled in Dale Martin's luxury transport, he would usually make sure that he was the last one to enter the van before it left. That way he seemed to make a Star like entrance. All he would have to do then was to just stand inside the van, give the occupants one of his cheeky grins, and the whole van would erupt just remembering the last joke or story Mike had told them when they were last together. Mike Marino had to be one of the funniest jokesters in the business, he could tell you a new joke on Monday, then retell you the very same joke on Tuesday that he had embellished. Then again every day of the week re-embellishing it each time with a knack he had for making the same joke funnier every time he told it. Then as we were traveling towards our destination, all he had to do was to turn his head, look back at any of us sitting behind him. Give us one of his cheeky grins, and everyone would be in stitches again without him even having to open his mouth. I had often said to him, between giggles, after he told his Monday joke, that I could hardly wait for the Saturday version of it. Damn, he could really be hilarious. Most of his stories were just as entertaining, but usually so unbelievable, that even amongst all us wrestlers he was known as 'Mick the Fib.' On this day Mike beat me to the punch, and dived right into his joke of the week before I had a chance to impart the great news I had for him. So I waited politely, but impatiently for him to finish his story, and for the other wrestlers to recover from the effects of it before I told my story. Well as to be expected, everyone laughed and laughed and the extra innuendos and such that he would add every time the laughter subsided kept the mirth and merriment going until we had left the outskirts of London behind us. As Mike had been telling the joke, and during the following laughter I had been measuring Him up size wise. I figured him to be close to 6 feet tall, and that he probably weighed somewhere between 15 to 16 stone, say somewhere in the region of 210 to 220 pounds. The Gypsies had told me that their Hughie, as they called him was almost 6 feet tall, but weighed over 17 stone, about 240 pounds. Finally when I thought that the tittering had died down enough, I began to tell Mike the news, and was rewarded by the full attention of everyone in the slow moving van. The first to break the silence was Mike himself, who startled me when he suddenly, shouted,

"Fuck of I'm not interested!!!!!" I couldn't believe what he had just said,

"Mike," I persisted, as though he hadn't grasped the full import of what I was telling him, "They said they would pay you 1,000 pounds!"

"I TOLD YOU I'M NOT FUCKIN' INTERESTED – NOW SHUT THE FUCK UP ABOUT IT!" He yelled at me – and that was the end of that. There was no more laughter or joviality for the rest of the trip, both Mike and the rest of the crew were uncharacteristically silent, Mike did turn and gave me a brief glance on a few occasions, but his cheeky grin was now completely gone, and replaced instead by an unfriendly glare. For whatever reason, things were never, ever the same between Mike and I again. He would still tell jokes in my company, and he would still laugh at my jokes, and listen to my stories, but from that time on there was definitely something missing. Mike got a lift back to London that night from another wrestler who had made his own way to the show by car, and it wasn't until the rest of us were on our way back to London in the van that the subject was brought up again. The other wrestlers, nosey to a fault began quizzing me. I probably made matters worse by admitting that I was not only willing, but eager to fight the gypsy king myself, especially for the kind of money they were offering.

To be honest it had crossed my mind not to mention the deal to Mike Marino at all, and then to tell the Gypsies that I had asked him, but Mike wasn't interested and that therefore they would have to let me fight instead of him. But I feared that the Gypsies were far too savvy for that and wouldn't believe me, especially when there was a 1,000 pounds in the offing. Now it seemed that that would be the story I would have to tell them whether they chose to believe me or not. I was now more determined than ever to fight the King of the Gypsies, as I felt I would also be fighting for the honor of professional wrestling as well as the money. I did hear that it was no exaggeration that Uriah Burton was notorious for his carnivorous ways, and that he did partake of a very substantial and nourishing snack, that was torn off the chest of the former 'King of the Gypsies' 'Big Jim' Nielson, when Uriah beat him for the Gypsy King title in the village of St Boswell near the Scottish Border a few years earlier.

Being the eternal optimist, I now began to persuade myself that since Mike Marino had flatly refused their challenge, the Gypsies had no other option than to let me fight, even though both the Gypsies had been so very adamant that they didn't want me. I even allowed myself to contemplate exactly what the 1,000 pounds would mean to me. A down payment on a house of our own for sure - a car? Probably not, for one thing I didn't know how to drive one, and I was never really that interested in cars anyway. 'A down payment on our own home for certain,' I thought, 'and whatever is left over after that can go in the bank against a rainy day.' In the early 60s 1,000 pounds was a small fortune. For the whole of the 2 years that I had worked 6 days a week in the coalmine I had not earned even a half of that amount. If I added up all the money I had earned boxing on the Fairground booths, and then added that to all of the money I had earned in every one of the professional wrestling matches I had ever been engaged in so far in my life, it would still fall short of 1,000 pounds. I knew that Mike Marino earned a lot more than I did as a professional wrestler, but even so, I could not understand why he wouldn't fight Uriah Burton. In Mike's early wrestling career he would have got into the ring at least 100 times with Bert Assirati to earn 1,000 pounds. If someone was brave enough to do that more than once, especially after the 'gentle' treatment he had received from the Islington ogre, to my mind he was brave enough to fight anyone. They say that its best to deal with the Devil you know, and even though I knew nothing about Uriah Burton, apart from what I'd learned from the Gypsies. If given the choice of coming to grips with him or Bert Assirati, I would have chosen The King of the Gypsies as an opponent over Bert any day of the week. So in spite of myself, I gradually became convinced that it was now my fight, and I began to plan my strategy based on what I had learned from the two Gypsies. I believed then as I do now, that all-in, no-holds barred street fighting is the most lethal form of combat, other than using some kind of weapon. One might be forgiven if they argued that a trained boxer, wrestler, or any other form of martial artist would have the advantage in such a contest. But the very fact that they had been taught in the process of learning their art, rules 'against using foul tactics' would be a very serious strike against them from the onset. Even in any form of Martial Arts that included submission holds, a competitor had the option of submitting rather than suffering broken bones or torn tendons. Or from losing consciousness from a strangle-hold, but in Street-Fighting, Mountain Fighting or Gypsy All-in Fighting, you would break bones first then accept their submission after. Gypsy 'Bare-knuckle, no holds barred fighting' had very little resemblance to 'The sweet science'; these fighters were Human Pit-Bulls, minus the humanity. When the Gypsies had told me about The Gypsy King's nasty biting tendencies as a way of dampening my desire to fight him, I had replied,

"Let's see how hard he can bite after I punch all his teeth out, I think I can recover from a nasty suck, don't you?!" But they responded with,

"Uriah can punch so hard that he could knock the skull right out of your head."

"So hard that your skull would be gone and your teeth would still be in what's left of you're napper!" added the other Gypsy in agreement."

"And he's stronger than 6 normal men, too strong for any of your wrestling tricks to do you any good!" stated the first Gypsy. They had given me plenty to think about, and I realized that I would have to completely restructure my usual back-alley brawling tactics if I didn't want to resemble a Frog in a blender when I fought their champion. Normally I was a rabid head-hunter, especially when pitted against anyone who was particularly handy with their fists. If you can control their head, you can usually control the rest of their body. When ever I had an all-in fight with a Boxer for instance, I'd be more than happy to risk a few smacks in the chops just to get into a clinch, then I'd go for his head, preferably a front chancery or choke hold. Once I had secured that, it was then very easy to drop onto my back, drawing my victim into a very powerful leg scissors. Then I could just tighten the choke, let gravity add to its pressure as I'd lean back and let the sharp edge of my forearm cut deeper and deeper into his windpipe. When he had lost consciousness, or was close too it, I'd roll him into a position where I could ground, gouge and pound, with little or no fear of retaliation. I always favored slamming the edge of my fist down onto his upturned face rather than punch down with my knuckles. I found that I could deliver a very much heavier blow that way, and wouldn't risk cutting my knuckles on any shattered teeth that may still be in his mouth. If he grabbed a handful of my hair, instead of fighting to free myself, I would allow him to pull my head down to where I would then bury my teeth into his nose. If you turn your head to right angles, and bite down hard on the thick bone of his nose, just bellow his eyes, the pressure can cause his eyes to swell up like two big black shiny plums. And if he can't see you, it's much harder for him to hit you, while you're hitting him.

'Not all these tactics,' I thought, 'would work at all well against Uriah Burton. For one thing, it would be totally stupid to risk taking a blow from someone with such an inhumanly powerful punch. And – after taking such a risk, to struggle and fight against a man who was inches taller and about 80 pounds heavier just to get my arm around his throat – and at the same time be putting my underarm in range of his lethal teeth, was, to put it mildly, fucking ridiculous. I decided it might be a very good idea to stay away from his head – at least initially, as that is where he probably kept his teeth.

'Well,' I thought, 'if I can't start at the top as I usually do, maybe I should start at the bottom, and if that proves successful, I can work my way up when it's a lot safer to do so.' I knew that my opponent would have the advantage of height and weight - strength also, if I was to believe my visitors. He could use his fists too, something I only relied on after I had placed my victim in a position where I couldn't miss, as I often did against an adversary who was standing, bobbing and weaving. So, if that was The Gypsy King's advantages, what were mine?

I had to make my lack of size my advantage, which I hoped would manifest itself with much more speed and stamina than the huge Gypsy might possess. If I was so much smaller than him, I'd crouch way down low and make myself smaller still, a smaller target for his big lethal fists. I'd crouch, but lean back rather than forward, so's to keep my head further away from him and his much longer reach. Then if I wanted to avoid his head, I'd go for his ankles, shins and knees instead. I was always very good at kicking, which I intended to make my main offensive, but only from the knees down until I toppled the whole great Oak. Then I'd have to play it by ear. If he managed to grab me I'd stab him in the eye, or both eyes with my forefingers - that was something else I excelled at. I could hit very hard and with deadly accuracy with the forefingers of either hand. By now I had already began to develop an impressive arsenal of submission holds, holds that were capable of choking or breaking the bones, and tearing apart the tendons of opponents. But Burton was an opponent who could possibly nullify a very large percentage of my arsenal of submission holds with his teeth. I had to be very careful of what part of me was anywhere in range of his powerful Gypsy fangs, whenever I got the opportunity to apply something horrific of my own. Not that I would be shy about using my own teeth now that I had been made aware that in this upcoming conflict, cannibalism was not only allowed, but mandatory. Even before I had ever left Wales behind me I had had a vast amount of experience in the kind of fighting I was expecting to engage in with the Gypsy King, and even though I used to joke,

'That I had so many ways to hurt someone, they had to invent new ways to scream', most of what I learned was taught to me by the countless mistakes I had made. Making mistakes are often the best way to learn, as long as you're tough enough to absorb them and stay the course. Every time I had been involved in a particularly rough fight, a fight where I had ended up receiving as good a hiding as the one I had administered to my opponent, I would always in retrospect, give myself a hard time,

"When he did this or that," I'd tell myself, "why the hell didn't I do that or this?" What I gradually began to realize was, if you got into fights as often as I did, then you'll eventually find yourself in the same position again. Then this time you can try 'that or this' on for size, and see then from experience if that tactic works well. If it did great, I'd learned something new, if it didn't, then back to the drawing board. I also realized that a certain strategy that worked great against one opponent could spell disaster against another, so having a number of tricks up one's sleeve was also very desirable. I have met many fighters who were so skilled in one tactic that they had never found it necessary to learn another one. For instance, if a fighter like my Brother was capable of ending every confrontation with one smashing left punch, why would he ever find the motive to learn anything else? BUT, what if you come up against someone who's specialty is making you miss and you can't land your big finish. Someone who's specialty puts you flat on your back in a submission hold, before you get that fist home. Or someone who is so damn tough, that even the hardest punch fails to faze him, what the Hell do you do then?!

One thing I knew without a doubt – the first mistake you made fighting against Uriah Burton 'King of the Gypsies' would most definitely prove to be your last. When I trained next with Mike Dimitri I quizzed him regarding what his tactics might be if he was engaged in a life and death contest with an opponent who was well versed in every foul trick the Devil himself might devise. But the main drawback with Mike's tuition was that everything I learned from him he taught the hard way. Very often after a session with him where I had been ragged, bagged and shagged, I'd come away no wiser than I had been before we began. I had been very tempted to confide in Mike, and confess the reason for my interest in developing a defense and offense against the kind of treatment I was expecting to experience whilst tussling with the Gypsy King of demolition. BUT, the very thought that Mike might expect 10-percent of my winnings for his trouble banished all temptation from my mind. There was something magic about the number 1,000, and I wanted it all. Nevertheless, thoughts of my upcoming war never left me; I ate, slept and drank the battle 25 hours a day. I even began experimenting and practicing moves against my professional opponents every night, imagining that each of them were Uriah Burton King of the Gypsies. Obviously, I didn't attempt to maim any of them, but I introduced kicking at the legs into my professional repertoire. Not in the knee cap, or below either, but with the flat of my sole against the thigh. I was soon able to make the kick look cosmetically devastating, although in reality I was able to hold all the force back and no severe injury or excessive pain would be suffered by my opponent. I was soon able to snipe my adversary's leg in a fraction of a flash from every conceivable angle. Knowing that if I had wanted to put my full force behind any of the kicks they could easily contain bone breaking possibilities - especially if they zeroed in on a knee, shins or ankle instead of the thigh.

One night when I was wrestling against Tony Costos, I told him what I was going to do, and to try to avoid my kicks to the best of his ability. Tony was a few pounds lighter than I was, and very fast too, but I still scored one hit in every three or four attempts. Just one would be enough to slow down the toughest adversary if I had kicked him with full force in a more vulnerable part of his leg or ankle. I also noticed that my new kicking attacks had an effect on the audience. I had taken my practice very seriously, and my newly found intensity seemed to add a very hard edge to my former persona. Everything I did in the ring during this period was very intense and very deliberate. In many arenas where the fans had previously cheered me on as the underdog now booed me as the vicious and cruel aggressor. The respect that existed between British wrestlers didn't always extend itself towards the foreigners, who seemed to be invading our shores in increasing numbers. Especially if the foreigner in question attempted to make himself a 'Star' at the Britisher's expense.

The Dutch Grappler Nick Van Heyden imagined that his extra size entitled him to dominate the match he had against me; he really didn't realize how happy that made me feel. Taking full advantage of the excuse he had handed me, I visualized Big

Uriah Burton in front of me instead of the dizzy Dutchman. I can't remember enough about the match to describe a blow by blow, but sufficient to say that he enjoyed the experience so thoroughly that he sailed back to the Netherlands the very next day.

Idris Musa of Turkey was an excellent young wrestler. He was about my age and size, but he was another victim of my vicious practice, as I primed my all-in-fighting strategy. Incidentally, the very rough treatment I administered so freely to Musa the Turk during that period paved the way for an unexpected dividend just a few years later, which I will describe in more detail at the time that the sequence occurred.

As I watched my opponent, The Zulu Warrior, Mir Zaffar Ealam climb onto the apron and into the ring, his wide, wild rolling eyes put me in mind of how I would imagine the madness in the eyes of a huge black Stallion who was tightly tethered inside a blazing barn. When the bell rang to begin our contest, the madness in his rolling eyes remained unabated as he charged me like an angry Wild Boar. The sight of his crazy stampede towards me sent a shiver of excitement from my heels to the back of my neck as I exploded out of my own corner and right into harms way. As we collided in the centre of the ring I threw an overhand forearm that even Pasquale Salvo would have been proud of. It struck the Wildman from Zululand so hard it turned him upside down. Like lightning the Zulu leapt back to his feet and charged again, even faster than he did to start our contest. But this time in the opposite direction with me on his arse like a Leopard on a Baboon. I noticed that his eyes were still wild, wide and rolling, but this time it wasn't caused by battle-lust but blind terror.

Talking of madness, I had wrestled with The Mad Mexican Joachim LaBarba before, and believe me it was no Sunday picnic. His wrestling style was even more unorthodox than my fairground boxing had been - if that was at all possible. The front of his head was shaved and in the back his hair was drawn into a pigtail. He had coal black eyes and a coal black Fu-Manchu moustache, which suggested an evil oriental sorcerer rather than a Mexican. It would be an understatement to say that there was no love lost between us, but on our way to our venue one day he successfully managed to really piss me off. We had stopped for a meal at a restaurant that served a very nice steak and salad, which was what I ordered, along with a pint of whole cream milk to help wash it down. No sooner than my meal and drink had been placed on the table, and the waitress had left, when I noticed that I only had a regular knife with which to cut my meat instead of a steak knife. So I went up to the counter to make the exchange. I got the correct knife and returned to my table and repast, to find my milk bottle empty and Joachim LaBarba whipping what was left of it off his droopy black moustache. In fairness, I must say that wrestlers were playing pranks on each other all the time. And if that was a prank, it was nothing at all to get excited about, compared with what most wrestlers were capable of. But, I have no sense of humor at all when it comes to anyone interfering with my food. Especially if I'm hungry, and even more so if I don't like the perpetrator to begin with. Although the arsehole didn't speak any English, I immediately ordered him to go and buy me a new pint of milk and to make sure it was the more expensive full cream variety. There was another Mexican wrestler named Tomas Riande with us that day who spoke English, and translated what I had said to the milk rustler. LaBarba did comply, and I got my milk replaced. But the loco-jerk-off made such a fuss that all the British were miserly, grabbing tightwads, that I decided that my honor and the honor of my country had been besmirched, and I would have to demand satisfaction. When later we arrived at the venue the posters revealed that my opponent that night was Joachim LaBarba. Then all I had to do after we had both entered the ring, was to visualize the Mad Mexican as Uriah Burton with a 1,000 pound bounty riding on his head. LaBarba became a Sombrero while I danced The Mexican Hat Dance all over him to the tune of 'The Mutilation Mambo' played at full volume in my brain by an imaginary Mariachi Rock Band. Both honor and full satisfaction was restored with a bloody big bonus.

The first promoter that I wrestled up north for was Wryton Promotions, and I worked for them for anywhere between a couple of consecutive days to a whole week almost every month. On this occasion I had wrestled in Altrincham, on the Monday night, and was wrestling at Solihull on the Tuesday. For Wryton Promotions I received 2 pounds extra, plus expenses, such as train fare and hotels – and a more elevated feeling of importance than I had experienced so far from Dale Martins. For Dale Martins, unless I was wrestling with a big name I would most likely be a preliminary. For Wryton Promotions I would often be billed in the semi-main event even when I was wrestling against a preliminary wrestler. At Solihull I was in my usual semi-main event slot, but this time I was billed against anything but a preliminary wrestler. In fact his pedigree was so impressive that if he'd been a Dog, he would have been the greatest all time champion that Crufts had ever seen. Hailing from Tokyo, Japan, Aikio Yashihara, as well as being a very accomplished freestyle wrestler had been awarded Black Belts in Judo, Jujitsu, Karate and Aikido. I remember wondering if he might also have a Black Belt for Origami, as he seemed to have completely ran out of anything else available in The Martial Arts department. The matchmaker, Martin 'Chopper' Conroy told me that they had picked up my Japanese opponent from the Hotel he was staying at in Manchester, and that he hadn't spoken one word to anyone else in their car for the whole of the 100 miles plus journey.

"I don't think he speaks English," explained Chopper, "although he seemed to understand what I said to him when I told him to put his wrestling bag in the trunk of the car." We were the second match in a semi-main event contest, of five ten minute rounds.

"What do you want us to do Chopper?" I asked.

"Do what you like," Chopper replied, "the Jap can't seem to understand a fuckin' word I'm saying to him!"

'Well that's novel,' I thought, 'I've never been told that one before, this ought to be interesting!' Very interesting indeed, the only thing I knew about Judo was from the little book that my young friend Paul James and I used to study and practice from when I was still attending the Grammar school. I had heard of both Jujitsu and Aikido, but didn't have a clue as to how they may differ from Judo. Then Karate was something else entirely. Although I didn't know much about that either, I had heard about all the devastating kicks, chops, breaking boards, and smashing concrete blocks, roof tiles and bricks, so, I thought once again, 'This ought to be interesting!"

I was already standing in my corner when my opponent approached the ring; his appearance caused a very impressive response from the fans who had packed the Civic Centre to capacity. The response he received, I gave credit to his use of his own country's national garb, as he looked quite resplendent in a very colorful and beautifully embroidered Kimono. His Magnificent presence seemed to multiply as he stepped into the ring and the gaudy silk and metallic threads in his Oriental gown gleamed and shimmered. As the Warrior of The Rising Sun basked below the bright ring lights, he Immediately became a prize. I felt that he had placed a jeweled crown on his head and was daring me to try to knock it off. In spite of my apprehension concerning any strange and exotic tactics he was sure to employ, I could barely wait to get the introductions behind us and the bell to ring to begin our contest. As the bell sounded the inscrutable, almost expressionless calm fell away from the Jap's face, and was replaced by a mask of shear viciousness. He leapt high in the air kicking, chopping, and screaming.

'Shit!' I thought, 'and I haven't even hit him yet!' In spite of my impatience to come to grips, I thought it might be wise to keep my distance while he was putting on such a savage display of violence. But then when I did approach, off he went again. My impatience to come to grips, caused me to put myself in range of his heavy artillery, I found that the force behind a flying kick aimed at the side of my head, that I blocked with my forearm would have been more than sufficient to knock me arse over head if I hadn't been blessed with the lightning fast reflexes necessary to block his attack.

'Right, you fucker!' I thought. 'I had been told to do what I wanted to do - so I did.' Although I knew that my own high kicks were as good as my Martial Arts trained opponent, I decided to remain completely faithful to my 'Uriah Burton Game-plan' and keep my kicks low. Especially as I now considered that the Jap had given me full license to deliver them with the force, and to the vicinity that I had in mind for my Giant Gypsy nemesis. By the second round the Japanese had completely ceased his high kicks, due to my counter moves which consisted of catching the leg that he kicked with. Then, either stepping in with a trip, or sniping his other leg right from under him with a vicious kick of my own to the side of his ankle. I then discovered another way of delivering a kick which turned out to be both offensively, and cosmetically effective, when I simultaneously dropped into a one legged squat as I kicked forward with the other foot. I was soon hopping around in a squat position and sniping out a kick straight in front of me reminiscent of the way that an agile Cossack performs his victory dance. Half way through the second round I took full advantage of the damage I had delivered when I dove in and scored a submission on his left leg. As the third round began, it did cross my mind to allow my opponent to take the offensive in order to make our contest look more competitive and exciting. But I didn't know him, and even more importantly, didn't trust him enough to take that chance. So all through the third I continued an unrelenting attack on the Jap's left leg. My concentration had never been more keen, his every attempt at any form of retaliation was thwarted before it had a chance, as his defenses evaporated by the second. Two minutes into the fourth round I brought our contest to a painful conclusion with another submission on his left leg. I did realize that I had left my very exotic adversary with very little drawing power in Solihull after I had greedily gobbled up all the glory, and left him with a two submission to zero defeat.

Under normal circumstances I might have felt guilty regarding my overwhelming monopoly over my opponent, but the continued encouragement I had been receiving all through the contest from referee Stan Rylands, such as,

"Wow that was terrific, let's see you do that again!" and then from 'Chopper Conroy as I entered the dressing room,

"Shit, that was a fuckin' great match – I didn't think you'd be able to do much with him!"

At last the big day came when the 2 Gypsies returned for the answer to their Champion's challenge, and without beating around the bush, I got straight to the point.

"Well it's like this," I told them, "I've got some good news, and I've got some bad news. The bad news is that Marino isn't interested in fighting. The good news is, I am!"

"Why isn't he interested in fighting?!" they wanted to know.

"I don't know," I told them truthfully, "he just said, fuck off, I'm not interested, but, as I just told you - I am!"

"You wouldn't stand a chance." One Gypsy replied.

"Not a snowball's chance in hell." Confirmed the other.

"How do you know that, unless you let me try?" I inquired.

"Uriah is twice your size and twice as strong, compared with him you're just a little kid!" The first Gypsy told me.

"That's what they said to David before he slew the shit out of Goliath?!" I argued.

"He's far too big for you!" he insisted.

"So what? I shouted, "I've fought bigger men, in and out of the ring, and I've beaten them, I've fought 7 different men in one day on the boxing booths and for only 1 pound a fight, so can you imagine what I'll do to your Gypsy King for a 1,000?!"

"You don't understand what Gypsy all-in, no holds barred, bare-knuckle fighting is all about," they warned me, "it isn't like boxing or wrestling with set rules, this is the most brutal style of street fighting, where anything and everything goes!"

"Oh yes I do understand what Gypsy all-in, bare-knuckle fighting is all about!" I contradicted loudly, "My Great-grandfather, Big Jim Arnold was a Welsh Mountain Fighter, which is exactly the same style and his Wife Caroline was a Romany Gypsy, so don't tell me I don't know what you're talking about – and I've fought on the Welsh Mountains too, same Mountains – same fucking results – I won. And – as far as Street fighting is concerned, where do you think Street fighting got its name? – It was named Street fighting after me, - Adrian Street!" I lied.

"If only Marino had your guts, we'd have ourselves a fight." The Gypsy stated.

"YOU'VE GOT YOURSELF A FUCKIN' FIGHT!" I insisted.

"Uriah Burton has never heard of you." The Gypsy told me.

"Well that makes us even," I countered, "I'd never heard of Uriah Burton before I met you two!" Then the Gypsy hit me with a bombshell when he replied,

"You're not big enough, or FAMOUS enough to fight Uriah Burton!"

BLUE VELVET

The truth can hurt very much, even more so if you have an ego with an appetite as large as mine to feed, in fact my ego and I were both in agony just thinking about the last thing the Gypsy said to me, before I told them both to,

"FUCK OFF!" – And don't come back until Uriah Burton has got the guts to fight me!" 'So I wasn't big enough or FAMOUS enough,' I thought over and over again till I thought my brain would burst. If I had become complacent and comfortable with my progress before the Gypsies came a visiting, I sure as Hell wasn't now. BUT, what was I going to do about it?! Who were the World's biggest wrestling Stars, and what did they have that I didn't? I asked myself. The answer as to who, came to me at once, the World Heavyweight Champion, 'Nature-Boy' Buddy Rogers. The wrestling Superstar who's illustrious mantle I imagined I had donned after being dubbed as such by famed wrestling writer Charles 'Spider' Mascall. As a result my wrestling had become much more deliberate, dominant and aggressive. My wrestling ability had also improved by leaps and bounds, but, I was still not 'Nature-Boy' Buddy Rogers. Buddy Rogers had proclaimed that he was 'often imitated, but never duplicated,' and although I would be the very first to agree with him, it sure as Hell wouldn't stop me trying. Especially in Britain where very few people had ever heard of the real thing, let alone seen him in action. Then the answer to the second part of my question came to me. I did have the ability and the attitude, but what Buddy Rogers had in spades that I lacked was 'THE LOOK!' True, I was a very good wrestler, but, I was a good wrestler in a land of great wrestlers. So what was I going to do to stand out from all the great wrestlers of Britain? That one was easy, - get my own 'LOOK'. I realized that the very first thing you have to do if you want to be a 'STAR' is to look like one. Then a whole myriad of pictures flashed through my mind as if to confirm my theory. All the things that had attracted my full and undivided attention going all the way back to my earliest memories. Pictures of the colorful costumes and uniforms of warriors from Red Indians and Zulus, to ancient Barbarians, Greeks, Romans, Saracens, Knights in shinning armor, and then the flashy uniforms worn by the Cavalrymen of Europe during the Napoleonic Wars. I was still determined to become a great wrestler, but I now fully appreciated that a great wrestler all done up in a pretty package would demand a whole lot more attention than just a great wrestler. As I have already stated, after watching my very first live wrestling show in Newport. I had been absolutely thrilled with the quality of the wrestling I saw that night, but quite disappointed with the color, costumes and showmanship displayed. Especially as everything I knew about professional wrestling up until that time, I had learned from the American wrestling magazines where every one of my favorites were colorful, brash, larger than life characters. With a mental image of the one and only original 'Nature-Boy' in my mind's eye, I set out on a quest to create my very own version of that 'Nature-Boy Look'. I had recently come across a Sports Store in Beak Street, near Soho, that I hadn't noticed before and assumed that it must have been newly opened. It was 'Lonsdale's' named no doubt after Lord Lonsdale, the man who promoted the first Boxing matches in 1891 where the contestants wore gloves instead of fighting bare-knuckle as they had prior to that time. I had only been in the store on a couple of previous occasions looking for boots. Although I had found the boots they sold too 'boxing' in style, they had assured me that they could custom make boots in a style more befitting a professional wrestler. I decided to pay them a visit, first to see what color ranges that might be available, and what kind of ideas I might derive as a result of that knowledge.

Well, I hit the jackpot! I had no sooner explained that I was looking for custom-made wrestling boots, preferably in a more unusual color than I was shown a beautiful pair of boots made of pale Baby-blue leather. It was love at first sight! I had never, ever seen wrestling boots that color before. My hands were shaking and my heart was thumping as I grabbed them out of the store assistant's hands in order to try them on for size. Again I hit the jackpot, these boots couldn't have fitted better if I had had them custom made. In fact, they had been custom made, but for another customer who had paid a small deposit and had then never turned up to collect them.

"We must have had them in the store for a year," the assistant explained. Then added hopefully, "the customer also ordered a ring jacket, and I'll bet that's your size too! Here I'll show it to you, and I'll give you a good deal if you want that as well." He then produced a blue and gold satin jacket that I didn't fall in love with. It was nice but looked to me too much like a sawn off version of the gowns worn by boxers. It was also very much in the style of the ring jackets worn by Jackie Pallo. The only difference being, Jackie's jackets was in different colors and made of a dull metallic fabric. Even if I had liked the style, I thought that it would have made a very poor match for the boots as the jacket was a deep royal blue and not a light Baby blue.

"I'll just take the boots," I told said, then a thought suddenly hit me and I asked,

"Who ordered the gown and boots?"

"It was a long time ago," the assistant told me, "I can't remember his name."

"Could it have been Tony Woods?" I suggested, as I remembered hearing Tony say that he had thought of an image and had ordered a costume to set the image off.

"That name does sound familiar." The assistant agreed vaguely, but then after I described Tony to him he thought that my theory was probably correct. I wondered then what had happened to Tony Woods and his big dream of becoming a wrestling Superstar, but as I have never heard of, or ever seen him again, I'm still wondering.

From Lonsdale's it was only a short walk to Borovik's fabric store near Soho Market in Berwick Street, where they seemed to stock every conceivable fabric in every conceivable color and shade. I was delighted, if not surprised to once again hit the jackpot and left Borovik's with a jacket length of Boot matching Baby Blue Velvet, and a similar length of metallic Silver lame to add a contrasting lining to my new Ring Jacket.

I had been given the estimate for the correct amount of yardage I needed from a Lady named Colette who lived in Brixton. She had recently began making wrestling trunks for Dale Martin's wrestlers. I had seen the array of fabrics suitable for making trunks she had available at her home which was also where she conducted her sewing business. I was once again proved to be correct with my assumption that she could match my new color scheme. She made my trunks to match and also made my new Jacket to my own design and specifications, just exactly the way I wanted it.

On the day I collected my new Jacket and Trunks I walked from Colette's home up to Dale Martin's office on my way home hoping to see some of the wrestlers outside that I could display my new outfit to. Just as I approached I met Mick McManus who was returning to the office from lunch, so I immediately accosted him, and showed him my new acquisition. His eyes popped wide open,

"How much did you pay for that Jacket?" he wanted to know, "I'll buy it off you!" he added before I could even reply.

"I don't want to sell it," I told him, "I had it made to match my boots and trunks." Mick seemed very disappointed that I wouldn't part with my new ring wear, but I was certain that it wouldn't have suited him, or fit his waistline even if I had been willing to sell it. I could only assume that he didn't really want it himself, but wanted to buy it so that I wouldn't have it. It was with that thought in mind that decided me to act on an idea I had only been toying with, and that was to pull out all stops and go for the whole 'Nature-Boy Look' hook-line and sinker. So, on my way back home I had just one more purchase to make to add the final touch, and that was from the nearest Chemist shop. Then as I burst into our flat I told Jean,

"Bleach my hair Blond!"

If I was going 'Nature-Boy' I decided - I was really going Nature-Boy!

****

The excitement I experienced in the dressing room as I waited to make my 'full Nature-Boy debut' must have exceeded the emotions I had felt as I made my way to the ring in my very first professional contest against Gentleman Geoff Moran. Or even in my Welsh Debut in Dumfries' Place Drill Hall in Cardiff. I had left nothing to chance. I looked magnificent and I knew it, in spite of the gauntlet of snide and jealous remarks I had lived through, made by all the other wrestlers who were still reeling from their first sight of my complete metamorphosis. I did have the same physique, but everything else was different. My chest still measured 48 inches, my waist was still only 27 inches, but I now sported a newly bleached blond mop and was clad in Baby-Blue. From my velvet jacket, to my Baby-Blue trunks, down to my Baby-Blue wrestling boots, which contrasted beautifully with the best suntan I had ever had before in my life. Cinderella had nothing on me; I likened myself to a magnificent blue Butterfly after it had emerged from a boring, dull Chrysalis. I could hardly wait for the fanfare to sound that would herald my triumphant procession from the dressing room towards my battleground.

I could just imagine the audience's reaction. At first they would just gasp at the very sight of me, then I would be completely enveloped in the deafening roar of approval, and I would be bombarded all the way to the ring with comments like,

"Oh, doesn't he look great?!"

"What a super young athlete!"

"Adrian is the greatest!" My brand new image had cost me a lot of money, much more than I could really afford, but the crowd's reaction and approval would be worth every farthing. The fanfare sounded, I burst out of the dressing room and into the spotlight that would follow me to the ring –

"Ahhhhhh!" – The mighty gasp of surprise that I had expected - but, from then on everything seemed to go south,

"Oh, isn't SHE cute!" Shrieked some stupid git in a loud effeminate voice.

"Ooowee – give me a kiss Mary!" some big fat bloke added.

"I'll see you outside after your match Darling!" boomed another male comedian. To say I was devastated, shocked and horrified would be like saying Adolph Hitler was very naughty - I was completely mortified!!! BUT! There was no way on Earth that I was going to let anyone in the audience, or even more so - in the dressing room, see how devastated, shocked and horrified I really was. So instead I did a complete one-eighty and in contrast to deflating like a punctured balloon, I puffed right up like a Bullfrog.

"Yes I am cute – thank you for noticing!" I replied to the

stupid git - then,

"Why on Earth would I want to kiss you, Fatso?!" to the big fat bloke – and,

"Sorry sweetie, you're really not my type!" to the male comedian, as my impersonation of the 'Nature-Boy' Buddy Rogers' manly strut evaporated, in favor of a graceful skip to the ring, and then all around it. After I had entered tonight's battleground the loud Wolf-whistles from all around the arena increased in volume until they hit a deafening crescendo. Then as the Master of Ceremonies began his introductions I heard a renewed snigger from the audience, and as I looked across the ring at my opponent I saw the reason for it. Scotland's Ted Hannon gave me 'that look' and did the limp wrist wave in my direction for their benefit. Well, the audience may have sniggered at Hannon's queer gesture, but not as much as they laughed at his obvious discomfort when I rewarded his salute with a blown kiss from pouting lips, and fluttering eyelashes. Then I approached him with my arms wide open as though I intended to embrace him. His response to that was to leap out of the ring as though Satan himself was after his sweet arse. The audience screamed with delight - as just like my peers in the dressing room, there was nothing they enjoyed more than someone else's discomfort. But now it was my opponent's discomfort they laughed at instead of my own. I was so very disappointed by the audience's reaction to my effort to wow them as they had never been wowed before. But there was no way that I was willing to lose face, especially in front of the jealous wrestlers who had scoffed at my new image with remarks like,

"What the fuck did you do that to your hair for - do you know how stupid you look?!" and "Bleed'n' Hell! You're not going in the ring looking like that, are you?!"

'Damn it! I thought, 'they all sounded like my Father.' How happy they would all be now, that I had obviously miscalculated the fans response, and had totally fucked-up. I knew I had fucked-up, but there was no way that I was going to admit it. Instead I viewed my predicament as a challenge. I was determined to turn it around, I was determined to make it work, I was determined to win. The only way I could think of preserving what little there was left of my badly dented dignity, was to go with the flow. While throwing all the innuendoes and insults right back into the faces of my treacherous fans and fellow wrestlers alike. I began to blow kisses to the more offensive men in the audience, and to my opponent. Then when I had him tied up in a debilitating hold, I would fuss with my hair or kiss my own biceps. I received mixed reaction from the fans, some loved it, some seemed highly amused, others booed for all they were worth - which wasn't much in my books. But at least I did have their full and undivided attention. When the match was over, and I walked back to the dressing room my head was in a whirl. I forced a very smug look on my face that was totally at odds with the emotions I was really feeling, but there was no way I would allow the wrestlers there to reap an atom of satisfaction at my expense. I had to pretend that the response I received from the audience, was the response I had been looking for. It was like this – Imagine that you had been invited to a party and wanted to make a big impression. You're all dressed up, and as you make your grand entrance you accidentally step on a tomato that one of the guests have dropped on the floor, and you fall face first right into the sherry-trifle. What do you do to save face? – Jump back up, you try to smile disarmingly through the whipped cream and desiccated coconut that's spread all over your chops and you say,

"I MEANT TO DO THAT – HA-HA!" Well that was the closest scenario that I can think of to describe my effort to deflect the derision that would have been meted on me wholesale, if I had allowed them just the faintest awareness of my true feelings.

I fully appreciated after a lifetime of deflecting ridicule, that even if the mockers and knockers didn't believe that you were not upset by their cruel jests. You could still deprive them of their full satisfaction if you simply refused to acknowledge that their mockery had even the slightest affect on you. Another invaluable weapon was a quick wit, which I had put to good use starting the day after I had learned to talk. As I mentioned, my Brother would amuse himself for hours, by telling me how small and ugly I was when I was a very young kid, but one day he made a frightful mistake in his effort to belittle me, when he told me,

"You're so ugly; you look like a Monkey's Brother!" He really didn't realize what he had actually said until I replied,

"Well that's hardly surprising – I am a Monkey's Brother!"

Thereafter, when ever Brother Terence felt he wanted to share his views concerning my lack of size and physical beauty, all I had to do was to repeat,

"Well that's hardly surprising - I am a Monkey's Brother!" to shut him the fuck up. Mind you, it would usually mean a severe pummeling, but a pummeling would most definitely be on the menu anyway, so why not give Big Brother a reason instead of getting a whacking for nothing?! As you can imagine, spending all my early school days posing as a Cherokee Indian War Chief, tended to invite a jib or two at my expense, but all that accomplished was an excellent opportunity to hone my own skills in verbal retaliation. Or if I couldn't think of a quick witty reply, a swift fist or a vicious kick would have to suffice. Either way, it was good practice and I always had the last laugh.

I have already spoken of the Coal Miners I worked with, sarcastic remarks about the sideburns, the hair style, the Teddy-Boy clothes - "You won't go to London." – And then after I did, "You won't last in London." – "You're too small to be a wrestler." – "A real wrestler would rip you in half." And then with Dad - shit, I'm not even going into that one! With all of them, I never ever felt as though I gave them as good as I got – I always thought I gave better. And – that was just as well, because when you enter the World of professional wrestlers you are throwing yourself on the mercy of the undisputed Princes of Piss-taking - where not an iota of mercy exists. There was just one thing that wrestlers enjoyed more than telling and listening to stories for hours on end – and that was piss-taking! Then, if the victim was to show even the tiniest signs of anger, embarrassment, or distress - or expose one microscopic chink in his armor. Then the sharp verbal daggers would find their way in, and there would be a mass feeding frenzy from every wrestler present. With no let up even after the victim's very heart, guts and brain had been sliced, spliced and diced. I am not attempting to put myself above that cruel and barbaric behavior, as no sooner had I began to appreciate their humor than I became a champion at it. If for no other reason than to deflect my own discomfort onto someone else when I found that I was the prey - preferably if possible onto the main and most offensive predator. Just as a physical bully will steer clear of you if you smash his chops, a verbal bully will soon learn not to get too sarcastic if you are capable of putting him in his place eleven times out of ten. When I had first began to wrestle for Dale Martins, in an effort to impress my peers, many of which I had idolized since I had first watched them in action in Cardiff. I made the terrible mistake of bringing the physique magazines to show them that I had appeared in over the last few years. Again I had miscalculated, instead of receiving the compliments and recognition I had expected as I passed the magazines around the crowded van, or dressing room, all I got was,

"Oh, look at all these naked men!" and "Damn – I can smell the Pansies from here!" also, "What a bunch of cream-puffs!" then another would add, "Don't you mean screaming poufs?" Was I disappointed and horrified?! – Well yes, as a matter of fact I WAS! – did I ever show it? – WHAT ARE YOU NUTS?!!!!

"All these Bodybuilders are queers - right?!" one would ask me,

"Well not all of us Dear," I replied sweetly, "I've heard there are a few who are not - although, I've never actually met any of them myself." You can't imagine how fast all those smug expressions just dropped right off every leering face.

"Hey let me outa here!" squawked the wrestler I was sitting next to, who was wedged between me and the window.

"Why Dear?" I inquired, "Are you uncomfortable?" I added, as I slid my arm comfortingly around his shoulder.

"Hey let me out - I'm not sitting next to a fuckin' Pouf!" he shouted.

"Oh sit still and don't be such a drama Queen," I told him gently, "you've got nothing to worry about from me my Dear - you're not even my type."

"What do you mean, I'm not you're type," he wanted to know, "what's wrong with me?!"

"Oh, you're far too effeminate for me my Dear petal," I replied, using my very best 'Lon of London' imitation, "I like my men more manly." Well his face dropped a foot, and all the other wrestlers laughed their heads off – AND AT HIM – NOT AT ME! – Just the way it ought to be. So even though I was upset at not receiving the sort of 'reaction' I had wanted, and had expected from the wrestling audience. I found that all the mockers, knockers and piss-takers from my childhood, right up to – and most especially the other wrestlers, had strengthened my armor to an almost impenetrable thickness and had made me 'appear' completely invulnerable against the audience's most hostile and offensive reaction to my new image. And then the word 'REACTION' slid right to the forefront of my mind - that sort of reaction may not have been the sort of reaction I had expected or hoped for from the crowd, BUT, it was still more reaction than any other wrestler got that night. 'So', I thought, 'that may not have been the sort of reaction I had been looking for, but it had been more than I had ever received before, so who cares what sort of reaction it was? – I WANTED MORE OF IT!'

ADRIAN STREET
SETS OUT TO PROVE
APPEARANCES CAN BE DECEPTIVE. - Russell Plummer.

Adrian Street trotted into the ring amid a somewhat mixed reception from a crowd rather stunned by his appearance – in pale blue, complete to his boots and it was some minutes before a few derisive whistles and shouts could be heard. By that time Adrian, beneath his familiar mop of blond hair was cheerfully grinning at all and sundry and it was left to Master of Ceremonies Bobby Palmer to sum it all up when he turned to the crowd and asked them: "Can you help but like him?"

If any doubts persisted by the time the contest on this particular evening started they had disappeared half an hour later after Adrian had turned in a smart display to come back from a fall down to level the match and hold British Lightweight Champion Melwyn Riss to a draw. Although the opponents and crowds have been different this is fast becoming the regular entrance for the young welterweight from Wales and Adrian made it quite clear to me that the stir caused by his appearances is no accident.

"You can call me something of a "Nature-Boy' Buddy Rogers disciple if you like," said Adrian, "although there is a difference between me and most of this school." He added "I like to think I can hold my own by wrestling, but if that is not enough, I'm out to make sure the crowds remember me by my appearance." Not that Adrian formally billed as 'The Welsh Adonis' and now the 'Nature-Boy' and one of the best built young men in wrestling needs to worry on that score, but his fast growing wardrobe of ring jackets and dressing gowns is certainly making him a man few fans will forget. Now a professional for something more than four and a half years Adrian has been making good progress recently and has turned in some particularly good contests in Southern halls since the start of the season and is now seen often in televised matches. From Brynmawr, near Cardiff, Adrian feels he is now sufficiently well established and experienced to team up in tag combination – and quite naturally would like nothing better than to be featured with his talented countryman Tony Charles. A Charles-Street combination could soon establish itself among the leading teams in the country and Adrian hopes that some enterprising promoter will soon hit upon the idea of a 'Welsh Dragons' team and put it into practice. Adrian has a number of interests out of the ring, among them still and cine photography, painting and sketching. He is also well known as a model for physical culture magazines and has often been a 'cover man.' When he hit upon the idea of an extensive array of ring wear he set about building up his wardrobe. Now he is determined to arrive with a different outfit on each appearance at any hall – and by hook or by crook, make sure that the crowds will remember him.

Any suggestion for a best dressed welterweight competition? – Russell Plummer.

As it seems, in many arenas I was making a favorable impression, but I wasn't looking for favorable any more, I was looking for WOW!!!!! I do think that this might have made for a better story if my transition had been more immediate, but it wasn't an overnight rags to rhinestones success, it was more of an evolution than a Eureka. Nevertheless my impatience did make it a fairly rapid evolution. In some arenas the audience almost got the point, but only almost. In other arenas they missed the point entirely, and I had to bare the full brunt of their ignorance. But as I may have mentioned before, if I really go out of my way to do something that I imagine people would very much appreciate – and they don't – just you wait and see what I'll do next!

My TV debut wearing my new 'Look' I felt had really paid off, so much so that I wondered what I could possibly do to top it next time. I realized that it would only be a matter of time before the fans got used to seeing me in my new-blue outfit, and that eventually, familiarity would breed contempt. So even the splendid figure I cut would all too soon become commonplace or part of the scenery – I was not going to allow that to happen. So, in order to counter this, I determined to wear something different each time I made an appearance at the same arena, after of course giving each new look a TV debut.

At first, in order to give myself the time to come up with a new look I modified the Baby-Blue trunks and replaced the original ones with a new design. They were the same color and fabric, but the new design had both sides of the trunks completely removed and the front and back of the trunks joined together with only very thin Baby-Blue straps. I did wear G-String briefs underneath them to keep everything in place, but they still looked as though I was naked down both sides of my body, apart from the very thin strips. Did they get the attention and crowd reaction I hoped for as a result? – Well I'll let the reaction and statements made by Stan Stone, the very conservative, ex old-school wrestler turned referee answer that one,

"What in Hell's name do you call those things you're wearing?! He spluttered when he saw them for the first time, "Those are not wrestling trunks - you can't wear those - I won't go in the same ring with you and referee your match if you're going to wear them - you'll get us all arrested, they'll close this arena down!!!"

"Okay, I'll go and ask Jack Dale what he thinks of them in that case." I sighed, so off I went to ask Jack what he thought about them,

"Hey Jack!" I called to him when I found him in the box-office, "What do you think of my new design wrestling trunks?"

"They look great," Jack replied, "I wish more of the Boys would use a bit more imagination with their ring-wear - if you don't watch them, they'd all go in the ring wearing the same colors." He complained.

"Well Stan Stone said he wouldn't referee my match if I wear them." I told him.

"I'll be in the dressing room in another 10 minutes," he replied, "I'll sort it out with him." I shot back to the dressing room like a rocket, and told Stan Stone myself,

"Jack said these WRESTLING trunks are great, and it's okay to wear them whether you approve or not – so there!" Stan was livid, but that was okay too, as there were not many referees that I was particularly fond of anyway. The trunks shocked everyone as they were meant to do; they also bought me time to begin my creation of another brand new look. I wanted something that would prove to be a total contrast in color and style to my Baby-Blue number, but still be in character with 'The Nature-Boy Gimmick.' I decided to stick with the velvet and metallic lining, but completely change the style and color. For color, I chose jet black velvet for the outside of my gown with a metallic gold lining. For style I thought I would like to emulate one of the many Light-Cavalry regiments of the Napoleonic period, such as the Hussars. My personal favorites were Napoleon's Elite Body Guard, The Chasseur a de Cheval, or anything worn by the flamboyant and dashing Marshal Joachim Murat. But the colors worn by these particular warriors were not what I had in mind. Instead I would choose something along the lines of The Prussian Death's Head Hussars, or The Hussars of The Black Brunswickers, but modified to suit my own needs. These Hussars wore a close fitting tunic they called a Dolman, and then a looser fitting braided, fur-trimmed jacket called a Pelisse that was usually worn more like a cape than a jacket. It was fastened over the left shoulder in order to leave their saber hand free for slashing. I kept the design of the Dolman basically as is, but altered the design of the Pelisse so that it was more like a short, sleeveless cape which sat squarely on both of my shoulders instead of being draped over the left. I also replaced the military style braiding with designs made up out of gold sequins, and large Emerald Green Rhinestones in order to suggest a flashy Male Peacock when I held the edges of the cape and raised both hands. What I particularly liked about that jacket was that the hands could be raised and the cape spread as a gesture of impending victory, or triumph when an audience were cheering my efforts. Or if the same gesture was employed combined with a haughty sneer, and arrogant pose it could suggest instead a two finger, or middle finger salute to all those who chose to boo me. I already had black boots and trunks to wear with it, but very soon became dissatisfied with that arrangement. As no sooner had I dispensed with the fancy jacket to begin my match, than I would once again find myself clad in clothes that were no flashier than any of my opponents - and that would never do. I decided to try to match the gold lining of my jacket instead of the black outside. So I took another trip to Borovik's for metallic gold fabric to make my trunks and then took a pair of my old white boots and spray painted them a bright metallic gold. - Now that was very much flashier than any of my opponents – and that would do very nicely thank you. As soon as I was told that I had another TV show coming up, I set to work on my third creation. This time I went back to a similar style jacket to the Baby-Blue velvet one, but with much fuller, puffier sleeves. Then instead of velvet, it was made of metallic silver lame` with a bright red satin lining. After I brought the jacket home from Collette's I drew a design of a big Welsh Dragon that I got Jean to embroider large enough to cover the whole back of it, and she really made a beautiful job of it. It was embroidered in a glossy red silk with the details all picked out in black. Each scale covering the Dragon's entire body and wings were stuffed with padding so that the whole of the finished design looked, and felt more like a base-relief than a one dimensional picture. With this jacket I would wear silver metallic-lame` trunks, and I spray painted yet another pair of boots in metallic silver to match everything else. Although the jacket made its début on a Television show held in London's Bermondsey Baths, I was really looking forward to the first time I would wear the outfit in Cardiff – capital City of Wales. That way I could shamelessly flaunt my Welshness in front of all my fellow country folk, and if they didn't choose to accept me as their hero, then I could throw my patriotism, and their lack of it right back in the traitorous faces with the beautiful emblem of Wales emblazoned right across my back. Unfortunately that was never to be, as when I returned home that evening after my TV match in Bermondsey Baths, I found that my beautiful, brand new Welsh Dragon Jacket had been stolen out of my case. Obviously the jacket couldn't be used, and was of no use to another wrestler, but it just goes to prove the degree of jealousy that my new image was already beginning to provoke.

****

So, according to my Gypsy visitors, I wasn't big enough, or famous enough to fight their King. As a result I was now working diligently on my new look that would hopefully help to take care of 'The Famous' aspect, but in the meantime without consciously trying I was also getting a lot bigger. When I had first arrived in London from Wales I had managed to build myself up to 179 pounds. I had hoped to increase it further to at least 200 pounds, but after loosing my job, and then training 11 times a week on a starvation diet, I had dropped down to 144 pounds. When at last, I could once again afford to eat, and had halved my training regimen, the weight had slowly crept back up, by the time I had got married I weighed 155 pounds. But by the time Jean was just about ready to give birth to our first child I weighed in at a hefty 199 pounds! In just 6 months I had gained 44 pounds, which I attributed at the time to feelings of sympathy for Jean, who too had steadily been gaining weight as a result of her condition.

Although it could have been partly sympathy, the fact that I now lived just a few miles from where I would be dropped off each night, and I would only have to walk that distance instead of all the way across London must have contributed somewhat to my increasing size too. Yet another contributing factor was due to the Mammoth sized meals I would consume every night, or early morning when I arrived back home from where ever I had been wrestling.

Jean must have been the laziest person I had ever met in my life, by this time I had purchased a television set for her, and each morning or afternoon when I left the flat to go to Dale Martins, she would be sitting in her chair watching it. Very many hours later, when I returned home she would still be sitting in the very same position, usually gazing at a blank screen, as though time had stood still for her since the time I left. As her Beehive hairdo seemed to have got higher and higher, since we had got married and the fact that she very seldom seemed to move. I began to wonder if the increased elevation of her hairdo was actually caused by hair, or dust. But, in her defense what ever time of the night or morning I came back home, there would either be a large cooked meal waiting for me, or she would be sitting there ready to cook one. – And to that I would give the most credit for making me heavier than I had ever been before in my life. I had always wanted to be very much heavier, at least from the very first time I had made my mind up to become a professional wrestler. I had been told time and again that I was too small, but now that I seemed to be capable at last of easily putting on as much weight as I thought necessary, I began to experience mixed feelings about getting too heavy. All I remember hearing as a youngster when living in Wales was you're too small to be a wrestler, even when I met Reg Trood and Pasquale Salvo in the YMCA before I had ever had my first professional match, Pasquale had told me,

"You'll never make any money as a wrestler - little guys like you are ten a penny, - ha-ha-ha!" As a result I had tried to gain weight but had been very unsuccessful, until now, but as they say, 'be careful what you wish for.' In my eternal quest to make as much money as I possibly could, I had still been posing for physique photographs, for anyone in London with the desire, the cash and a camera. With of course the exception of Lon of London. As well as all the regulars, I had been introduced to Royale, Vince and Spartan by Ray Fury, who had also posed professionally for physique magazines. Then I was contacted by Galaxy Studios in Richmond, who not only paid better than all the rest, but put my photos in new magazines like 'Scan' – and used my real name in them instead of Kid Tarzan Jonathan. Galaxy it seemed couldn't get enough of me. On almost every one of the very few days I had free from wrestling, I was able to schedule a lucrative session in front of the camera. But, when my weight began to increase so dramatically, my muscular definition decreased in the same fashion. By the time my weight crested at 199 pounds and my waistline had increased from 27 inches, to very portly 33, it spelled the end of my physique posing, and the end of a lucrative source of income. So already I was beginning to have my doubts about swelling up to a full blown heavyweight. Especially as I was only 5' 7" tall, and at the age of 21, I was certain that there was very little hope of gaining any more height to warrant carrying all that extra baggage. The reason that so many professional wrestlers wanted to join the heavyweight division was, that up until that time it was the heavyweights who were the undisputed rulers of the roost. They were at the very pinnacle of the food chain, with all the lighter-weights being regarded as the third class citizens of our profession. An example of the heavyweight's attitude towards their smaller piers occurred on the way to a show one day when I got out of the van for a 'Melvin Riss' – 'piss' and when I returned to the van found that 'Mr. Universe' Big John Lees had moved out of his own seat into my more comfortable one. As I already knew that complaining would be a total waste of breath, I just bided my time until we stopped to eat, and Big John went into the café with the rest of the wrestlers. As usual I had brought my own food with me, so as soon as the van was empty, I moved back onto my original seat. When Big John returned to the van with the rest of the guys, he glared at me and ordered,

"Get out of my seat, Street!" I had just put a fork-full of food into my mouth, so I just chewed away slowly while Big John towered expectantly above me. After I had swallowed I replied,

"It's not your seat, so piss off!"

"If you don't get out of that seat right now, I'll drag you out of it!" he threatened.

"If you want me out of this seat, you'll have to drag me out of it," I told him, then I added, "but I guarantee that you are going to bleed if you try!"

"This is your last chance!" He roared, "Are you getting out of that seat or am I going to move you!"

"You are going to have to move me!" I replied, as I popped another mouthful of food into my chops.

"Fuckin' lightweights need to know their place in this business!" He told both me and everyone else in the van, as he walked away and sat down again in his original seat – at the back of the bus. Former Mr. Universe winner, Big John Lees ended up backing down after threatening me, but I would not have backed down, and Big John would have bled if he had laid his hand on me just as I had promised him. For one thing I don't respond well to threats, and on this occasion Mr. Universe's timing couldn't have been worse, as this incident occurred at the same time that I still thought that I might be going to fight Uriah Burton. In fact, all the time Big John Lees had been standing in front of me issuing his threats, I had been sizing him up as I chewed on my lunch. Uriah Burton, I had been told, was a little less than 6 feet tall, and weighed close to 240 pounds. John Lees, I estimated would have been a few inches taller, but approximately the same weight. Which I thought at that time might have proved to be good practice for me if he had made good on his threat, and attempted to remove me from my seat.

Almost all of the big draws, or Main Events in those days were in the heavyweight division. The biggest crowd puller of all at that time, was the Canadian, Mohawk Indian, Billy Two-Rivers. Billy who entered the ring in a full Indian headdress and sported a Mohican scalp-lock hairdo, was reputed to be earning a whapping 40 pounds a match, at a time when very few of Britain's top heavyweights were earning more than 10 or 12 pounds.

The huge, Scottish bearded behemoth, Wild Ian Campbell, who stood 6 feet 4 inches tall and weighed in the region of 300 pounds, was also an overnight sensation. I have seen a crowd of fans who had been lining up outside a wrestling arena for hours to ensure a seat. When the sudden appearance of the mammoth Scot after he had squeezed himself out of his self driven Bentley, wearing his matching Deerstalker hat and cape. They left their places in line in a hurry to disperse and stampede down the road terrified out of their minds as he approached the arena.

The first time I ever set eyes on the giant American Sky-Hi-Lee was in Cardiff. I had arrived early and as I entered the dressing-room I felt as though I had walked through a magic portal and into the Jurassic age. Perched on a wooden chair that was made for a modern human being was the nearest thing I had ever seen to a prehistoric Pterodactyl. I said "hello" and almost felt the ground vibrate as he turned towards me and replied in a low growl that was as primeval as his appearance. I shook hands with a paw the size of a Frogman's flipper, and noted that their owner was at least as tall as I was while he was still sitting down. I was quite amazed to find that when he did stand up, his head didn't crash right through the ceiling, as his legs were hardly longer than my own. Although at the height of 6 feet 10 inches, he was the tallest human being that I had ever seen up until that time. Of all the giants I have seen since, not one has come close to having a rib-box as long as his, it was the size and shape of a large trashcan, and began from his hips which were level with my own and seemed to end inches above my head. Big Sky had come over from the States originally to wrestle for Paul Lincoln's promotions. As well as a hefty payoff, included in his contract was two bottles of whiskey a night which he would drink like I would drink a bottle of milk. Before he became a wrestler Sky-Hi-Lee had worked as a Geek in the American Carnivals, and would stick skewers and needles through his face and arms. He would eat electric light bulbs and chickens heads. If you drank with Sky in a pub or a night-club, always the showman after he threw a slug of whiskey down his throat, he'd eat the glass that the whiskey had been served in, and then wash down the glass shards that he had reduced to powder with his next glass of whiskey. After enough booze had blurred their better judgment many wrestlers in Sky's company would sometimes attempt to emulate this feat, mostly with dire consequences.

The most extreme example Sky told us, had occurred when he was touring Japan. When one night after the matches Sky and a number of other wrestlers including the legendary Korean born, Japanese superstar Riki Dozan was relaxing in a Tokyo Nightclub. A few rounds of drinks into the evening, and Big Sky decided it was time for his party piece, and after downing a double Scotch he began munching on the glass. Riki Dozan's eyes must have popped 10 inches out of his head. He really could not comprehend what he was witnessing, and when Sky took another shot of whiskey to wash all the crunched up glass away, he was completely speechless. Right up until the moment before Sky had began his whiskey glass trick, Riki had been holding court, and had been the central figure at their table. He was not the sort of person who took kindly to being upstaged. He at once ordered 2 more whiskeys for Sky, and then ordered Sky to repeat his party piece. Big Sky being more than happy to perform an encore, indulged him to the full. Sky had hardly finished swilling down the shards of the first glass, with the whiskey from the second. Before Riki Dozan grabbed up the glass ask-tray that was sitting on their table, and attacked it with his teeth like a starving Hyena would tear into a baby Gazelle. Within one minute there was blood splattered all over the table, as the rabid Riki chewed on a small amount of glass he had managed to crack off the ashtray. Along with a couple of his own teeth that had also cracked off as a result of his determination not to be outdone.

I had first heard of Riki Dozan about 10 years earlier, as a result of his name cropping up amongst many of the foremost wrestlers in the Middle and Far East being invited to compete in the yearly 'Champion of the Orient Tournaments.' They were held in Malaysia and Singapore by the 400 pound plus, Hungarian born Emile 'King Kong' Czaja. As was usual, the tournament was extremely successful, so much so, that the 'Japanese Mob' connected Riki Dozan decided it was time for Japan to invade Malaysia and Singapore for a second time in a quest to take over the wrestling there.

Emile 'King Kong' Czaja who had earned his nickname after playing the Giant Ape in a movie shot in India, had ran the wrestling promotions in the Singapore area for many years. But after a death-threat from Riki Dozan and his Japanese mobsters, that they promised would be carried out, posthaste if he remained in Dodge. Czaja and his Australian born Wife Ellie, went into a forced exile in Sydney, where he once again began promoting wrestling.

Riki Dozan had initially begun wrestling in the Sumo style, but by about 1950 he began his career as a Freestyle professional. His timing couldn't have been better, as so close to the end of the war, demoralized Japan was in need of a 'Super-hero' and Riki Dozan was there to fit the bill. American 'Villains' were imported to face the Japanese Champion, and Riki would vanquish them one after another. This not only avenged Japan's wartime defeat, and boosted Japan's moral as a result, but in the process elevated Riki Dozan to an almost mythical and Godlike status. Both in the eyes of the Japanese public and even more so to Riki Dozan himself. In December 1963 while partying in the same nightclub in which he had broken his teeth on the ashtray. Riki was stabbed in the stomach by a rival gangster named Katsuji Murata, with a knife whose blade had been soaked in urine. But being a God, Riki then retaliated by beating the crap out of his would be assassin, and throwing him out of the club. He then returned to his table and continuing his partying as though nothing had occurred. Later Riki was admitted to Shannoh Hospital, he got himself stitched up, and probably would have easily recovered. But for the Doctor who told Riki that under no circumstances was he to drink any fizzy drinks. It was a shame that the Doctor didn't know Riki Dozan better, as no one ordered a God about, and no one told Riki Dozan what he could, or couldn't do. To prove this point, Riki sent one of his gofers out for a case of 7UP – he proved his point alright – and in the traditional Japanese ritualized form of suicide, he sat in bed and drank the lot. His stomach burst, as he accidentally but equally painfully performed Seppuku, and died using a case of 7UP instead of the traditional Japanese blade.

Another of Ski-Hi-Lee's party tricks entailed his boozing buddies drawing a full sized dartboard on Big Sky's huge bare back, and then playing the very popular British pub game, by throwing a set of 3 steel darts, one at a time right into his naked flesh. There were a number of us, thus engaged in Sky's Old Compton Street flat after the matches had ended one night, when Dave Larson who by this time was armed to the teeth with Dutch courage, and decided that he was up to emulating Ski-Hi-Lee's bizarre feat. Jon Cortez was also present that night, and he liked Dave Larson about as much as a cosmetic model liked acne. He insisted on being the first to hurl a dart at Dave Larson's bare back. Whether it was too much drink, whether it was too much excitement, or whether it was great dart playing, only Jon Cortez would have known for sure. As after throwing the dart with all the force he could muster, Dave Larson was leaping around the flat screaming like a Soho Tart who's latest John had pissed off without paying, with Jon's dart embedded deeply right into the back of his head.

Big Sky was just one of many Americans wrestling in Britain at that time, there was also 'Texas' Buddy Cody who was no taller, but much heavier than I. There was 'Texas' Jack Bence, who was also heavier and not much taller, 'Cowboy' Kenny Ackles, the 6' 4" ex Marine Frankie Townsend, 'Catalina' George Drake who was a particularly good friend of mine, so was The Masked Zebra Kid and 'Lucky' Somonovitch. Each of them had a great sense of humor – very mischievous, but not as vindictive as our home grown variety. Lucky had told me lots of stories of my American Idols, many of whom he had wrestled against himself, including 'Nature Boy' Buddy Rogers. He earned my undying friendship when he told me that I reminded him very much of a younger Buddy Rogers. He was one of the very few wrestlers who seemed to be aware of what I was endeavoring to achieve with my new and fast evolving image. He told me to stick to it, as he really thought that my ideas and imagination would eventually pay off. I really treasured a glossy 8x10 inch photo of himself that he gave me, on which he wrote 'from your good friend Lucky Somonovitch, to the one and only 'Amazing Adrian'.

Mostly the Americans, like other foreigners would wrestle against British wrestlers. But one night I was on the same card when 'Lucky' topped the bill against one of his fellow countryman 'Catalina' George Drake, and they agreed to give us a typical American wrestling contest. The ring was set on a stage, which meant that the whole audience was only able to sit on one side of it and view the action in the same way that they would watch a play or a movie. That gave all the rest of the wrestlers on the bill the ability to watch their match from the wings that surrounded the other three sides of the ring and us hidden from the fans by the stage's curtains. As soon as the bell sounded to start their contest their antics had me alternately laughing out loud, or cringing with embarrassment.

"How do I look, Baby?!" Lucky asked his opponent as he strutted around the ring.

"You look frigin' great Man - how do I look?!" Replied 'Catalina' George.

"Magnificent Baby - you've been on the weights – right?!" answered Lucky.

"Never touched a barbell in my life, Honey, all this is natural!" Claimed George indignantly, as he puffed up his chest and flexed his biceps to emphasize the fact.

"WOW MAN! – Don't do that again, you're making me hard!" Gasped Lucky.

"Okay, that's nothing, just watch me get out of a wrist-lock!" challenged George as he offered his left arm to Lucky by putting it in a perfect position for Lucky to apply the appropriate hold. Lucky obliged, which made George scream,

"WAOW MAN, YOUR KILLING ME – NOT SO FRGGIN' TIGHT!!!"

We could all see from our vantage point that Lucky was hardly touching him, but as loud as he screamed, the audience, who from their vantage point imagined George was being crucified screamed and cheered even louder. It seemed that we wrestlers were watching one version of their match, and the fans another, with both sets of audience being thoroughly entertained. But as clever as I appreciated both contestants to be, I was certain that if Jack Dale had been standing with us that night that both my American friends would have been on the first plane back to the USA the very next morning.

After watching the All-American match I thought I must have seen it all. But just a few nights later I was wrestling in one of the Bath's Halls, when the main event contest saw 'Texas' Jack Bence pitted against 'The Dazzler' Joe Cornelius. Before their match even began, the audience knew exactly who was the villain and who was their hero. They booed and hooted at the snarling, scowling Texan, and cheered loudly for the handsome, smiling Dazzler. Their cheers hit a crescendo as The Dazzler was introduced and he pirouetted theatrically in the middle of the ring causing his glittering cape to swirl out all around him. Texas Jack responded badly towards the adoration that was being showered on his hated adversary when he charged across the ring, grabbed the top rope and viciously kicked the bottom one as he screamed abuse at the fans, and ordered them to,

"SHUT UP!!!" Which I was soon to discover was setting the scene for the whole contest. The bell sounded, both wrestlers burst out of their corners and began to circle each other. A hush of anticipation fell over the audience, broken only by a scattering of hollers of encouragement from various corners of the hall of,

"GO GET HIM JOE!" After a few more circuits the two warriors clashed in the middle of the ring, the battle was on, and the fans exploded. Both contestants trembled with exertion as they pushed and pulled at each other in an attempt to gain advantage, and bit by bit the heroic Joe was forced to give ground as the grumpy, growling Gremlin from Texas forced him backwards towards one corner of the ring. The audience screamed their encouragement a decibel higher as The Dazzler slowly but surely gave more ground. HA! But that had only been a ruse, and the arrogant American fell for it. In the last split second Joe cleverly sidestepped and using the full force of the Texan's impetus sent him hurtling face first into the corner-post – once again the audience exploded in unison.

"HA-HA – GO GET HIM JOE!!" And once again the tenacious Texan hurled himself at the ropes and ordered the fans to,

"SHUT THE HELL UP!!! As he covered both his ears, with both his hands in response to their loud defiance. This sort of scenario continued, as every single one of the American's legitimate but aggressive onslaughts failed to bear fruit. And he was again forced to cover his ears with his hands, as he was bombarded by wave after wave of brain numbing jeers from the jubilant fans. But, as fair means had obviously failed him, he began to foul, a little at first, and then in earnest and soon he had the Dazzler dazed, dizzy and in deep shit. Poor Joe was now systematically dismantled, and for the first time since the match had began a hush fell over the audience. They watched in horrified dismay the destruction and pending demise of their own shining hero. Torn, battered and helpless, Joe lay at the feet of his victorious, but vindictive conqueror. Everyone knew he could have put an end to his adversary's misery any time he chose, but instead chose to draw out the agony in order to satisfy his own sadistic pleasure. And to punish by proxy every one of his hated, unsupportive, British fans. The brute from Texas simply drooled with satanic satisfaction as he dug his powerful, talon like fingers deeper and deeper into the trapezius muscles of his now motionless opponent, who he had propped up into a sitting position in the middle of the ring. He controlled Joe easily, with one knee in his back whilst he knelt on the other so that he could gloat and beam victoriously at the audience. He would turn his opponent's head in various directions in order to display the agony that was etched on the Dazzler's face to each and every one of the hero's distraught fans.

Well, he taunted and sneered, as both his opponent and the fans groaned in unison, while enjoying every second of their mutual dismay. BUT! All of a sudden Joe thrusts his fist into the air, and everyone in the audience holds their breath - then Joe stamps hard on the mat with one foot – silence – then he stomps again – and again – AND AGAIN!

Soon everyone in the audience is stamping in time with their hero – then they begin to chant – softly at first and then louder – and LOUDER – AND LOUDER!!

"JOE – JOE – JOE – JOE!!!!!" The stamping and chanting gets louder and louder. The Texas Tornado is unable to stand the colossal, deafening racket and he leaves his victim and scrambles to his feet screaming at the audience,

"SHUT UP – SHUT UP – SHUT – UP!!!" But all the entire crowd did was to stomp harder and shout louder and LOUDER!

"JOE – JOE – JOE – JOE!!!" 'Texas Jack is beside himself with rage and distress - he just couldn't stand the awful noise. Joe leaps back to his feet as his confused and concussed nemesis hurtles around the ring holding both ears as hard as he can. In his confusion the Texan rushes straight into one mighty forearm uppercut that sends him flying about 4 feet into the air before depositing him with a crash flat on his back in the middle of the ring. Without another second's hesitation, Joe smashes down on top of him and scores the first pin-fall, serenaded by the loudest cheering yet.

Bewitched, bothered and bewildered, 'Texas' Jack Bence staggers back to his feet as the crowd once more begins to chant,

"JOE – JOE – JOE!!!" And with that the Texan screams at the referee,

"HOLD IT – HOLD THE MATCH – I'LL BE RIGHT BACK!" And with that he leaps right out of the ring and runs as fast as his legs will carry him back to the dressing room. Just a minute later he popped back out and scurried up into the ring, in his hand he carried a small package, which he held out in front of him at arms length before tearing it open and emptying the contents into his hand. Then with a flourish he popped one earplug into one of his ears and then the second one into the other, before throwing the empty earplug packet out into the crowd where the fans could examine it and confirm their worst fears. The bell rang loudly to begin the next round, but the Texan had to be prodded into action by the referee as he now appeared to be unable to hear anything – thanks to the earplugs. The Dazzler began to orchestrate another avalanche of noise, the fans were only too eager to comply, but now the crafty Cowboy just chuckled horribly, pointed to his ears and shook his head with glee, but only for long enough to piss the fans off. He then went after the people's favorite with a vengeance, and in no time flat he reduced him to a heap of rubble. Again, in order to prolong Joe's agony the terrible Texan tortured him horribly, sneering and grimacing at the audience all the while. Now all their stomping, shouting and chanting had not the slightest effect on him. Eventually after at last growing tired of tormenting his victim, who by now seemed to be too shattered to even groan in agony. Texas Jack tore him off the mat, lifted him into the air and smashed him back down to the canvas with all the brutal force he could muster. As the crowd screamed in dismay, the Terror from Texas dived down after his desiccated victim and easily scored the second and equalizing pin-fall. The fans groaned, as deaf 'Texas' Jack Bence laughed and poor Joe Cornelius couldn't even drag himself back to his corner without the help of his second. All too soon the bell rings again, and poor Joe has to stagger out of his corner and back into harm's way. The fans groan for him as his opponent explodes out of his own corner and smashes into the Dazzler with such force he sends him crashing back into the corner he had just vacated. And then it was all the Texan as he ground Joe into hamburger meat. He alternately teased and taunted the crowd whilst sadistically toying with the fan's fast failing favorite. Then to add painful insult to torturous injury, the Terror from Texas places Joe once again in a sitting position in the center of the ring. He repeats the excruciating hold he had tormented him with earlier in the match by digging the fingers of both hands deeper and deeper down into Cornelius's trapezius muscles. Joe squirmed and then screamed out loud, but there would be no respite this time round. Nevertheless, in one supreme effort, Joe once again raised his clenched fist - the crowd began to murmur. He stamped one foot, the crowd began to rumble - he pounded the mat with his fist – with one foot – with two feet, the crowd joined in, then once again as though sensing that a miracle might take place they began to chant,

"COME ON JOE – JOE – JOE – JOE!!!" Obviously, the deafened Texan was unable to hear the awful noise. But he could feel the vibration of the whole hall rocking. Although he was still immune and unaffected by the audio, Joe wasn't, and unlike his opponent, instead of being debilitated by the dreadful racket he was rejuvenated by it. Then the miracle did take place as the Dazzler suddenly came back from the dead in a way that would have put Lazarus to shame. In a blur he spun out of the hold and behind 'Texas' Jack, first grabbing him in the identical hold that he had just escaped from and forced him down to his knees. He nodded and smiled triumphantly to the loudly screaming fans. Then in a second act of triumph he pointed to the Texan's ears, and he looked all around the sea of faces as if soliciting the fan's approval,

"YES JOE – YES JOE – YES!!!" They all screeched loudly. And Joe obliged by first pulling out one of Jack's earplugs, and then the other and throwing them both as souvenirs to the deliriously happy fans. Startled, 'Texas' Jack leapt to his feet; Joe simply looked around the hall, smiled and stamped one foot – that was it – ALL HELL BROKE LOSE!!! The noise was unbelievable, SCREAMING – STOMPING – CHANTING AND CHEERING! 'Texas' Jack was panic stricken. Like a Scorpion trapped in a ring of fire he rushed from one side of the wrestling ring to the other. Eventually colliding with another devastating forearm uppercut from Joe, which again sent him into orbit before crashing down to the canvas, where Cornelius covered him for a fall and a quick – 1 – 2 – 3 count. The Dazzler leapt up the victor – I thought the noise would blow the roof right off the building!

Although The Masked Zebra Kid stood an inch or two shy of 6 feet tall, he must have threatened to crush the scales with a bodyweight of 350 pounds or more. His real name was George Bollas and was an American with the strongest of Aegean flavoring. He even spoke Greek fluently, and still had more family and friends in Greece than in his new home in the States. Big George was one of my best friends in the wrestling World at that time, and it was he who first introduced me to great All American Breakfast. Although when I say 'great', I refer more to the quantity than to the quality of this strange gastronomic monstrosity. By strange, I mean that as well as a large quantity of eggs, which I recognized and heartily approved of. There was what they called sausages, but were more like flat burgers. There was also what they called bacon, but what the British would call streaky-bacon, and was only used in Britain to baste things like turkey breast, or fillet steak whilst it cooked, and was then discarded. But under the rules of the great American Breakfast it was devoured with gusto. Then what really made it strange was the fact that they also ate what I considered to be a desert on the same plate, at the same time. And that was a mile high stack of pancakes, or what they called flapjacks, smothered in a half gallon of maple-syrup. Then strangest of all – a half bucket of wallpaper paste which they called grits?! BUT – as I said, their breakfast might have lacked quality but did not lack quantity – I really do like quality, but I can do quantity very well too, thank you!

George would always travel to all the Northern shows in his little dark green Volkswagen, and would always offer me a ride free of charge back to London where we both lived. Then if we arrived back, as we usually did in the early hours of the morning, George would treat me to a huge American Breakfast at an 'American Club' that he belonged to in London. If we arrived earlier he would share a meal with me that Jean would cook for us at home. Whichever occurred, my good friend George Bollas would always take me right home to my own door and would never leave me in the middle of nowhere as most of the other wrestlers would do.

My most memorable recollection of the powerful Russian-Canadian, George Gordienko was when he had totally blitzed my wrestling hero of that period Mike Marino. That was on the night that the conversation that I had with Mike in Cardiff led to my leaving Wales for London in order to pursue my ultimate quest.

In Coventry one night I witnessed a contest between George Gordienko and 'The Butcher of Budapest' Joseph Kovaks, which all but blitzed that recollection. George Gordienko was rated by many wrestling authorities as one of the best wrestlers of all time. The Hungarian Champion, Joseph Kovaks was an Olympic Medalist before turning professional, and possessed a wrestling pedigree that must have rivaled, or even equaled that of the Herculean Russian-Canadian. I felt a strange atmosphere the moment I walked into the dressing room that night, and was disconcerted even further when I saw there were a number of

Joint's promoters present that were totally out of their own respective territories. I also learned that there were probably a few more promoters who were sitting amongst the audience who never made an appearance in the dressing room that night. They were all waiting for the history making clash of the Titans that was going to be tonight's Main Event. Les Martin was also present, and although Coventry was a Dale Martin's arena, and Les Martin did attend some of the shows, I had never before seen him as far afield. When Kovaks and Gordienko left the dressing room to make their entrance to the ring there was not a soul left in the dressing room. Everyone, both wrestler and promoter were out amongst the audience in order to watch what promised to be the match of the decade. Les Martin had 'suggested' to George and Joseph that they should 'maybe' wrestle to a draw, but speculation was running high as to whether either of them would abide by his 'loosely phrased' suggestion, and might instead attempt to score an unscheduled victory over the other. Obviously both the Russian-Canadian and the Hungarian would be very protective of their respective reputations, and a win for either would swell their status to almost mythical proportions. But of course at his opponent's expense. Even as the Master of ceremonies began his introduction, a sensation so palpable began to envelope the whole arena. A feeling of unreality ensued, anticipation was riding high, more especially amongst the wrestlers and promoters who all understood more fully than the fans did what we were all about to witness. At last the bell rang to sound the beginning of a contest that had the potential to make wrestling history and both the mighty Mat-Men turned to face each other. Slowly, so very slowly The Canadian Behemoth and The Butcher of Budapest strode towards each other, it was as though they were walking in slow motion through a morass of thick treacle. Then the moment they were close enough to come to grips, the Hungarian Ogre lifted the Canadian Colossus up high as the crowd roared with excitement. The mighty roar suddenly degenerated into a whimper and then complete silence as Kovaks laid Gordienko down onto the mat as gently as a loving Mother would lay down her newborn offspring. Then just as gently he lowered himself on top of the prone Canadian, as the referee counted to 3 which gave the Hungarian a one fall lead.

With a display of no emotion whatsoever, both contestants got to their feet, walked back to their respective corners where they both waited expressionlessly for the bell to sound to begin the second round. The bell sounded to begin a round that could have well been an action replay of the first – if there had actually been any 'action'. The second round only differed from the first in that on this occasion it was George Gordienko who slowly hoisted up Joseph Kovaks, and very – very gently laid him on the mat, and very – very gently covered him to score the equalizing pin-fall.

Both men stood in their corners until the bell tolled to commence the third round which signaled blistering action from each of the contestants as they charged at each other with all the speed their huge ponderous frames would allow. They crashed together in the centre of the ring with an impact that seemed to rock the arena. Both men bounced off each other and landed flat on their backs and lay there while the referee counted them both out. As soon as the referee had finished counting the double knockout, both men leapt to their feet, shook each other's hand, got out of the ring and marched back to the dressing room. A roar of complete silence from a bewildered audience perused them every step of the way.

Blistered with embarrassment all the wrestlers got back to the sanctuary of the dressing room even before the contestants. Big George Gordienko had hardly sat down before Les Martin burst into the dressing room, - he was absolutely livid,

"WHAT WAS THAT ALL ABOU ---?!!!" That was as far as he got, before the mighty Russian-Canadian was out of his seat and right into Les Martin's flustered face.

"I KNOW WHAT YOU WANTED TO SEE!" George growled, "YOU AND ALL THE REST OF THE PROMOTERS - BUT IF YOU WANT TO SEE THAT – BE PREPARED TO PAY FOR IT – IF YOU WANT A REAL FIGHT – IT WILL COST YOU REAL MONEY!!!" Complete silence reigned as the mighty George sat back down, and that seemed to be, very much that!

The Canadian 'Gorgeous' Terry Garvin fancied himself as Canada's answer to the great American originator of 'The Gorgeous Gimmick', the one and only 'Gorgeous' George Wagner. I just remember seeing Garvin on only one occasion, when we both wrestled on the same card in Purley Orchid Ballroom for Dale Martins. He only wrestled for Joint Promotions for a short while after that before returning home to Canada.

He had come over to wrestle in Britain originally for Paul Lincoln's Promotion, and only wrestled for Joint's a few times before he left Britain. Most of what I learned about 'Gorgeous' Terry Garvin was second hand, and for that I will be eternally grateful.

Many in our business were known for their cruel and outrageous jokes and bawdy behavior, but I never heard of anyone who could compete with the crazy Canadian for downright crudity. Wrestlers were always mooning other wrestlers who might be traveling in another vehicle to the matches. But when Garvin stuck his arse though the window of the car he was riding in, he wasn't satisfied with a conventional moon, he would actually take a crap! When he wrestled at Paul Lincoln's Metropolitan Theatre one night he took a crap through one of the upstairs windows onto a crowd of wrestling fans who were lining up outside the Metropolitan waiting to buy their tickets.

The Gorgeous one became lonely and lovesick for the love of his life, who turned out to be a handsome young Canadian wrestler named Roger Bollett. Garvin persuaded the promoters to bring Roger over to Britain to wrestle. To say Roger Bollet's, skills as a professional wrestler was extremely mediocre would have been very kind indeed. So much so, that the promoters were inclined to send him back where he came from a short while after he had arrived. He didn't possess a scrap of appeal to the British wrestling fans, and poor Garvin was beside himself with grief at the very thought of loosing his young lover so soon after being reunited. But, Terry came up with a solution.

The biggest box-office draw to ever come to Britain from Canada was the great Mohawk wrestling superstar, Billy Two-Rivers. So in order to add instant charisma to his colorless boyfriend, why not make him into a Red-Indian? They would give him a Mohican hairdo, a feathered war-bonnet and re-name him Billy Red-Cloud. The promoters went for it, and although Roger was no Billy Two-Rivers, his transformation did help enough to give him a new lease of life and keep him wrestling in Britain. Everyone would have been happy and Roger probably would have continued to remain wrestling in Britain for the entire duration of his mentor's tour. But for Roger's infatuation for a six-foot tall, Red-haired Lady named Rusty, who came up to London to spend a day with him after their meeting at the matches held in Margate a couple of nights earlier.

Garvin had woken up very late that day, and had already discovered that he was sleeping alone. When he arose there was no sign of Roger anywhere in the Old Compton Street apartment they shared. After showering he made his way to Coffeeville expecting to find Roger partaking of some refreshments, only to be told that he had been there earlier, but had left with a very tall, Redheaded Lady - Garvin was livid! He hurried around the corner to 'The Masquerade' Gay Club,

"Yes," he was told, after his inquiry, "Roger had been in – WITH A VERY TALL RED-HAIRED WOMAN, NO LESS - BUT HAD LEFT SOME TIME AGO!"

Garvin insane with jealous fury rushed to 'The Straggler's Club',

"Yes, Roger had been in - but!" – Well you get the picture. Garvin who was beside himself by now rushed from one club to another searching for his wayward lover, who was doing, he didn't know what with a Woman! Only to be told the same story over and over, he searched and searched in vain but Roger was forever two Clubs ahead of him. Then he eventually disappeared completely off the radar screen, and the frantic Fairy feared the worst. After many hours of total frustration, the distraught and dangerously jealous Garvin made his lonely way back to his empty apartment. But, when he arrived the apartment wasn't empty, and the Roving Roger Red-Cloud was back on the reservation. Roger may have only been a pretend Indian, but the Firewater he'd consumed had been very real, and he was out like a light. Snoring loudly, Roger was laying flat on his back with his mouth wide open sprawled all over the large, stuffed settee that dominated the lounge. Garvin's relief at finding his unfaithful lover soon evaporated back into a jealous fit of fury, as he visualized what his lover had been up to and with whom. Quickly and quietly he stripped off all his clothes, and gently climbed onto the settee, so's not to disturb the sleeping beauty. He then squatted over him and took a crap right onto poor Roger's upturned face - SPLAT!!!

The pending impact immediately woke the sleeping Brave, who shot to his feet, and after a very brief war-dance, threw a mighty punch from the backyard which caught the prancing pervert flush in the chops. He was sent hurtling right across the room where he collided with a resounding crash into their booze cabinet. Bouncing off the furniture the 'Gorgeous Gargoyle' flew back at Roger armed with a bottle of Canadian Bourbon. Which he was holding by the neck, he swung the weapon overhead in a huge arch, like an Indian War-club. The bottle exploded right on top off Roger's head – and another Redskin bit the dust. Drink administered in that fashion can have a very stunning effect. An ambulance had to be called to transport the bloody shit splattered Warrior to the nearest infirmary in order to get cleaned up and then stitched up. Unfortunately in the process all the hair had to be shaved from around the gash on top of his head, which completely cut his Mohawk haircut in half. The poor warrior now had stitches going one way and the remnants of his Mohawk going the other, his head looked like a hot-cross-bun. Even before the damage Roger had not really made a very convincing Red-Indian, now with a Bunny-tail of hair on the back of his neck and a little pom-pom tuft in the front the magic was well and truly gone. And so too was Roger. The promoters decided they couldn't use a Mohican without the Mohican hairdo, so Billy Red-Cloud was sent back to the reservation in Canada, and very soon a very lonely and lovesick 'Gorgeous' Terry Garvin disappeared into the sunset in his wayward lover's wake.

The giant 6'4'' 260 pound Maori Warrior John DaSilva was the proverbial 'Gentle Giant' – outside the ring. If you faced him on the inside of the squared circle it would be a much different story. John was huge and all muscle, I was amazed when he told me that he had never in his life trained with weights,

"I get all the exercise I need wrestling in the ring every night." He told me.

"Well if you have never lifted weights before, and you are already that big and muscular, just imagine what you'd look like if you began body-building." I suggested, as I hated to see such incredible potential not being exploited to the maximum.

"No Adrian," he grinned, "if I lift weights, I'll get really big - if I get really big, I'll have to spend more money on new clothes that I would prefer to save." And that was that, but Big John was one of the nicest people I have ever met in our business,

Prince Peter Maivia of the Samoan Islands lived about ten minuets walk away from my flat with his Wife Leah and young Daughter Ata. Ata would grow up to marry the American wrestling muscleman Rocky Johnson, whose son Dwayne would grow up to become better known as WWE superstar and film-star 'The Rock'. Peter was also featured in a movie when he appeared in the James Bond film 'You only live twice', which was shot in Japan. When Peter came to Britain the first time, he arrived from New Zealand where he had been a champion in both the amateur and professional ranks. The first time I met him during his first British tour he barely weighed 200 pounds, when he returned for a second tour he weighed at least 280 pounds, and usually hovered between that weight and 300 pounds. Although he had gained an incredible amount of weight, it was weight that looked good on him, unlike many other wrestlers who had done likewise just to be able to call themselves heavyweights.

Although there were a fair number of genuine homegrown heavyweights in Britain at this time, I would estimate that they would be vastly outnumbered by the number of lighter-weights who had force fed themselves into the heavyweight division. To me, both their physical condition and appearance was unappealing and uninspiring and although I did give the heavyweight division a brief tryout, I felt it was not for me. I decided that I would much prefer to be a big lightweight than a little heavyweight.

I was always known for my speed and agility, but being heavy slowed me down. Even worse, the new 'Nature-Boy look outfits' that had cost me so much money were threatening to split their seams, and looked much less elegant on a chunkier physique.

An extreme example of a natural middleweight's desire to enter the elite heavyweight force was 'Dangerous' Danny Lynch, from Shipley in Yorkshire. Wrestlers who knew him when he first turned professional, told me that in his early days in the business he stood 5' 9" and weighed about 175 pounds. He had quite a good physique, in spite of looking as though he could have looked much better if he had weighed about 10 pounds less. I met Danny after he had moved down South to wrestle for Dale Martins, by that time I estimated that he weighed about 185 pounds, but he insisted that he weighed at least 200. Although he was obsessed with gaining more weight, adding the bulk he desired seemed to elude him, until he went on a fool proof diet which consisted of gallons of beer which he used to wash down anabolic steroid tablets by the handful. I had never heard of anabolic steroids before that time, and I remember asking Jack Dale about them one day when he was traveling to the show with us in the van. Danny Lynch had told me about them first, but I thought that it was just something he had made up to fool the gullible, like a Jackalope or some other mythical Beastie.

Jack assured me that they did in fact exist, and that American Bodybuilders had been using them to build bigger muscles for more than a decade. Naturally that got my attention, until he added,

"They do put on size and muscle, but they also have some negative side effects, including shrinking the testicles." Then he laughed for an hour after I replied,

"Fuck that Jack – I'd rather have skinny arms!"

But shrinking testicles or not, 'Dangerous' Danny Lynch continued to gobble up Dianabol as though they were M&Ms. So much so, that I began to wonder if they also shrank the brain. Yorkshire wrestlers claimed that it was Danny's childhood dream to become a monster. He actually longed for cauliflower ears, as he thought that possessing them would make him look more like a wrestler. To further his quest in that direction, he had his fellow wrestlers hit his ears with the heels of their shoes, squeeze them, pinch them, punch them and even slam a door on them. But to no avail, Danny seemed to have un-cauliflowerable ears, and the poor Devil had to go through the whole of his life wearing nice ones. Nevertheless, he found a new way to horrify his fans when he began using a razor-blade on himself in the ring. I had been on the same card as Danny on at least a couple of occasions, when he Chickened out after he claimed he was going to take a blade into the ring. After beating up his opponent for a period, the opponent would rally, then come back at Danny, and at the opportune moment, he'd sneak the blade from it's hiding place in his leotard. He would cut his forehead in a way that looked as though he had received the injury from his opponent and bleed over everything and everyone in the ring. I had never witnessed this feat, and I went out and found a good vantage spot on both occasions, but when it came to the crunch Danny was unable to find the courage. However, I was once again on the same card in Carlyon Bay in Cornwell, when Danny tried and this time succeeded in drawing his own blood - by the pint. That was just the beginning of it, with the howls and screams of shear horror from an audience who were not used to all that blood and gore. Danny now became as addicted to the crowd reaction as he had become addicted to beer and anabolic steroids, and every night he wrestled he bled – and bled - and bled. To say that 'Dangerous' Danny overdid the head cutting would be like saying Vlad overdid the impaling, and the more he did it the less it meant to the audience. It was a clear case of familiarity breeds contempt. Fans would sometimes mention him, and say things like,

"You know the wrestler I mean - he's got short blond hair, and has really thin skin - you only have to touch him and he bleeds all over the place, ------"

Even the promoters asked Danny not to cut himself anymore, cut it out, or at least 'cut' it down, and only in a special match where it once again might actually mean something. but Danny couldn't stop cutting himself, he was even nicknamed Mr. Gillette by everyone in the wrestling business. Eventually, he had cut various parts of his head so often and so badly, that the hair on the front of his head, and even his eyebrows would only grow in tufts. Rather than wear that really moth-eaten look, he shaved off what was left of his eyebrows and all the hair on his head. Except for one patch like a Bunny tail on the back that he dyed jet black to match an Oriental style mustache which made him look like one of 'The Mighty Chang's' ugly Sisters. By this time Danny's Guinness and Dianabol diet had puffed him up to a fat waddling 280 pounds. It was as a result of his addiction to seeing his own blood too often that finally got him fired from Joint Promotions for good. It was a few years later when I once again met 'Dangerous' Danny, who had been wrestling meantime for his own, and various independent promotions. By this time he weighed in at a whopping 350 pounds, and by carrying all that weight he must have shrunk in height to at least an inch shorter than I was, rather than about two inches taller as he had been when I met him first.

It was during this period that Heavyweight dominance in British professional wrestling took a body-blow from which it would never fully recover.

BONAPARTE INCARNATE

There were two main reasons why smaller wrestlers were beginning to invade – and then eventually surpass the Big Men's dominance of pro wrestling. The first was thanks to television. Just as the Giant Dinosaurs who were unable to successfully adapt to the changing climate which favored the pending dominance of the much smaller Mammals. Many Big Heavyweights found that they were unable to successfully adapt to the changing climate in professional wrestling brought about by television. On TV all you can view is a small, flat screen, on which every wrestler, whether they stood 5' 4" and weighed 140 pounds, or 6' 10" and exceeding 300 pounds, they all look the same size on TV. Therefore on television being really large has no advantage at all, in fact, in many cases it has a number of disadvantages. For instance most of the smaller wrestlers were better proportioned, which tended to make them look bigger than most of the big men when viewed on a small screen. Then of course there was the matter of both speed and agility, which once again is more in the little man's domain. Even mentally the smaller men were much better equipped. As unlike their bigger peers they had had to fight tooth and nail to gain just a glimmer of the attention and recognition that a huge wrestler would receive for no other reason than the fact that he was huge. There would usually be more content in a small wrestler's contests, in fact big wrestlers were soon complaining bitterly that the Lightweights were doing too much in a match. They also accused Lightweights of using what used to be known as big heavyweight finishes to a match, as a mere 'high-spot'. Or to cleverly counter, or reverse what had been considered in the heavyweight ranks as an unbreakable finishing hold.

"Fucking Lightweights are going to kill this business!!!" was something I heard uttered by the disgruntled Heavyweights again and again. Of course, I, like every other Lightweight heartily disagreed with their assessment, and instead maintained that at last we were claiming some of what we so rightly deserved. We wre certainly not killing the business; on the contrary, especially on television where wrestling had so recently gained its unprecedented popularity. It was the Lighterweights who were really attracting the viewers with their speed, agility and more extensive repertoire. So from this time on the Lightweights were both demanding and receiving the attention that for eons the Big Men of the sport had taken for granted. - An old poem, obviously composed by a Lightweight wrestler went like this -

Bees do the work, Drones get the honey;
Lightweights have the skill, Heavyweights get the money.

There were very few Lightweights who were considered Main-event Grapplers before television, and of the very few exceptions the most prominent was World Lightweight Wrestling Champion, George Kidd. But, even he would not have consistently topped the bill anywhere else but in his native Scotland. South of the border he would rarely wrestle in a contest above the semi-main event, unless it was a World Lightweight Championship title defense. After TV, the first Lighter-weight to put a serious dent in the Heavyweight's formerly impregnable armor was 'Mr. TV' Jackie Pallo, with his very unique and patent television loss. But the wrestler who I would credit, more than any other for finally leveling the playing fields of British Professional Wrestling was the one and only Mick McManus, of New Cross, London. Mick was probably at least a couple of inches shorter than I was, and in those days maybe just a few pounds heavier. His appearance, in addition to sharing a very similar stature to Napoleon Bonaparte was his facial features, set off by an identical hairstyle; he could have easily passed for a twin or even as a reincarnation of the Great French Emperor himself. And, the similarity didn't end there. Mick also possessed all the ambition, talent, ruthlessness, strategy, tactics and genius of the self styled Conqueror of most of 19th Century Europe. Nevertheless, even armed as he was with all those invaluable assets, it was not until he became the possessor of the all powerful and unbeatable 'Office-Hold' that he was able to exploit all those invaluable assets to their full potential.

In the mid-fifties a number of Dale Martin's wrestlers, led by

Paul Lincoln and Ray Hunter, planned to break away from Joint Promotions and create an independent wrestling Promotion of their own. Most prominent amongst the score or more wrestlers who were involved with them was 'Judo' Al Hayes and Mike Marino. McManus, who was first sworn to secrecy, was also invited to join their Exodus. But instead he walked into Les Martin's office and blew the whistle on the renegade's plot before it was fully hatched. This resulted in Mike Marino, who had some kind of contract with Dale Martin's, hovering in limbo-land for three months, before he was officially and legally able to Join and wrestle for Paul Lincoln's promotion.

It also resulted in Mick McManus being rewarded by Les Martin who gave Mick an office job which included matchmaking for Dale Martin's Promotions. From that time on it was now Mick McManus who would decide who would wrestle who – and who would be the winner and who would be the looser – and from that time Mick McManus didn't loose a match!

Well in actual fact, he did eventually lose a couple, but that is another story. That was how Mick McManus was given unlimited access and use of 'The Office Hold' and as a result became absolutely invincible. As matchmaker he was also in a position to award himself top-billing on most of the cards he appeared on. He was also able to put himself on television even more regularly than 'Mr. TV.' Jackie Pallo. From then on McManus wrestled in all the biggest and best paying arenas. He would only wrestle for the Northern Promoters on TV, or big spectaculars. He would very carefully chose his opponents, and just as carefully chose opponents for all his closest rivals. If a rival appeared to threaten his exalted position, a few loses to lesser rated opponents would very soon weaken their profile a tad. When he appeared at an arena one week, he would pad out the rest of the card with the biggest draws available, guaranteeing a packed house. The next week in the same arena his closest rival might be billed against a complete nobody, with the weakest draws available. Then he could boast to Dale Martins,

"Look how many fans I drew in to that arena compared to Jackie Pallo who wrestled there the next week!" What he wouldn't mention was that Jackie Pallo may have been just one of the big names who Mick would have had padding out the show that he had packed out the week before. This state of affairs caused a huge amount of jealousy from every other wrestler in the business. But in fairness to Mick McManus, there was not another wrestler in the business who wouldn't have exploited Mick's position to a lesser or greater degree if they had been given the opportunity to do so. Also in fairness to Mick, as a wrestler he deserved top billing. His crowd psychology was as good as it got, a great tactician, he could stir up the crowd like no other. After giving his 'good-guy' opponent the most savage of thrashings, he could turn the loud boos and jeers into ear shattering cheers the second he allowed his opponent to snatch the incentive away from him. Then with his famous cry of despair,

"NOT THE EARS – NO – NO – NOT THE EARS!!!!!" He would dash all around the ring screaming, as his opponent grabbed and twisted Mick's large cauliflower ears spitefully and for all he was worth, while the crowd's screams of delight blended with Mick's screams of agony. But, in the end, always after the closest of calls, Mick would always win. Then once again, the fans would leave the arena telling each other the very same thing they had said after the last time they had watched Mick wrestle, and the same thing they would be destined to say for very many years to come,

"WAIT UNTIL NEXT TIME – SO AND SO WILL GET HIM THEN FOR SURE – AND I'M DEFINITELY GOING TO BE THERE TO SEE IT!!!" As I stated we all resented 'Niggely Mick' very much, but in hindsight, I think every British Lightweight owed him a huge dept of gratitude for being so instrumental in smashing down the weight barrier in what had become 'The Golden Age of British Wrestling.

****

It was late morning on the 26th of September 1962, and as I was halfway through my breakfast, Jean announced that the cramping pains that had started much earlier that morning, but had since faded, had now began again in earnest. I phoned for a taxi and we were soon on our way to South-London Hospital for Women. After our arrival, and Jean had been admitted and was sitting 'comfortably' in bed, I announced to the nurses in charge that I wanted to be present during the birth of my Child. They explained that it would probably be at least a few hours before Jean reached that stage, and suggested that I should go away and make myself scarce for most of that time. I left the Hospital, but really did not know what to do with myself to pass the time. First I thought that I would go home and finish my breakfast, but I soon found that I had no appetite after I arrived there. Then I remembered that the movie 'The Vikings', starring many of my favorite film stars, Kirk Douglas, Tony Curtis, Janet Leigh and Ernest Borgnine, was playing in Brixton Odeon. So I imagined that it might occupy my mind for a while. I had seen the movie when it had first come out, and had enjoyed it very much. 'If that doesn't take my mind off what was going on at the Hospital nothing would.' I thought. I was right – Nothing would take my mind off what was going on in the Hospital. After fidgeting in my seat for an hour, and looking at the large cinema clock every 20 seconds for the whole of that time, I decided at last that even an epic featuring the famous, fighting Norsemen couldn't hold my interest under those circumstances. I left and rode the Underground to Clapham Common Tube Station, which was directly opposite the Hospital. Next door to the Station was a very conveniently placed Flower Shop, where I purchased a big bunch of very pretty Flowers. I reached the floor where Jean's room was situated, and asked the first Nurse I saw what the status was. She told me that she would inquire and disappeared into Jean's room. Almost immediately she reappeared and announced,

"Mr. Street, you have a Son!" I had a Son, it was impossible to come to terms with the surreal feelings that surrounded me. Feelings that would be impossible for me to describe to someone who has never experienced it. But also unnecessary to try to explain it to someone who has. I walked into Jean's room enveloped in a huge bubble of unreality with a pathetic bunch of flowers in my hand. Jean looked tired but smug, as well she might – and then I saw my Baby Son, the loveliest creature I had ever set eyes on. Jean had done an excellent job.

****

A combination of occurrences put a temporary halt to my training with Mike Dimitri at the YMCA. Firstly Mike, who was now refereeing full time, seemed to be in too much pain most of the time. True he was no longer taking the bumps that had been necessary every night in his role as a wrestler, but as a referee he would now be in the ring for at least 4 matches every night instead of just his own. To be honest, I was glad of the excuse not to go to the YMCA at that time. In order to get there I would have to leave home early in the morning after very little sleep, and I'd have to pass by the office on my way there. Then when I left the YMCA I would have to pass the office again on my way home. I'd grab something to eat, and some grub to take with me, and then travel down to the office to catch the transport to that night's venue, after already passing it twice the same morning. And then the main reason. I was now a proud Father, and I wanted to spend as much time with my brand new Son. Even though, at that time of his life, he spent most of his time sleeping. His name was Adrian David Street. Adrian after me and David after the patron Saint of Wales. I had already counted all his fingers, toes, eyes etcetera to make sure they were all present and correct, but then how could he possibly go wrong with two such pretty parents?

For a period Leon Fortuna and I began weight-training with 'The Cardiff Strongman' Johnny Yearsley in his own gym, which was in the back yard of his home in Dartford. Leon would pick me up in his car each day, and we would sometimes drive first to a sports store, and buy a 10 pound dumbbell/barbell disc each. Which would then give to Johnny Yearsley as weekly payment for the use of his gym. Johnny was a tremendous piss-taker. But as many piss-takers are, he did not take kindly to the smart retorts he would always receive from me in return for all his smart arsed sarcasm. That coupled with the fact that I was fast catching up to the immense poundage that mighty John would use during his Herculean workouts, made the duration of our training period with the former British weightlifting record holder and former 1957 Mr. Universe contender fairly short-lived. Yearsley used our occasional absenteeism as the excuse to banish both Leon and I, from continuing to use his gym, as we would sometimes be absent for days or even weeks owing to our wrestling commitments. John was obviously well aware that we had no choice as to where we would be booked and it was not our fault that we were sometimes unable to join him every day. Nevertheless, we were both fired, so I had to find another place to train. Preferably close by, that would be open for business at the time I needed it. They did have a limited amount of weights at the gym in Dale Martin's offices, but even a limited amount was much better than none. I began leaving home earlier, and training there before I left in the van to the venue I would be wrestling in each night. About half the weights they had at Dale's gym used to belong to the legendary 'Old time' Strongman Eugene Sandow, and were better suited for performing feats of strength, than for regular weight training. The heaviest of the Sandow barbells only weighed about 200 pounds, but the weight was like two solid cannonballs joined by a bar that was not only badly bent, but at least as thick as my wrist. With the result that it was almost of no use to me at all. My body was very strong, but my grip wasn't, and my hands are not large. I was unable to come anywhere close to wrapping my fingers around the thick and bent bar with enough gripping strength to lift the bloody monstrosity clear off the floor. I could easily lift far more weight than that particular barbell above my head – if it was a regular, modern barbell. But with that lump of metal, the only thing I was able to do with it was to lay on the ground, drag it onto my chest using a bent arm pullover, and then press it off my chest for a number of reps. Many of the bigger wrestlers had attempted to lift it above their heads, but I never saw anyone succeed until a short, fat Irish heavyweight named Ivor Barrett did it. Fatty Barrett was very strong, but all he ever did when he worked out at Dale's gym was with that barbell. He trained and trained for over a year with it until he was able to get it up to his chest, then he carried on with iron determination until at last he was able to jerk it up to arms length above his head. Even then, he was not satisfied, and his full satisfaction would not be realized until he was strong and able enough to lift the heavy, clumsy barbell anytime and every time he attempted it. When at last he was satisfied, the reason for his quest became apparent, all that grueling work was for no other purpose than to impress Jack Dale, who was always very impressed by any feat of physical strength or prowess.

On the day he decided to display his super feat of strength for Jack Dale, there were a number of wrestlers in the gym, waiting to ride the vans to their various venues. I was the only other wrestler besides Barret who was actually training, and was bench pressing at the opposite corner from the Irishman. He told one of the waiting wrestlers to go and ask Jack Dale to come downstairs from his office in order to witness Barrett's feat of super strength. Jack came down and we all gathered around the modern-day Sandow expectantly. Ivor Barrett strode powerfully up to the grotesque and ancient barbell, took a number of deep breaths, squatted into position with his hands gripping the thick, bent bar and dragged the bar right up to his chest in one giant effort. He gasped another huge lungful of air before slamming up the heavy, awkward barbell to arms length and then shook and trembled under it as he fought to control it.

Everyone gasped and applauded as Barrett with his fat, freckled face as red as an overripe tomato threw the weight down to the ground with a loud resounding thud. Just then the gym door opened and in stepped George Gordienko, the Russian-Canadian powerhouse. He was wearing a very heavy overcoat, a very, very large brimmed hat and a very, very, very long cigar sticking straight out of his mouth. As the huge barbell that had just been discarded by the Irishman landed on the ground in front of George, without a seconds hesitation he bent over picked it up to his chest as though it was made of toy balloons. Then he pushed it outwards in order for it to clear the long cigar and the large brim of his hat, then back again to arms length above his head. He brought it back down to his chest then repeated, this maneuver in such a blur of repetitions that I for one lost count. Then he dropped the weight back on the ground making the thoroughly outclassed, amazed, dismayed – and still gasping Irishman jump back out of harm's way.

A very similar scenario took place one night in the dressing room at Watford Town Hall. We were all sitting and getting changed when the door opened and in walked Jack Dale. In a flash, Big Bill Verna who had been sitting right opposite me leapt to his feet and dropped down into a full Indian squat, and as he rose back up he began chanting,

"343, - 344, - 345" – it was just for Jack's benefit, as though he had been performing Indian squats for the last half hour. But, unfortunately for Big Bill, sitting right next to him was Big George Gordienko, and as Bill began his squats, Gordienko just slid forward out of his seat and into a handstand. Then began keeping pace with Bill Verna's squats with shoulder dips from a handstand position. That would have been a very impressive feat if it had been performed by a lightweight, but Big George Gordienko weighed around 260 pounds or more!

I myself had been enjoying Jack Dale's approval by merely training most every day at the office where he would see me working out every time he entered the gym. He came in one day, where between sets on the bench I had been having a chat with Johnny Yearsley who was waiting to catch his ride in one of Dale's vans. Before Jack Dale had entered the gym, Johnny and I had been having a normal amiable conversation but as soon as he saw Jack, Yearsley's tone changed and in a very loud voice to ensure that Jack Dale could hear him right across the gym, he said,

"Huh! Is that all the weight you can use on the bench? I thought you were supposed to be strong!"

By now Jack had approached us and was in the process of counting the poundage of the plates I had piled on the bar when I said to him,

"Hey Jack, listen at Yearsley trying to belittle my warm up weight for your benefit, Leon Fortuna and I used to train with him, but I'll bet Yearsley never told you that he wouldn't let us workout with him anymore because I was catching him up on most of his lifts."

The smirk disappeared off Yearsley's face, but he wouldn't miss a chance to show off in front of the Boss, so he challenged me,

"Okay, let's have a bench-press completion right now and we'll see whose the strongest!"

Johnny Yearsley was a fully fledged heavyweight, as well as being one of the strongest men in the World at his weight. He had broken 22 British weightlifting records, 14 of which still stood, including the Crucifix Record which is in 'The Guinness Book of Records. He performed this superhuman feat of strength in London's Scarla Theatre when he held a pair of 76. 3/4 pound dumbbells out for one minute. The effort earned him an almost unbreakable record and 10 broken tendons in his chest. He was only a few inches taller than I was, but must have weighed more than 220 pounds; he was also the possessor of the first pair of genuine 20 inch upper arms that I had ever seen, so I replied,

"Hey John, you outweigh me by more than 40 pounds, if you want a fair competition then we should use our own bodyweight, not a barbell. You issued the challenge, but I'll still give you the choice of weapons between pushups, chins, or parallel bar dips."

By this time I had become tired of the extra weight I had gained and had got my bodyweight down to about 175 pounds, so I knew that it would be me who had the advantage with any of the exercises I had given Yearsley a choice of. Yearsley chose parallel bar dips, but insisted that as I was the one to dictate the choice of weapons that I would have to go first. Thus giving him the advantage of knowing before hand how many repetitions he needed to perform in order to win. I had no problem with that, as I knew I was extremely good at all of the choices I had given him, and could easily tally up a total that he would find impossible to emulate.

"Jack will be the referee," I explained as I took my position on the parallel bars, and "that only a full dip would count." And off I went - 100 easy repetitions later I swung myself back to the ground and with a flourish and invited Yearsley to,

"See if you can do better than that Mate!"

With Jack Dale refereeing, and I sitting on the bench as the best vantage spot where I could look up and enjoy the distress that would soon begin to register on Big Johnny Yearsley's face, the count began. Well I certainly wasn't disappointed, with the distress factor, 30 reps – 40 reps - I was surprised that a 220 pound plus man had got this far. 50 – 60 – 70 reps. I was amazed, but his huge, 20" arms were trembling now, the sweat was dripping off his face like a tropical thunderstorm, and I wondered if he could possibly maintain this Herculean effort and reach 80 reps. 80 – 81 – 82. Damn I have to say I was impressed, but the end was close now, any second I expected him to fall off the bars and onto the gym floor. 90 reps – 91, Shit! I couldn't believe he was still going - 99 reps – 100 reps – 101 reps. Then he collapsed off the parallel bars, onto which he then had to cling to prevent himself from falling flat on his face. - BUT! The big muscle-bound Bastard had beaten me!

"Okay, John," I suggested, in order to save face, "what about the best of 3 sets?"

"No way, fuck off!" Big Johnny Yearsley eventually managed to gasp, "I won and that's it!" And fair play to him, I guess he had.

****

It was the 7th of December, the 21st Anniversary of the Japanese attack on Pearl Harbor, and as I was traveling home from Northampton where I had been wrestling that night. I began to feel worse than the Hawaiian Harbor looked on the morning of the 8th. Just two days after my 22nd Birthday I was sitting miserably in Dale's ice-cold, Hell on wheels of a van, simultaneously shivering and then burning up with the flu. Saturday night I wrestled again, and it wasn't until the Sunday that I had a night off when at last I could lay in bed all day and enjoy being horribly ill in peace,

Or so I thought. There was a knock on our door, Jean went down to answer it and after a few minutes she came back up stairs and told me,

"Hey Street" - Yes, we'd been married 9 months and she still called me Street instead of Adrian. "Hey Street," she called, "that was Jo' at the door, she's in a terrible state, will you go and sort Tom out? He's drunk, and he won't leave her alone.

"No, I won't go and sort Tom out!" I replied indignantly, "Tell her to phone the Police if he won't go on his own, her ex-Husband is a Policeman, let him sort it out!"

Josephine was our next door neighbor, who Jean had made friends with soon after we had moved to Brancaster Road. We had never met her ex-Husband at this time, as according to Jo, he had left her a year or so earlier and was now living with an under aged Girl. Since we had become friends with Jo she had met her current Boyfriend Tom, who as a result had also become a good friend of ours. Tom was from Australia, he was a really nice guy with a great sense of humor, and made excellent company. The problem now was that Jo's ex-Husband had been making romantic overtures towards her, with reconciliation in mind, and much to Tom's disgust and despair, Jo had decided to give her ex another chance. So, on this night Tom had got himself blind stinking drunk. He came around to implore Jo not to return to her ex, but his gesture had soon degenerated into a flaming row, which in turn prompted Jo to seek my help.

"She can't call her Husband," Jean explained, "She doesn't want him to know that Tom has been around!"

"Well that's just too bad," I replied, "I'm laying here sick, and if you think I'm going outside in this cold weather, you're as daft as Jo is for going back to her stupid Husband!"

"Just go and talk to him." Jean implored.

"No I won't!" I insisted, "It's none of our business – and if it comes to the push, I actually like Tom more than I like Jo - so do me a favor, leave them alone and let them work it out for themselves – now keep quiet," I added, "I'm trying to watch the television!" Closing the subject once and for all - or so I thought!

Everything was nice and quiet and I thought that the episode was over, when Jean imploded into the room screaming,

"QUICK – QUICK – HELP – HE'S TURNED VIOLENT – I JUST WENT NEXT DOOR TO TELL TOM TO LEAVE JO ALONE, AND HE THREW AN ELECTRIC FIRE AT ME!!!!"

"Why the fuck can't you mind your own bloody business?!" I shouted, as I jumped out of bed and pulled on a pair of trousers, slid on a shirt, and stepped into a pair of rubber flip-flops. As far as I was concerned, anything between Jo and Tom was strictly their problem. I was certainly not looking for any kind of confrontation with Tom on Jo's behalf - but, nobody threatens my family with any kind of violence. Even if they were poking their noses where they didn't belong. I marched into Jo's ground floor apartment, and found a very belligerent Tom sitting on the floor with his back propped up against an armchair. The electric fire he had thrown at Jean was lying in front of him, after narrowly missing her and bouncing back off the wall.

"Tom!" I told him, "I don't give a flying fuck what's going on with you and Jo, but no one is going to throw things at my Wife and get away with it, so get up and fuck off!"

As far as I was concerned he was getting off light, he had crossed the line, but under the circumstances I wasn't going to get violent.

That was when Jo came in screaming,

"DON'T HIT HIM ADRIAN – PLEASE DON'T HIT HIM!!!!" And grabbed my arms to prevent me from doing something I had no intention of doing in the first place.

"I DON'T NEED TO HAVE A FUCKIN' WOMAN TO PROTECT ME!!!" Roared Tom, as he picked up the electric fire and smashed it down as hard as he could onto my bare foot. Now it was Jo's turn to bounce off the wall, as with a scream of pain and rage I threw her away from me, and dropped onto Tom like a ton of bricks – no make that two tons of bricks! Then as I proceeded to use Tom like a Tom-tom. Jo ran next door and upstairs into MY apartment, and used MY phone, to call the police. And tell them to 'come as quickly as they could, as a professional wrestler was beating the living shit out of someone in her apartment.' – What was that thing I said about friends?!

It was only Jean coming to warn me that the police were now on their way that 'arrested' my blitzkrieg on Tom, and induced me to return next door. I had no sooner closed the door and began to walk upstairs when a loud knocking once again 'arrested' my next move. I was standing on my doorstep explaining what had occurred to what seemed like a whole street full of policemen, when yet another police car arrived carrying a Police Captain. It turned out to be none other than Jo's ex husband – and after he had introduced himself as such, I thought it best to begin my story over again for his benefit. Emphasizing the fact that it was his own rival in love, that had caused the disturbance in the first place. It was just then, that what little there was left of Tom was escorted out of Jo's front door by a couple of cops. As he saw me, he struggled free and charged right into my face, and although he was immediately restrained from attacking me, he sprayed me with bloody spittle as he growled viciously out of a shattered face,

"I'm going to get you for that – you watch your back cos' I'm coming for you!!!"

I was gratified that Tom had issued his threats in front of the police, as if he did make good on his threat, I could hardly be held responsible for what would surely happen to him on that occasion.

"Well you know where to find me." I replied with a sigh.

So, instead of being arrested I was actually thanked by Jo's ex, and I was allowed to go back to bed where I could continue to be horribly ill in peace.

A week or so later I was just coming out of the front door, when I saw standing over the other side of the road none other but Tom; he stepped off the curb and strode swiftly towards me as I felt both of my hands ball into fists.

"I'm glad I caught you Ade," he told me, "I wanted to apologize to you and Jean, and thank you for not damaging me too badly - I know you could have really fucked me up if you'd wanted to." He held out his hand and added, "I hope we can still be friends, it was the drink, not me."

I checked out the very extensive damage still evident on his swollen, multicolored face as I shook his hand and replied,

"I'm sorry too Tom, I really wish it had never happened." Be that as it may, Jo's ex Husband moved back in with her and I never saw Tom again.

Although that was not the end of the story, as I was told that years later Tom and Jo got back together, they got married and had a couple of kids – poor Tom!

So once again tranquility reigned in our household, but unfortunately not for long!

A month or two into the New Year another couple with a young child moved into the flat above ours. The lady was a tall, skinny blond, her husband was a short, very dark skinned East Indian, and their child was an olive skinned boy who would have been only a few months older than my own baby, Adrian.

I have always been very fond of young kids, probably shared the same mentality, but I had never really taken much notice of young babies, until I had one of my own. Then I seemed to be very much more aware of them than I ever had been before in my life. The upstairs little boy was named King, as I said; he had olive colored skin, the biggest, glossiest black eyes, and a huge mop of slightly curly, jet black hair. He was so pretty, that I thought at first he was a girl, and made the mistake of asking his parents what 'HER' name was. I was told that he was a boy, and his name was King. The mistake I made turned out to be a very bad one indeed, as the next time I saw the child he was as bald as a Q-Ball.

"What happened to King's hair?" I asked his Mother. Her husband had shaved it all off, she explained, as he didn't like the Baby-Boy being mistaken for a Girl.

"I'm so sorry," I told her and then asked, "was that my fault?"

"No, it wasn't," she assured me, "he has been threatening to do it for a long time."

That was just the beginning, the little Indian turned out to be a great big bully, and would smash his wife in the face, or whack the Baby for almost no apparent reason whatsoever.

Then I made my second mistake.

Our nice quite evening was suddenly shattered, when Sabu the bloody Elephant-Boy began shouting at the top of his voice, his skinny wife began screaming. Which in turn woke Baby Adrian out of a nice sound sleep with a start, which caused him, in turn to join in the chorus of the loud screaming, which created a horrid screeching stereo effect. The mistake I made was by calling upstairs and telling them both – very nicely,

"TO SHUT THE FUCK UP!!!!!"

My complaint instead of shutting them up caused them both to come scuttling downstairs, and for some strange reason they seemed to mistake me for the wise King Solomon, and both began reciting their mutual grievances to me at the same time. He had obviously punched her in the face. Her top lip was swollen, and tears, mascara, blood and snot ran tantalizingly down her chops.

"He keeps on beating me up!" she sobbed.

"She didn't bring the correct change home out of the money I gave her to go shopping, Mr. Street," He countered, "look at this," he continued, waving a grocery bill and a handful of change at me, "count it yourself, it's 4-pence short."

"WHAT!!!" I replied, "You punched your wife's chops off, just because she was 4 pennies short with the change?! I put my hand in my pocket, pulled out a handful of change, handed him a sixpenny piece out of it and told him,

"There you are, you just made 2-pence profit, now piss-off and shut up, the both of you!"

"You don't understand Mr. Street," he persisted irritably, as he popped the money, including my sixpence back into his pocket, "how do I know what she's doing with the money?!"

"What fucking difference does it make what she's doing with it?" I replied, "It was only bloody 4-pence in the first place, and now you've made 50 percent profit, so go away and shut up, I don't want to hear any more about it!"

"You don't understand Mr. Street," he told me once more, "how do I know that she's not using the money to phone her Mother?!"

"What fucking difference does it make if she is, surely she can phone her own Mother can't she?! I asked.

"How do I know what she's telling her Mother about me?!" he wanted to know.

"Nothing that's any good, if she's telling her the truth!" I replied.

This scenario soon became an almost daily occurrence. Even if I was away wrestling and didn't witness their lunacy myself, I would get it second hand from Jean who would complain to me,

"Those fuckers upstairs were at it again, they woke Adrian up three times last night! So then I'd complain to them.

"He keeps on hitting King on the head with a pencil!" She whimpered.

"What?!" I inquired, thinking that I had mistaken what she said.

"He keeps hitting King on the h-----!"

"I WANT HIM TO BE TOUGH! Sabu interrupted, "She keeps picking him up all the time, I don't want him to get soft!"

"Babies are supposed to be soft, you fucking idiot!" I told him, and added, "You ever hit him on the head again with anything – and I'll hit you on the head with this!!! I said, while placing my clenched fist in front of his nose, "then we'll see how bloody tough you are, won't we?!"

Things would sometimes calm down a little for a few days after I had shared my views with them both, but would soon erupt again in earnest, especially if I was away for a while. The whole episode came to a head one day while I was in the kitchen pouring myself a cup of coffee. First I heard Baby King begin to cry, then I heard Sabu - who I later learned had been in his kitchen shaving with the same open razor he had used to scalp his offspring, yelling furiously. I stepped out of my own kitchen and was in the process of filling my lungs in order to do a little yelling myself - before the racket he was making disturbed my offspring. ButI was beaten to the punch when I heard Sabu's Wife screaming hysterically,

"NO – NO - - PLEASE LEAVE HIM ALONE YOUR KILLING HIM!!!!"

I looked to see where I could very quickly put my coffee cup down without spilling it, but dropped the lot on the floor when the woman came out of their room onto the landing and called to me,

"MR. STREET – QUICK – HELP, HE'S KILLING KING – HE'S STRANGLING HIM!!!"

I was up the stairs and into their room in a flash - and as the scene in front of me came into focus, I was certain that this had to be a dream. Sabu was leaning over King's crib with both his hands around the Baby's face and throat while he simultaneously shook and crushed the little Boy with all his might. I was so shocked by the total lack of reality, that I seemed to tip-toe quietly up behind him, placed my hand softly onto Sabu's shoulder, and turned him towards me, as gently as though I was handling his Baby Son. Just as gently I pried his fingers from around the Baby's neck, gently picked the Baby up and walked out of his room, and down the stairs to my own flat. The Baby's Mother had ran downstairs ahead of me, and was now cowering in my flat behind Jean, who was attempting to calm her down, while I just stood there, completely bewildered with the Child still in my arms.

I was suddenly awakened out of my stupor by Sabu's loud demand,

"MR. STREET – BRING MY SON BACK UPSTAIRS RIGHT NOW!"

I handed King to Jean, and walked out of my flat to confront the little Baby's irate Father, he was standing on his landing glaring down at me,

"Bring my Son, back upstairs right now, or I'll call the Police!" he warned me.

"That's good – phone them right away," I responded, "that will save me doing it!"

He disappeared into his kitchen, then reappeared brandishing the razor he had been shaving with,

"BRING MY SON BACK RIGHT NOW, OR I'LL CUT YOU, YOU BASTARD!!! He screamed as he began slashing at the air in front of him in emphasis.

It is possible that I may have already mentioned that I don't respond kindly to threats - he was about an inch shorter than I was and wasn't so heavily built, but not only had he threatened me, but the tool he had threatened me with, I considered would not only suffice as an equalizer, but would also justify what was about to happen next.

I was up those fucking stairs three or four steps at a time, where his razor went was anyone's guess, but he certainly didn't use it on me!

What did I do to him?!!! Everything you can think of and more – twice!!! And as I began an encore, his wife came running out of MY flat, screaming that I was to leave him alone – and announcing that she had just used MY phone to call the Police, and told them that a professional wrestler was beating her husband up! Talk about Déjà-BLOODY-Vu!

I was so disgusted with both her, and her shit-head of a husband that I dragged him off the floor by his hair with my left hand, grabbed a handful of the arse of his trousers with my right, and launched him right at his wife who was now standing below us at the foot of the stairs. She squawked and ran back into my flat, but poked her head back out just in time to see me launch myself right after her husband where I landed on top of him feet-first. Unfortunately that caused her to erupt into a fit of hysterics, and in an attempt to calm her down, I told her that I would take Sabu back upstairs and lay him on their bed. So, I picked up her husband and carried him upstairs as gently as I had brought his Baby down. But upon entering their room, the very sight of King's crib brought back such a vivid memory of this beast's brutality, that instead of laying him gently on his bed as I had promised, I turned him upside-down and hurled him at the wall as hard as I could.

Great timing, here came the police again – in force!

I explained the situation to a very tall, skinny, grizzled, graying Sergeant, and showed him the bruises on the Baby's face and neck, which were, as if to confirm my claim, by now quite livid. We then walked upstairs together where I showed him the scene of the crime – or crimes, according to who you chose to sympathize with, and the Sergeant told me,

"Chuck the Bastard though the fuckin' window next time!"

Sabu was still in sweet repose on the floor where I had left him, but I strongly suspected that he was only pretending to be dead, and that he heard and appreciated every word that the Sergeant had just suggested to me. That prompted me to tell King's Mother, who had just entered the room with two more Policemen, that she should tell her husband that if I ever caught him abusing King, if I ever heard him make any loud noise, or even if he were to pass me in the hallway close enough for me to touch, that I wouldn't hesitate for one split second, than to begin again exactly where I had just left off.

I made my statement for the Police as the sad trio left in a squad car for a trip to the Station; I heard King and his Mother return later that evening, while Sabu was spending the night elsewhere. When I returned home from wrestling at a local London show the next night, I was aware of an eerie silence as I entered the house, and was informed by Jean that our noisy, upstairs neighbors were gone for good.

Within a couple of days we got an unscheduled visit from our Landlord Mr. Sikorski, who was somewhat miffed that he now had an un-rented apartment to re-let, and wanted to share his frustration with who he thought was the cause of his problem. I told him exactly what happened, and suggested that he was at liberty to go and check my story with the Police if he doubted my word. He just sniffed and responded with,

"Humm! I believe you were involved in a similar incident next door just a couple of months ago?!

"Why yes I was!" I told him irritably, "Would you like me to tell you about that too, or would you prefer to check that police report while you're at the Station, checking on the latest one?!"

He sniffed again and then changed the subject,

"Oh, by the way Mr. Street, I don't have a key to this flat, do you think you could get me one cut?" he asked.

"Why do you want one?" I inquired.

"I like to inspect my properties from time to time." He explained.

"Why don't you inspect it now," I suggested, "I believe you'll find there's nothing damaged – or missing."

"I like to make random inspections." He told me.

"You can make whatever inspections you see fit when ever you come to collect the rent." I told him.

"Are you going to get me a key cut or not?" he wanted to know.

"No, I'm not." I replied.

"Why not – don't you trust me?!" he snapped.

"That's not the point," I told him, "we value our privacy, and we don't want anyone snooping around while we are not present."

"I'm the Landlord," he insisted, "It's my property, so I don't consider you have any right to object to my demands!"

"Who the fuck do you think you are – 'Polish' Peter Rachman?!" I wanted to know. I was gratified to see by his expression that he recognized the name, and so I continued, "my family, or I, will not be harassed or bullied by any damned Landlords - while I pay the rent, this space belongs to me, and we demand our privacy, so if you ever get the urge, and you want to inspect OUR flat – phone first and ask for an appointment!"

"I'm very sorry you feel that way Mr. Street." He replied meekly, and left, but he had certainly left a bad taste in my mouth.

The ever present urge to own my own house returned tenfold, but I was well aware that I was probably years away from saving enough money to even cover the deposit on one.

'What the Hell could I do in order to generate more income?' I wondered for the thousandth time.

****

In spite of my desire to save as much money as I could, I refused to even consider cutting back on my ever expanding collection of exotic ring wear, as I firmly believed that investing in my own image now would eventually pay dividends.

For my next gown I designed a thigh length Burgundy Velvet Cape, lined in a silver satin and trimmed all around with an off white fur. With that I usually wore my metallic silver trunks and boots. I had mixed feelings about it after I unveiled this outfit for the first time, as a number of wrestlers actually told me that it looked smart and that they liked it, I wasn't happy about that at all. As if to confirm my worst fears, the audiences in many of the arenas where this new look made its debut also seemed to approve, so I quickly dove back to the drawing board.

I began to search my mind for historical figures who had gained fame through controversy as well as ability, and the first to come to mind was my all-time favorite Boxing Star and first Black World Heavyweight Champion. The great Jack Johnson. In one of racially charged America's most racially charged periods, the Black King of Boxing had a God-given gift for rubbing everyone up the wrong way. The more they roared their disapproval, the more he would rub their noses in it by brutally, but skillfully battering each and every new white hope into sweet oblivion who attempted in vain to wipe the ever-present 'golden smile' off his face.

Then he would tell the World,

"I'm Jack Johnson – Heavyweight Champion of the World. I'm Black – they never let me forget it – I'm Black alright – I'll never let them forget it!"

Then there was Manfred Von Richthofen – 'The Bloody Red Baron,' Kaiser Wilhelm's number one Air-Ace of the First World War.

Was he skillful, was he deadly? Well the 80 British and Allied Pilots that he shot out of the sky couldn't all be wrong.

But, as great as an Air-Ace as he was before, he never earned his infamous nickname 'The Bloody Red Baron' until AFTER he had painted his flying machine a bright blood red. This not only added greatly to his legend but must have also purposely painted a great big bright blood red 'come and get me – if you dare' target on his own head. I greatly admired that kind of audacity, and in my own way decided to emulate it to the very best of my ability.

This time I was taking no chances whatsoever, I designed a close fitting velvet jacket that hugged the torso, exaggerating my small waistline which was thankfully once again below the 30 inch mark. This contrasted greatly with the fullest, puffiest sleeves yet, it was a very fetching, eye-catching design. But, just like 'The Bloody Red Baron's Flying Machine, it was not the design itself that would be the 'Main-Event' attraction, but the color of it. The Baron's color was red, mine was – HOT NEON PINK, with a heavy black wet-look satin lining, and the sleeves liberally sprinkled with metallic jet stars, then to complete the ensemble, Hot Neon Pink Trunks with matching Hot Neon Pink Leather Wrestling Boots.

Just like Manfred Von Richthofen, I was well aware that I was painting an irresistible target on my own head. And even though I knew full well that there would be no actual bullets flying in my direction, there were still many 'Shooters' in my business who would not hesitate to take aim, and use their own lethal arsenals to score a 'Bull's-eye.' Well I may have had mixed feelings concerning the Burgundy cape, but the reaction I received for the Neon Pink number, confirmed immediately that I was back on track and had definitely scored a 'Bull's-eye of my own.

Even as a child, my demand for attention always seemed to land me in very hot water, so what was new? – Well - quite a lot actually, even though continually pushing the envelope may have invited trouble, at least now I was getting paid for it!

The dressing room and van time criticism escalated as never before, this time I had done it right. When Master of Ceremonies, Bobby Palmer saw it for the first time, in a loud dressing room dominating voice he asked me,

"Is that another new wrestling gown?!"

"Why, yes it is." I replied.

"HA-HA-HA!" He laughed, and when he was sure that he had everyone's attention, he added, "Well, Adrian Street won't have any money left by the time he's finished with wrestling - BUT, he'll certainly have some dressing gowns!"

"HA-HA-HA!" Everyone in the dressing-room laughed obligingly; very soon I found that Bobby Palmer had definitely coined a phrase, as every time I added another gown to my ever expanding wardrobe, a hundred and one other dressing room smart-arses would repeat it,

"Adrian Street won't have any money by the time he's finished with wrestling - BUT, he'll certainly have a lot of dressing gowns – HA – HA – HA!!!!"

Damn – if I had just one pound for every time I heard that said, not only could I have afforded to leave our humble, rented apartment, I would have had enough money to buy Buckingham Palace, and still have plenty left over to purchase a few more wrestling gowns. The crowd response was immense, I may have looked 'Pretty in Pink' but everyone was seeing red, and needless to say, as a result, jealousy amongst my peers was once again rearing its ugly head. As soon as they realized that ridiculing my appearance had no effect on me at all, except maybe feeding my ego, they began to alter their tactics,

"He was probably a homo all the time," one of them would speculate as though I wasn't there.

"How come it took you so long to come out of the closet?" another of them would ask me.

"Do you remember all the girls he used to chase?" one of them would remind the others, "well he doesn't bother with girls any more does he?!"

"Yes, that's right," another agreed, "and do you remember all those queer magazines he used to pose for?!"

I had explained that I was now married and a Father, but that was not what they wanted to hear.

"Being married never used to stop you chasing everything in a dress!" they accused. "Probably wanted to try them on himself!" added another, "Ha-Ha-Ha!"

"Yes, tell us!" they demanded, "How come you don't chase Girls anymore?!"

'Time to change my own tactics.' I thought – and so I replied,

"Well, Girls are alright Dear, - but they are not like the real thing!!!"

In truth, I wasn't chasing Girls anymore, but if I told you that they were easy to resist, then I would be a bigger Liar than Charley Fisher, Jackie Pallo and Mike Marino combined, and as any wrestler who knew any of these three would attest to, that was really saying something.

What made things so much more difficult was that since giving birth, Jean seemed to have lost all interest in sex, and I was getting somewhere between very little and none at all. And, the very little I did get was totally unsatisfactory. Now, I am not completely stupid, or unusually insensitive, and I do realize that giving birth is no walk in the Park for any Woman. Especially the first time. I had also learned that as a result a Woman's hormones could be doing cartwheels, and back-flips, causing mood swings from Hell. But at age 22 almost total abstinence was causing my own hormones to perform some pretty spectacular acrobatics of their own, not to mention a slightly less than favorable disposition. We would talk about it, I would state my case as gently and as reasonably as I could – and sometimes if I was lucky I would get the 'go ahead.' And then the libido crusher of all times would often occur, when directly after agreement had been reached, it would be accompanied by the rolling of eyes, and the sigh of a martyr which would send me screaming out of the house as fast as I could run. I refused to accept a reluctant favor, there was so much more that I wanted than someone who would stick an ankle behind their head, and then lay back and think of England, while posing like a sacrificial Lamb. Well thanks, but no thanks, for me it was with maximum enthusiasm or not at all, I was desperate, but not that desperate - Well actually I was, but what was I supposed to do about it?

Hobbies helped a lot, and I did have a few, even though I was now 22 years old, my love of Military Miniatures had not diminished, in fact if anything my interest had increased, probably due to the fact that I had been looking at flashy antique uniforms for ideas while designing my own unique wrestling wear.

At first I had sculptured a Spartan and an Athenian Hoplite and had got Uncle Fred to make moulds of each of them out of aluminum. It took a lot of trial and error before I found that I also needed to hot the mould up, as well as melt the lead before I began producing perfect figures. But even then, they were never as well detailed as I would have preferred them to be. After that I was soon turning out Archers, and Horses for my Cavalry figures and Chariots, using my own moulds that I made out of Plaster of Paris. But even though my techniques improved and my Ancient Grecian armies grew I was still not satisfied with the definition on my models. I began to spend more time studying the beautiful Miniatures in a store named 'Tradition' and another store in Sloane Square, whose name I can't recall, but who's artwork was fantastic. Bit by bit I began to pick the proprietors brains and leaned very many ways of improving my own miniatures. In return I began doing homework for both stores, by cleaning up their figures of 'flash' and other debris after they had been cooled and removed from their moulds after casting.

Two of the most important things I learned were for one, regular Plaster of Paris would never reproduce the fine detail I was looking for, and that I would need to make my moulds from Dental Plaster instead. And two, that the pure lead I had been using to cast the models in, would not produce a finely detailed figure whatever I used to make the mould out of. What I had to do was mix the lead with tin. But, where could I get tin from? That problem solved itself one afternoon when I paid a visit to Dale Martin's Printers, which was situated in the basement of their offices.

A fact that I may have already alluded to once or twice, was that Joint Promoters were disgustingly mean. So mean in fact, that rather than bear the cost of making a new photo block of my 'new look' for their posters and programs, they were still using the first photos I had supplied them with from my dark-haired, 'Kid Tarzan Jonathan days. Without the fancy dress, and without the bleach blond mop. In order to remedy their deliberate faux-pas I decided to foot the bill myself, and took in a much larger photo wearing the 'new look' and ordered a new block to be made in my own choice of design and dimensions. While I was there, I had been waiting patiently for some attention whilst one of the printers was removing a handful of damaged metal letters out of a tray and replacing them with new ones. He casually passed the damaged ones to me, and asked me to throw them into a small waste sack that sat in the corner, and then laughed out loud because I had fallen for his little joke, and I now had printer's ink all over my hands. I remember him being disappointed that instead of being upset by his childish ruse, I was more interested in examining the little broken letters, and learning what kind of metal they were made from. BINGO! I learned they were a mixture of metals whose ingredients contained a large percentage of tin. I knew Malcolm, one of the printer's apprentices quite well, and after a quiet chat and a few shillings passing out of my hand and into Malcolm's. I was soon staggering homeward under the weight of a small, but very heavy sack of scrap metal. Now, not only did my armies grow by regiments at a time, they were now sharper, smarter and more detailed than ever before.

My Homework for the Military Miniature Stores, and my own growing armies didn't only help to keep me sane at home, but I now began bringing some of them with me in order to while away the hours and relieve some of the boredom whilst traveling to my wrestling matches in Dale's dreaded van. I began bringing two cases with me each day. One containing my wrestling gear, the other containing, my lunch, models, needle-files, metal clippers, small saws and a myriad of dental instruments, acrylic paints and brushes.

Now even my hobbies seemed to attract the media, this is an excerpt from a magazine interview during this period,

ADRIAN THE ANCIENT GREEK IS A BORN WINNER.

On my visit to Adrian Street's home in Streatham, London, I was given a peep into the past from which he believes he was reborn. Out came nearly 500 toy Greek Soldiers – from Spartan infantry to Athenian Charioteers he has spent years making.

And the Battle was re-staged to show me how Leonidas with only 300 Spartans and several thousand allies heroically defended the Pass of Thermopylae against mighty Xerxes and the Persian Army in 480 BC.

Adrian's pretty wife Jean, whose domestic bliss is shattered when he takes over the kitchen for another toy-making session, said:

"It beats me how he remembers those names. He's always saying he's living in the wrong age."

As a reminder the house has a Greek style décor and plaques of Hercules and Olympus in the Hallway.

EXPELLED.

Adrian expelled from Grammar School for lack of interest in any subjects but Art and History – said: "Yes, I feel I should have been an Ancient Greek, then like Alexander the Great, I'd be conquering the World."

"I'm made like him, you know, I always have my own way. I'll face any challenge and I let nothing stand in my way, and I'll always achieve what I say I will."

Thumping his chest confidently, Adrian the Greek prophesied: "I've always said I'll be rich – and that means I will be."

Under the gaze of Alexander the Great, staring down at me from an Oil Painting by artist 'Adrian' I tried on Adrian's prize possession – a Greek Warrior's Helmet, that he made himself.

Former Welterweight Champion of Wales, he wears dazzling gowns and strikes vain and precocious poses, fussing with his golden locks like a Pretty-Boy.

He insists on being introduced as Adrian 'Nature-Boy' Street and claims his MAYHEM ROUTINES, Which often have the crowds howling hate are inspired by the Ancient Greeks.
ARTIST.

They trained on forced marches, Adrian a weightlifting fanatic, goes in for hill-climbing and Marathon country walks, which initially earned him the ring nickname of 'Nature-Boy'.

His family wanted him to be an artist,

"But I felt wrestling was something I could do better than anything else." He said. "They laughed at me and said I'd never make it."

To prove himself he headed from Brynmawr, Breconshire, at the age of 16 and at an amateur club was befriended by referee and ex-World Champion Wrestler Mike Dimitri. "Mike," said Adrian, "is the only Modern Greek I can compare with the old ones and I owe him a lot."

While training, he met living expenses by Boxing in Fairground Booths.

"I reckoned that by keeping my fists up I could avoid being hit." He said, "But I was wrong, I became so fed up at having a leather glove banging in my face, in frustration one evening I picked up an opponent and slung him across the ring in a wrestling move – I was disqualified and sacked on the spot. – END.

The inspiration for my Oil-Painting of 'Alexander the Great' that was referred to in the magazine article came from a most unlikely source, - My friend Bill Jones, better known as my first physique photographer, 'Mark' rang me one day and told me that he had taken his very last physique photo.

"Why?!" I wanted to know.

He explained that he had now retired and intended changing most things concerning his lifestyle. It was only going to be a matter of time after tying up all loose ends before he left Britain and spent 4 months of the year in Greece and the other 8 in the West Indies for rest of his life.

"I have decided I want to paint instead of taking photographs," he explained, and then went on to tell me, "funny really, as I couldn't even draw a straight line when I was in school, but now I really have the urge to become an artist, I have completed a few pictures and I would like to show them to you, when you have the time."

I had always fancied myself as an artist, so I told him,

"Why yes I'd love to see them," and then added self importantly, "I'll also be happy to give you a few pointers." A few pointers indeed, my jaw dropped the first time I examined Bill's artwork, as it was far better than anything that I had ever produced, and almost immediately it was I who was asking Bill for pointers. His paintings were all in oils, a medium that I had never used, but now intended to, after the huge amount of inspiration that I derived from viewing the artwork of a self confessed novice.

While I was with Bill that day, he asked me if I knew that 'Sean' had been chosen to play the major role in a movie about 'James Bond'?

"Who's Sean and who's James Bond?" I wanted to know.

"Sean Connery – Oh, you probably know him better as Tom." He told me, "He's playing Ian Fleming's Super Spy in a movie called 'Dr. No.' – Milton Reid is in it also."

At that time, I had never heard of James Bond, or Ian Fleming, and I only knew Tom Connery as one of 'Mark's' physique models and as a former Mr. Universe contestant.

The 'oil' painting of Alexander the Great that domineered a wall in our lounge that I was so very proud of, was my first attempt, and probably the worst oil painting that I ever produced. I didn't understand the medium; I had no use for linseed oil, and used turpentine so liberally that the resulting 'work of art' was more like a watercolor on canvas than an oil painting.

When Mike Dimitri, who incidentally was a great artist himself saw it, his major criticism was that it contained too much detail, the same criticism that I had received from my Art teacher at an Art School I had attended 3 nights a week, just before and a while after I had left day school. In those days, my view on the subject differed greatly from my more knowledgeable critics, as I thought my fanatical attention to detail was my strong point rather than my weakness. But Mike explained that by omitting much of the detail and instead 'suggesting' it, would give each and every person who viewed the picture an opportunity to use their own imagination, and read into it their own version of what they actually saw.

Initially that was too hard a pill for me to swallow. If my subject was a soldier for instance, I was so taken with every tiny aspect of his garb, that I would even take pains to perfect the pupil in the eye of a Lion insignia on the tiny brass buttons on the jacket of his Battle-Dress. Old habits die hard, and at first it was almost impossible to convince me to 'suggest' rather than to continue to hammer the point home. But once I learned to appreciate and even master the concept, it then began to dawn on me that 'suggestion' could also be a great asset in the 'Art' of professional wrestling.

****

When wrestling fans, or predators of either sex wanted to contact their favorite, or most despised wrestler, all they had to do was to drop him a line at Dale Martin's Office, 313 Brixton Road. There was a very large board in the passageway that led to the gym where the mail was left, usually in alphabetical order. From Monday till Saturday the first thing a wrestler would do when arriving at the Office, to catch their ride would be to check their mail. The letters were most often from fans who requested autographs or photographs of their wrestling Idols. Wishes of wellbeing and success to the 'Blue-eyes' wrestlers. And anything from 'I hope you drop dead' to actual threats of violence, or even death to the hated 'Villains' of the sport. As I was still loved in some arenas and hated in others, I was receiving very large quantities of both varieties.

One afternoon while in the van and on my way to Peterborough I began looking through the mail I had received that day. It contained the usual array of letters from autograph and photograph collectors, to explicit propositions from naughty young Ladies. I then opened an envelope which contained a photo as well as a letter; I first looked at the photo, and then read the letter that had been written to me by someone named Steve. This Steve explained that I had first attracted his attention as, according to him, I stood out from all the other wrestlers like a pretty School-girl would stand out from a herd of Bulls. He went on to tell me that I had inspired him to write a sonnet, which he had included in his letter; the sonnet went like this –

'Adrian Street is a lovely Lad – and his bottom I'd like to pad.

Forty pounds at least I'd pay – with his 'orchestras' to play.

Adrian I love you Dear, - cos' you're pretty and I'm queer.

'Orchestras' are another example of the rhyming 'Cockney Slang' – 'orchestra stalls' – Balls. The photo was a physique shot of a very naked man holding a sword at the same erotic angle as his own erect weapon. He wasn't the young, trim Adonis type that one might find in some of the more questionable physique magazines; in contrast he had a heavier build, and formidable facial features that reminded me a lot of 'Iron-man' Steve Logan. And as luck would have it, The Iron-Man himself was sitting just across the van from me and I decided to have a little wrestler type fun at his expense.

"Steve!" I called to him, "This is a lovely sonnet you've written for me, but you shouldn't send me naked photos of yourself - what if any of the other wrestlers saw it – I'd hate to imagine what they'd think!" Of course, I immediately had the undivided attention of every wrestler traveling in the van, so I passed the photo to the wrestler seated in front of me and said,

"Oh no, he snatched the photo right out of my hand before I could stop him - sorry Steve!"

Steve Logan was a great prankster, really funny, but didn't appreciate a joke if he was the brunt of it.

"Damn it does look like you Steve," all the wrestlers agreed as they passed the photo around the van, "have you got any more we can look at?" they asked him.

The photo was passed back to me and I handed it to Steve to get his reaction to it, and invited him to,

"Own up Steve – it is you, isn't it?"

The Iron-Man took the photo, held it up to the light, and after scrutinizing it for a full minute, then he took a long drag from his ever present cigarette, and growled in his gravel voice,

"Na, it isn't me – I ain't got a sword."

"Come on Steve," I insisted, "it is you isn't it? You've even signed it Steve" then continued by reading out loud the sonnet which amused everyone – except Steve, then I added,

"Would you really give me forty-pounds just to play with my orchestras Steve?"

"Yes!" he replied, taking another long drag, "Wiv' a fuckin' big hammer!"

We all laughed. Then without missing a beat, he completely changed the subject by describing the wonderful meal he had enjoyed the night before in a Mexican Restaurant.

By the time we arrived at our venue in Peterborough I was dying for a 'Melvin' Melvin Riss – piss, but still took time to sign a dozen or so autographs before entering the dressing room. Upon entering I dropped my wrestling bag and made a B-line for the toilet, which I found to my dismay was locked.

"Wait your turn," one of the wrestlers told me, "we've got a line up here, we're all waiting to go!"

Well we all waited ages, but eventually, who should stagger out of the toilet with torrents of sweat running all down his scarlet, steaming face was the Iron-Man.

"What have you been doing in there, Steve?" I demanded suspiciously, "I knew I shouldn't have shown you a photograph of a naked man!"

He ignored the innuendo and replied,

"It was that fuckin' Mexican food!" he complained, "Those fuckin' Jalapeño Peppers don't 'arf burn yer bleed'n arsehole!"

"You are supposed to put them in your mouth Steve!" I told him.

I think it was about a month later before 'The Iron-Man' spoke to me again.

Still on the subject of letters sent to wrestlers at Dale Martin's Offices, we were on our way to another night's venue when the portly Irishman, Ivor Barret began to boast about how many Valentine cards he had received,

"14 Saint Valentine cards I got sent to me today Boys!" he announced to the whole van load of wrestlers.

"Have they been written in ink, - or are they in brail?" one wrestler asked him, "They must have all come from a school for the blind!"

"Huh! You're all jealous, 'cos you probably never got any!" He retorted.

"When did you get them all, Ivor?" I wanted to know.

"I got them all today," he replied, "I'll probably get a load more tomorrow!"

"I don't think so," I told him – and the rest of the van load of wrestlers, "you only wrote and addressed them to yourself a couple of weeks ago!"

"What are you talking about?!" he asked as his pale freckly face began to turn the same color as my latest wrestling outfit, "these cards are from all over the country!"

"What's the betting that each card was posted from each venue that you have wrestled at over the last few weeks?" I asked him, "I remember seeing you writing them all out in Dale's Gym – got them back quick didn't you?!"

"What a load of bollocks!" he claimed.

But that didn't stop the wrestlers ribbing him unmercifully, and just to add to his discomfort I decided to share an observation with the rest of the van,

"Ivor?" I asked him, "How come you expect us to believe that you didn't write those Valentine cards to yourself, when I for one have never – ever seen you with a female of any description?!"

That of course started a feeding frenzy, as everyone in the van agreed that they had never – ever witnessed that phenomenon either. Unable to muster any verbal retaliation, he chose instead to ignore the gibes, and throw all his concentration into glaring at me with all the hostility he could muster. In order to accomplish this feat, the silly Irishman had to twist around in his seat, while I sat back as comfortably as one could in Dale's dreadful vans, and accepted his childish challenge to a staring out contest.

"YOU BLINKED!" He would shout periodically, "LOOK!" He would invite the other wrestlers, "LOOK HE BLINKED!"

The gibes he attempted to avert were still heaped upon him by the other wrestlers, but he completely refused to respond, taking refuge instead in supposedly vanquishing me with the hostility of his glaring eyes. The contest ended after we had arrived at our destination. Instead of continuing to torment 'Freckle-Chops' I contented myself in the dressing-room by painting some of the Military Miniatures that I had brought with me for that purpose. BUT – I had decided that the Irishman had not been punished nearly enough, and solicited the aid of a couple of other likeminded wrestlers to help with the little plan I had in store for him. After the wrestling show was over and we were once again in the van, and had began our return journey to London, one of the wrestlers tapped 'Irish Ivor' on the shoulder and told him as he pointed at me,

"Hey! Barret – he's starring at you again!" – And even though darkness had already fallen the contest was back on with a vengeance,

"Bet you can't make him blink!" they told the Irishman, as he glared for all he was worth.

"He's beating you this time Ivor," another observed, "he hasn't blinked once!"

Ivor Barret glared and stared, absolutely determined to win, even if he lost his eyesight in the process, but stare as he did, he could not get me to blink even once.

Hours later we stopped at a greasy-spoon café on the outskirts of London, and we all piled out of the van in order to get a late night bite. I made a point of standing in front of Ivor Barret and studying the condition of his eyes, which I found to be extremely watery and very red,

"What's wrong with your eyes, Ivor?" I asked him, "You look as though you've been crying - those nasty wrestlers haven't been teasing you again have they?!"

Before he could think of a suitable reply, I closed my eyes, which exposed the big Owl-like eyes I had painted on my eyelids with my acrylic paints - the very same big Owl-like eyes that this gullible, Gaelic Git had been staring at all night, while I slept.

Gullible or not Ivor Barret was very knowledgeable, in fact he knew more about some of my favorite subjects than I did in those days. I thought I was an authority on everything Bonaparte, but Fatty Barret knew more. I don't know what brought that particular subject up one day as we traveled to that night's venue, but we were suddenly discussing Orangutans. I happened to mention that my Father had actually seen them in the wild when he was a prisoner of war in Sumatra, and that the locals had told him that the word Orangutan meant 'Wild Man of the Woods' in the Sumatran language.

"OH, NO IT DOESN'T," screamed Fatty Barret, "IT MEANS 'OLD MAN OF THE WOODS!" And to prove his point he began carrying an encyclopedia around with him with the pages concerning Orangutans marked out in order to prove that he was right and my Father was wrong.

My only retaliation was to quote French Physiologist, Claude Bernard,

'Mediocre men often have the most acquired knowledge.'

By far the best letter that I received at that time could not have come at a better time; it had got my attention 3 seconds after I opened the envelope and found it contained a 5-pound note as well as a letter. The letter was from Ipswich and was signed by someone named Jack Robinson, who described himself as a great fan. He had only ever watched wrestling on TV, but intended to attend St. Matthews Baths Hall, in Ipswich where I would be appearing on the Friday night of the very next week. He expressed the wish to meet me and to watch wrestling live for the first time in his life.

I was watching the first match whilst signing autographs when Jack Robinson approached and introduced himself, he was quite heavily built, balding and a couple of inches shorter than me. I estimated that he would have been in his mid-fifties and looked to me as though he might be a retired Army Colonel. Nothing could have been further from the truth, after chatting with him for a while I learned that he was in fact an ex Tailor – obviously, that also got my attention. We began talking about clothes and he immediately offered to make me some shirts out of some very colorful silk fabric that he had come by. I gave him my measurements and my phone number, and he said that he could bring them to my home in London on the next day I had free.

If ever I did have a day free from wrestling, which was becoming more and more of a rare occurrence, that day would usually be on a Sunday. It was probably about a month after the Ipswich show that Jack visited me at home, bringing with him a suitcase full of goodies. He had brought me 5 multi-colored silk shirts, 4 pairs of trousers and a Burgundy colored Blazer they all fitted me perfectly, and best of all they were all free!

From that time on, Jack would visit our house in London about once a month, and every month was like Christmas. He would open up his suitcase, and out of it would come tailored clothes galore. He was thrilled one day when I asked him if he was able to make me a new jacket for the ring, and made to my own design. I sketched out the design I had in mind and a few weeks later I was trying it on for size. It was by far the best wrestling Jacket that I had ever seen, and that included the very best that I had ever seen in every American wrestling magazine that I had ever owned. It was made in a heavy white satin, lined in a heavy red, black and metallic gold brocade, and the whole of the white satin was studded in white pearls and multi-colored rhinestones. The sleeves were not big and puffy, but roomy enough to enable me to slip out of it easily when I disrobed in the ring. The body of the jacket was closefitting, it hugged the torso and fitted like a glove. With white being a neutral color, but studded with a multitude of different colored rhinestones, it enabled me to wear almost any color trunks, and boots with it.

The third time he visited he brought with him a few more silk shirts, a few more pairs of trousers, a royal blue blazer, and we talked about a new Ring Jacket that I had designed.

THE LITTLE ZEBRA

I was whittling away at one of my Miniatures with a tiny file as we rode along in the van one day, when The Zebra Kid, who was spread over the two seats next to mine, asked me where I had got the little Soldier from.

"I made it myself George." I told him.

"How?" he wanted to know.

I explained the process to him as best I could, and then he asked,

"Could you make a mould of this little Zebra Kid, and then cast it in metal?" as he produced a little plastic figure of a masked wrestler.

"Yes I could," I replied, "but it doesn't look like you."

"Maybe it would if you painted the mask with Zebra stripes like mine." He suggested.

"That would help a bit." I admitted, I didn't want to get personal and point out that unlike Big George, the little figure actually possessed a waistline.

"When can you do it?" George wanted to know.

"I'm not wrestling on Sunday," I told him, "I could start it then." So we made a date. Early Sunday morning a loud banging on our door woke me from the deepest sleep; I checked the clock and found that I had been in bed for less than 4 hours. Jean answered the door to admit the large, loud, animated Zebra Kid, who totally succeeded in shattering and shredding my sleeping nerves with,

"COME ON – WAKE-UP – TIME TO MAKE MY LITTLE ZEBRA!!!!!"

"Okay, just give me time to wake up," I slurred sleepily, "I haven't even had my breakfast yet."

"I've had mine already," he told me, as he held the little plastic model in front of my blurry eyes, "c'mon I want my little Zebras!"

"I'll look at it while I'm eating and drinking my coffee," I replied, and asked him, "do you want something to eat, or some coffee, George?"

"NO-NO!" He yelled, "I JUST WANT MY LITTLE ZEBRA!"

"Okay just let me look at it – and don't keep shouting, - you're giving me a fucking headache." I told him.

"Why do you want to look at it?!" he wanted to know.

I took the figure and showed him the very faint flash lines all around it,

"See that?" I asked, and explained that the faint line was where the two sides of the mould met, and therefore would most probably be the best way for me to duplicate the original mould by using the line as a guide.

I must stress at this time, that I had already surpassed the patience of a Chinese Jobe, as I am not amiable after being noisily woken out of a very deep sleep. I am not tolerant of being pestered when I am both tired and hungry, and I don't like insistent demands being issued while I'm trying to enjoy any meal – especially my Breakfast!

As soon as I finished my second cup of coffee, I picked up the little wrestler and took it into the kitchen, where I kept the plastercine that I would use to imbed one half of the figure in.

"How long is this going to take?!" asked Big George impatiently.

"As long as it takes," I replied, "you want a perfect figure, don't you?"

After imbedding the figure in plastercine up to the old flash-line, I then built a wall all around it and began mixing the dental-plaster in order to pour the first half of the mould.

"How long is this going to take?!" Big George asked again.

"As long as it takes!" I replied with a sigh. I won't bore you with the whole process, but hours later after enduring endless moaning and groaning from my extremely impatient guest, I announced proudly that the mould was now complete and I predicted it would produce an excellent metal duplicate of George's little model wrestler.

"WELL – GO ON THEN – MAKE ONE!!!" He demanded.

"Don't be silly George;" I told him, "it will take days for the plaster of Paris to dry out enough to be able to pour molten metal into it!"

"NO – I WANT IT NOW!!!" He demanded.

"Well, you can't have it now;" I replied patiently, "the mould is not ready!"

"I WANT IT NOW – I WANT IT NOW – I WANT IT NOW!!!" He wailed.

"Well you can't have it now George," I insisted, "If I try to cast it before the mould is dried out, the fucking thing will explode!"

"I WANT IT NOW – I WANT IT NOW – I WANT IT NOW!!! He sobbed – and I'm not kidding – he was crying and carrying on like a great big Baby!

To cut a very long, and even more frustrating story short, I agreed to attempt to cast a little wrestler for the huge distraught 360 pound behemoth, who half filled our small flat with his bulk and the other half with his loud childish sobbing. BUT – I agreed for no other reason than to prove to him once and for all that it couldn't be done successfully that quickly. After removing the original prototype, I clamped both sides of the mould together, melted down a quantity of printer's type and lead, poured it into the mould and was immediately showered with an explosion of molten metal and steam. Some of it hit me on the side of my face, but most of it landed on the back of my left hand that had held the mould steady during the pouring.

"SEE WHAT I MEAN YOU DAFT TWAT!!!" I told him, as I ran my burned hand under the tap, and tugged a scrap of hot metal out of my singed sideburns. – did he offer any sympathy?

"I WANT A LITTLE ZEBRA – I WANT A LITTLE ZEBRA – I WANT A LITTLE ZEBRA!!! Was all I got.

There must have been more steam coming out of my nostrils and ear holes than had just gushed out of the wet mould, but with a superhuman effort I succeeded in tempering my outrage, and suggested having a look at the result of casting molten metal into a wet mould. Strangely enough the head and torso was almost perfect, but from the waist down, and especially the legs were just distorted spindles,

"OH NO," He sobbed as he examined the deformed little wrestler, "I WANT A LITTLE ZEBRA!!!" – And so on and so forth!

He carried on like a big, nasty spoiled Child, then,

"TRY IT AGAIN! – TRY IT AGAIN! – TRY IT AGAIN!!! He demanded.

At first I refused, - then I relented – what did I get?! – A whole action replay and another deformed model wrestler, followed by,

"I WANT A LITTLE ZEBRA!!!!!" And so bloody on!!!!

"GEORGE!" I told him, "YOU'VE COME OVER HERE - WASTED MY WHOLE DAY – THE ONLY DAY I'VE GOT OFF FOR WEEKS – I AGREED TO DO YOU A FAVOR, AND ALL YOU DO IS BAWL ALL DAY LIKE A FUCKING BABY – NOW DO ME A FAVOR, AND FUCK OFF HOME!!!"

"I'M NOT GOING UNTIL YOU MAKE ME A LITTLE ZEBRA!!!" He threatened.

"NO?!" I replied, "WELL JUST WATCH THIS!!!" – I picked the mould up opened the window and threw the mould half way around the World!

"DON'T SLAM THE DOOR ON YOUR WAY OUT!!!" I told him,

Needless to say he did.

A few weeks later the exact situation that I had patiently waited for presented itself, and I was traveling to a show in the van with the huge surly Zebra Kid sitting just a few yards away from me. We had already crossed paths a few times since my failure to produce 'his little Zebra' but the timing had not been right – today it was.

Like two overgrown Children we former 'Best friends' were not speaking to each other anymore, but I had a lot more to offer the big American Baby than my mere silence.

"What are you making Ade?" Peter Kelly asked me as he leaned over the back of his seat and watched as I whittled away with a tiny hacksaw.

"I'm just cleaning up a Cavalry Horse for one of my Cuirassiers," I replied, then added, "What do you think of this one?" as I handed him a figure I had hidden in my case.

"WOW! – That's fantastic!!! He exclaimed and then to The Zebra Kid, "Hey, George, have you seen this – it looks exactly like you?!"

I watched the amazed expression flash onto Big George's face as he gazed mesmerized at the little figure that Peter held towards him.

"Show it to Tony." I told Peter quickly, as I didn't want it to get within reach of George. I had sculptured the little figure of the Zebra Kid, in proportion, and in full ring regalia. Every tiny detail was present from his Zebra striped mask, to his huge Zebra striped Ring Jacket, right down to the picture of his masked countenance that adorned the buckle of the huge, wide belt that fastened his jacket together. It was a little masterpiece.

The little figure was passed from hand to hand all around the van, with everyone expressing their shear amazement as to how realistic and how close to the real character my little Zebra Kid was. Eventually, I allowed it to be handed to George, who simply drooled over it, and in spite of himself, in a voice of sheer awe seldom heard outside the confines of a beautiful Cathedral, he whispered,

"It's fantastic." Then he turned to me, and with eyes mimicking the appeal of a Kitten begging for a caress, he asked me,

"Can I have it?"

"No you can't!" I replied spitefully, as I leaned forward and plucked it out of his hand, "I need the metal - so I'm going to melt it down and make a whole regiment of Carthaginian War Elephants out of it!"

Poor George, I swear his lower lip trembled with sadness and pent up emotion, the way my own probably did as a young kid when I was told by my Mother that,

"No Adrian, you can't take Henry VIII's Suit of Armor home with you from The Tower of London."

But, by the end of our journey I relented and gave him his little Zebra Kid - even I couldn't remain that cruel for long.

For once my kindness repaid me tenfold, George, just like the overgrown Child he was, waddled around the dressing room that night, showing his new treasure to all the other wrestlers on the card who had not traveled down to the show in the van.

Big Bruno Elrington was the first to ask me,

"How much would you charge me to make one of those of me?"

"One pound." I replied.

"Could you make one of me too?!" asked Joe Cornelius, then added, "I'll give you a pound each for one of myself, one of The Zebra Kid, one of Big Bruno and any one of the wrestlers that I have wrestled against, I'd like to have a whole collection of them." He stated.

Over time I eventually sculptured, cast and painted little model Wrestlers for Joe Cornelius which included, as well as himself, Big Bruno and The Zebra Kid, also The Wildman of Borneo, Dr. Death, Samoan Peter Maivia, Ski-Hi Lee, Dangerous Danny Lynch, Billy Two-Rivers and Masambula the West-African Witchdoctor. Most of these wrestlers wanted to buy their own figure too, and some like Joe Cornelius wanted some of their favorite opponents also.

The reason I chose the aforementioned wrestlers to immortalize in metal, was due to the fact that they all stood out from the other wrestlers, in either their physical characteristics, or in the way they dressed to enter the ring. Which made it easy for me to duplicate their look. There was obviously a hundred or more famous wrestling Stars I could have chosen to sculpt, but they were far too nondescript, as Jack Dale had told me when I had shown him my new style wrestling trunks,

'I wish more of the wrestlers would use a bit of imagination, they'll all go in the ring wearing the same colors, if you don't watch them.'

Quite honestly in those days I could have made a generic wrestling figure and called it whoever I had wanted to, there were some fantastic wrestlers, but their fantastic wrestling skill was only surpassed by their lack of imagination when it came to ring wear. Correction – it was also surpassed by their lack of desire to spend any money, on ring-wear. Mind you, I wasn't complaining, their shortcomings only worked to my advantage, when it came to ring-wear, I had very few, if any rivals.

****

During one of my increasingly frequent metal scavenging forays to Dale Martin's Printers, I was watching the poster printing in progress whilst waiting for Malcolm, who had become my own personal 'metal merchant' to return from lunch. I had watched this exercise many times before, but on this occasion there was the added interest. Watching the larger photo of the 'New Look' appearing on Dale Martin's Posters for the first time - the photo that I had paid for myself.

'It looked much better than the original one.' I thought – 'the wrestling fans will really take more notice of that' and then it occurred to me. 'That if I were to once again foot the bill, and invest in a much bigger photo block still – and the crafty, penny pinching bastards in the office, decided to steal the use of it, as I was certain they would. They would not really be able to use it on their posters, without featuring me in a more important match than in just a preliminary position. If a much larger, and more prominent photo on the posters succeeded in elevating me to Main Event, or even only Semi-Main Event. The extra money I would receive as result, would not only repay my investment over and over again, but would also add considerably to my prestige, not to mention the increased attention it would generate with the wrestling fans, whenever they checked the new posters in their own town or city. This was one idea that I realized was just too good to pass up. I tried it and it turned out to be one of my best investments yet. With the exception of my new fabulous ring wear of course!

By this time I had already christened the beautiful new ring Jacket that I had designed and that my own private Tailor, Jack Robinson had put together for me. It was made in a Neon Lemon Yellow satin, and lined in a bright Purple satin. The front of the jacket was decorated on the right side, from the shoulder, vertically down to the waist with large rhinestone encrusted letters which spelled out 'NATURE BOY'. On the left side of the jacket, from shoulder to waist was a large copy of the Peacock I have tattooed on my right forearm. And covering the whole of the back of the jacket was a huge Peacock with it's tail feathers spread out like an exotic fan. Both Peacocks were made from rhinestones, sequins and bugle-beads, all in the exact colors that one would find on a real live Peacock. With that Jacket I wore Neon Yellow Trunks with matching leather boots.

I had never really found Dale Martin's Gym a very satisfactory place to workout, so that when a 'Universal Health Studio' opened in Brixton, I thought I would give it a whirl.

Almost every day I would try to make time to get a session in there on my way to catch my ride from the office. I had never seen such an array of barbells and dumbbells before in my life. Row upon row of chrome steel exercise equipment all laid out with the precision of one of my own metallic regiments. Instead of the dirty rusty heap of junk metal that I had worked out with ever since I had quit lifting buckets of rocks in my own back garden in Wales.

One whole side of the gym was wide, wall to wall windows, the rest of the walls were mirrors. It was light and blindingly bright, not at all like the dark, dirty, dungeons of torture that I was more used to, and loved passionately. But it suited my purpose during the period that I was a member, even though I can't truthfully say it was a place that I felt at home. One of the trainers/instructors was a young, well built, guy whose name was Mickey Muldoon, and we soon became good friends. Mickey was a little taller than I, but about the same weight, fair hair, and a smile that lit up the already dazzling studio. He had a great sense of humor, and we seemed to compete every session I spent there, not on how much we could lift, but on how much we could make each other laugh.

Mickey knew exactly who I was the first time I walked into the gym, as he was an avid wrestling fan, and had seen me on TV on a number of occasions. Of course that in itself appealed to my ego enough for me to remember him, but what made an indelible impression on my mind at that time was the handful of photographs he'd brought to the gym one day to show me. They were of a very pretty, dark haired Lady, posing completely naked, in the most unladylike poses one could imagine. Now although they were very pleasant to look at, they in themselves would not be something I would particularly remember. Except, about a week or so later, I was busy exercising when I caught sight of a young Girl standing in the entranceway to the studio and she asked me,

"Is Mickey here?" after receiving my affirmative reply she asked me,

"Could you tell him Sandra is looking for him?"

"Okay," I told her, "I'll go and fetch him for you." –

'Now where had I seen that Girl before?' I wondered. It

didn't dawn on me until after I had found Mickey and told him that a Young Girl named Sandra was waiting to see him and was standing by the entrance.

"Oh, that's my Wife," he told me, "come," he beckoned, "I'll introduce you,"

She was very quiet, seemed shy and looked much younger in real life than she did in the photographs that Mickey had shown to me, although I was not surprised to learn that Mick's wife Sandra was just barely sixteen years old.

A TICKET TO RYDE

Usually when we wrestled on the Isle of Wight we wrestled in Ventnor, a town on the southern part of the island, which meant a train ride across the island after we had sailed from Portsmouth harbor on the Ferry Boat to Ryde. But on this occasion we would be wrestling on a late afternoon show in a football stadium in Ryde. The morning and early afternoon had been taken up with a big town festival, where awards were presented to everyone who was thought worthy, from sports men and women to the choosing of 'The Beauty Queen of the Isle of Wight' the contestants would be chosen from amongst the winners who had each been crowned Queen of their own respective towns on the island.

I was wrestling in the last match against Jon Cortez, with whom I had become friends in spite of our very iffy introduction to each other when I had wrestled against him on the one and only Paul Lincoln show I was ever to appear on in Finsbury Park a few years earlier. Jon's popularity with a very enthusiastic crowd immediately colored him as the Hero and me as the villain of the peace, and we both went with the flow. The cheers for Jon would have lifted the roof right off the stadium – if it had had a roof to begin with, the boos and jeers I received during, and especially at the end of the match as the referee raised my hand in victory would have done likewise.

In the corridor leading back to our dressing rooms I had to pass by all the Beauty Queens, who had previously been sitting in a place of honor watching the matches after the Queen of Queens had been crowned, just before the wrestling had commenced. I supposed that they had all rushed from their seats down to the dressing room area in order to obtain an autograph from the handsome and dashing hero that I had just vanquished. They really were very pretty; their beauty set off by their gorgeous dresses, reminding me so much of 'that wedding dress' – YES – that wedding dress. But, remaining in character, I stopped in front of them and regarded them all in mock contempt,

"Damn! If all you haggard, old crones actually won a beauty contest - I'd hate to see what the losers looked like!" I informed them with a sneer, shaking my head to emphasis my mock disbelief, I then added, "You are lucky that I didn't compete – none of you would have stood a chance!" My very rude retort caused an avalanche of verbal response from the irate beauties. I just turned walked a couple of steps to my own dressing room, and after opening the door, I turned towards them once again, in order to impart a final insult – WHEN SHE STRUCK!!!

One of the beauties leapt forward, grabbed me and then shoved me forcefully right through the door and into the dressing-room, slamming the door with a bang behind her. I must admit I was shocked, but not so shocked as I was when she pulled up her dress, pulled down her draws and told me,

"You'll have to be quick – my Husband is on his way here to pick me up!!!!" Did I fall off my self imposed celibacy wagon? – NO I DIDN'T – I WAS DRAGGED OFF IT!!! - The beautiful girl – the Dress – THE ENTHUSIASM!!!!!!

HEY, COME ON – IT WASN'T MY FAULT!!!

Within 20 minutes she was gone and I just sat there puffing and wondering if I had just had a wild and weird dream induced by partly self imposed sexual starvation. But just like a reformed alcoholic – just one drink and ------

I allowed my very strong and natural selfishness to resurface once more – and resurface with a vengeance – From that time on, I decided to live life to the full – I would not, under any circumstances deprive myself of anything that might appeal to me – everything – anything I might want was out there for the taking and I was going to get my share and then some – from now on, every night at every wrestling arena, to me, would be just like another day in the orifice!

But, there was a problem – I had been working very hard at 'suggesting' an image of effeminacy, so how would the wrestling fans react if I was once again to be observed flirting and fraternizing with the flocks of Females who were ever-present, ever-willing and always available around the arenas? After much thought, I came to the conclusion that it might prove to be a bloody good idea.

I realized that if I did succeed in convincing the public that I was nothing more than a 'Prancing Pansy' it would only be a matter of time before they accepted the image and took it in their stride. It's not that it still wouldn't have attracted a certain amount of interest, but I wanted to create more than a one dimensional character, that could be easily labeled and placed neatly in an appropriate box.

I wanted to create a Masterpiece and to do that I would utilize Mike Dimitri's advice on Art to the full. I would purposely blur the edges, obscure details in shadow, make an obvious statement, and then 'suggest' the opposite, in an effort to shroud my persona in such mystery that each individual would have to come to their own personal conclusion, and see what they wanted to see, and when they did I would do whatever it took to confuse the issue all over again. If anyone asked me directly for an explanation concerning my sexuality, my standard answer was,

"OH REALLY!!! When anyone tries to infer, in any way, shape or form, that I am effeminate – it makes me want to SCREAM!!!"

As usual I found that my fellow wrestlers were great sounding boards, I had already learned that the best way to frustrate their efforts to ridicule, was to not only agree with them, but take everything they said a step and a half further. And then on occasion, by vehemently denying another accusation or effort to ridicule, I could wind them up cause confusion, and keep them entirely off balance, as a very forceful denial was a sure fire way to ensure that they would believe the complete opposite, and if it could work with the wrestlers, it would most certainly work with the wrestling fans.

So instead of sneaking and hiding in the shadows, which would 'suggest' I was attempting to hide something. I would openly allow all the Ladies who would flock to the ringside at the end of most of my matches full access, and they would take full advantage by kissing and hugging me in full view of everyone in the audience. Now that, I thought would give the fans something to think about. As for the last half an hour or so they would have been booing and jeering as I had skipped, minced and flounced around the ring, patting the rumps of both referee and opponent alike, while alternately dropping a kiss or two on him for good measure. Then in order to blur the edges, I would lay the cruelest and most vicious beating on him that it was possible for me to administer. Fraternizing with the Ladies immediately after the contest would also provide food for speculation. Not to mention the satisfaction I would derive from gloating outrageously at all the lovesick local men and boys, who could only in their wildest dreams, imagine getting as close and personal with just one of those many pretty, Horney young Ladies.

****

One of my more memorable matches before the end of 1963 took place on November the 14th at the Café Royale in aid of 'The Younger Foundation for the Mentally Handicapped' where the audience would watch the action while they all dined in splendor at tables all set out around the ring.

I, just as all the other contestants on the card that night were very proud to be wrestling for such a worthy cause in such a prestigious venue, but, that for me was as good as it was going to get - with the result, my antics that night were wild enough for me to get called into the office the very next morning for a very severe reprimand.

I was wrestling against Leon Fortuna in the opening match and by the time the fanfare heralded our march to the ring we were both primed and ready to go. But, by the time M.C. Francis C. Blake had completed his welcome speech and introductions, both Leon and I had already lost most of our initial enthusiasm. By the time we were only half way though the first of 4x10 minute round contest, we had both lost all of it - the audience was total CRAP!!!

In spite of the wall-to-wall tuxedos, expensive jewelry and glittering evening gowns, I had never come across a more ignorant herd of Pigs and Sows before. Instead of at least giving Leon and I a chance to entertain them, as we were being paid to do, they all competed amongst themselves, as to who could make the most fun and shower the most ridicule on our very best efforts. They would stand up make jokes at our expense, punctuated by shouts and squeals from the Women of,

"IT'S ALL FAKE – GET UP, THAT DOESN'T HURT, HA-HA-HA!!!" And the more alcohol they consumed the worse they got. They were not a wrestling audience – they didn't have the slightest clue as to what they were witnessing – but ignorance of the law is not considered an excuse, and in my books neither is plain ignorance – I'd had enough! I grabbed hold of Leon and told him,

"Throw me off the ropes as hard as you can!" – Leon obliged. As Leon bounced me back into the ropes and hurled me across the ring I added as much impetus to his effort as I could possibly muster. Then after I had turned a somersault and hit the mat I used the full momentum to carry me completely through the bottom ropes, and after hitting the ground outside the ring I rolled over and over until I ended up underneath the table in the middle of the row. Once under the table I stood up with all my strength behind it, the table flew into the air emptying dishes and plates full of food and glasses and bottles of booze over all the diners. Immediately I leapt heroically back into the ring and told Leon,

"Do it again!" Leon repeated the maneuver and after taking an almighty bump, I flew through the opposite ropes and repeated the flying table trick. Then I ran part way around the ring in order to obliterate new pastures when I would fly out of the ring for the third time. On this occasion the need to prompt Leon was superfluous, as he was ready, and poised to aid my lift off and departure before I had even entered the ring. Then WHOOSH! The third set of tables went into orbit - back into the ring I dived and with a little help from my friend Leon, I committed a little blitzkrieg on the fourth section.

Well we may not have been able to get their attention before, but we certainly had it now. The whole place was in an uproar, the ringsiders were furious, the rest of the audience were in stitches - so were Leon and I, but next morning, before I had even finished breakfast, the phone rang,

Jack Dale wanted to see me in the office – AT ONCE!!!

Apparently, Francis P. Blake couldn't wait to report last night's unruly conduct – and, I suppose, as I deserved, I got the whole blame for the devastation. But, after explaining to Jack exactly what lead up to my little outburst, especially the bit where the audience were chanting,

"IT'S ALL FAKE!!!" Jack's belligerent attitude began to melt. What really helped turn the tide in my favor was the timely entrance into Jack's office by Mick McManus who had been wrestling against Julien Maurice the night before in the Main-Event.

"What was the audience like last night, Mick?" I asked him.

"A load of fuckin' piss-takers!" he replied.

I looked back at Jack; he looked appeased, so I told him,

"Some of those rich Tarts didn't look quite so glamorous with their tiaras decorated with Shrimp-cocktail and custard!" Jack was still laughing when I left his office and went down stairs to catch a bus back home,

'A lot better than getting fired.' I thought.

****

It was strange that 'Polish' Peter Rachman did not attain National awareness while he was still 'officially' in the Land of the Living, it was only after a couple of his ex-tenants who had also both been his ex-mistresses, Christine Keeler and Mandy Rice-Davis got themselves involved in a huge Government 'Scandal' that his name began to surface. Although I could not be certain of the fact, I believe that it was probably Mandy and Christine, who I saw with 'Nasty' Cassie and Peter Rachman in 'Esmeralda's Barn' on the night that Peter Rann had first introduced me to 'Mad' Fred the Ear-bitter.

Whether 'Polish' Peter was alive or dead was of no consequence – either way he was missing, and his absence had caused a vacuum which adversely effected all the thugs, rent collectors, enforcers and gangs of rowdies that he had once employed. Some like Peter Rann were now full time professional wrestlers, but many like 'Mad' Fred Rondell were not. Fred's reputation as ex doorman and bouncer at Esmeralda's Barn preceded him, with the result that few Club owners would willingly risk employing him in that category. But, with the number of vicious gangs that existed in London during that period, it would ensure that his talent would not entirely go to waste.

By this time Fred and I knew each other very well, so that he must have noticed that just lately, as a result of having my own private tailor I was becoming better dressed every time he saw me. That was probably what prompted him to ask me if I was in the market for buying some very expensive Leather Coats and Jackets. Which he assured me were legitimate and honestly come by, and would only cost me a mere fraction of their retail value. I assured him that I was very, very interested indeed. Fred told me of a huge shipment of leather garments that he was on the brink of acquiring, and I began fantasizing about what various styles, and colors of coats and jackets I would soon be purchasing for both Jean and myself. Like a Child waiting for Christmas, I waited for Fred's phone call to tell me that I could come and take my pick. I had made him promise me that I would have the first choice of his soon to be acquired merchandise. The phone call never came – disappointed I went to seek Fred out to find out why. His excuse was not only lame, but undecipherable. As I've explained, Fred talked in bursts, like an old rusty machinegun, changing the subject mid sentence and all I did understand for sure was that there was no Leather Coats or Jackets to be had.

The next time I was with Peter Rann I asked him what happened to the leather shipment, and learned the whole story. After laughing like a Snake and asking me,

"SSSSSSSS!!! Fred told you they were legitimate and honestly come by, and you believed him?! – SSSSSSSSSSSS!!!!" And then added, "Would you like to buy this antique ring?" The ring he showed me was not only beautiful, it was really quite unusual; it had a large rough, uncut Purple Amethyst set into a heavy Silver setting.

"Is it legitimate and honestly come by?" I asked him as I counted 8 pounds into his hand.

"SSSSSSSSSSSS!!!" He replied.

"So, what happened to the Leather stuff?" I wanted to know.

According to Peter's story, Fred had 'acquired' two huge coffin sized trunks of Leather Gear, and in order to cause as much confusion as possible as to where he picked up the merchandize and where it's final destination would be, Fred decided to ride a number of taxis all around London first. It was only after his fourth taxi ride, and after he had paid the Cabbie, that he found there were no coffin sized trunks to unload as there had been from the other three previous taxi rides he had taken. It was only then that he realized that he must have confused himself, and had forgotten to load them into the fourth taxi, and he had in fact left them on the pavement somewhere in London. He leapt back aboard the taxi, and they sped back to where he hoped the trunks would still be sitting – unfortunately they were not!

"SSSSSSSSSSSS!!! – Fred is a fucking idiot sometimes!" Peter concluded.

The next time I met Fred, the two trunks full of Leather goodies wasn't mentioned at all - but the Antique ring was,

"Where did you get that ring from?!" Fred inquired.

"I bought it off Peter Rann." I replied.

"How much did you pay for it?" he wanted to know.

"Eight quid." I told him.

"That ring belonged to me!" he informed me sullenly. He didn't ask for it back and I didn't offer it, but for the hundredth time I marveled at what Peter Rann was capable of getting away with in his dealings with 'Mad' Fred Rondell.

You may remember me saying that when I was first introduced to Fred by Peter, at the time he was bouncing outside Esmeralda's Barn, and I offered to shake his hand. Instead of actually taking a grip, he very quickly, and barely brushed my finger tips with his own. I thought it was unusual, but didn't dwell on the fact until Peter brought it up and explained the reason why.

"Fred is the most homophobic creature in the World," Peter explained, "the only time he will willingly touch a man is when he is beating, kicking, or biting the life out of him. If you try to pat him on the back or shoulder he'll move just enough to make you miss."

As a result of 'Polish' Peter Rachman no longer being on the scene, Fred at this time, Peter told me was wheeling and dealing – and probably stealing too. Or at least buying and selling stuff that had been stolen. Fred also knew a lot about antiques; Peter said, and told me that Kalman Gaston had introduced him to a Lady friend of his who had a small mansion full of old goodies that she wanted to unload. Fred was invited to inspect a small treasure trove of antique silver, glassware, Porcelain, artwork and furniture, while Kalman strolled around flirting with the Lady of the house. As Fred was bent over examining a vase on a very low shelf, Kalman was walking by him, and without giving the matter a second's thought, to amuse himself and his Lady friend he patted Fred on his backside. WHOOOOSH!!! – Kalman hit the wall upside-down on the other side of the very large room. As he bounced off the wall and onto the floor his life was probably saved by the Lady who threw herself over Kalman's prone body just a split second before 'Mad' Fred who's foot was poised above him, and was ready to stomp the handsome Hungarian's face into the intricate and exotic weave of the Antique Persian Carpet on which he lay.

"IF YOU HURT HIM, OUR DEAL IS OFF!!!" Screamed the Lady at Fred. Fred took off around the room punching the walls and kicking the furniture, while yelling at the top of his loud voice,

"IF I FIND OUT HE'S QUEER – I'LL HUNT HIM DOWN AND KILL HIM!!!"

I was sitting in the front passenger seat of Peter Rann's car one day. Peter was driving, and Fred was sitting in the back. Peter stopped to pick up Spencer Churchill who was wrestling that night on the same card as Peter and I, and after depositing his gear in the trunk he got in the back of the car with Fred. Spencer was also a good friend of Fred's, and was well aware of his ultra-homophobic nature. But as wrestlers often did, he delighted in teasing his fellow travelers. When Spencer had entered the car, Fred had instinctively put as much space between Spencer and himself as he possibly could. But instead of respecting Fred's space, Spencer closed the gap, attempted to put his arm around Fred's shoulder and said,

"Come on Fred, give Spencer a little cuddle!"

Fred's hands shot out so fast and powerfully hitting Spencer with the flat of his palms in his chest, so that Spencer almost exploded back out of the back door he had just closed.

"SPENCER!" Fred growled, "It's taken you more than 20 years to build up all your muscles – it will take me less than 10 minutes to rip them all off again, if you just so much as try to touch me!!!" Needless to mention – Spencer didn't try!

I did remember, as a result of Lon of London's strange behavior being a trifle homophobic myself, but Fred the Ear-biter seemed to have taken homophobia to a whole new level, I asked

Peter Rann why,

"We were together one day collecting rents for Rachman," Peter told me, "and after Fred knocked on a door, it was opened by what Fred thought were two elderly ladies. Instead they were two old transvestites, wearing sexy underwear and colorful negligees, with wrinkles showing prominently through their thick exotic face makeup. It wasn't until one of them spoke to Fred, in a voice that was as deep as the Grand Canyon that Fred realized they were men – and he screamed, leapt down the steps and ran down the street still screaming."

"Why did he do that?" I inquired, "Had he suffered some bad experience that that incident reminded him of, or did the transvestites just scare him?"

"I don't know," Peter replied, "all I know is, that when I found Fred he was a mile or more down the road beating lumps off a telegraph pole just to calm himself down!"

Peter was a fantastic cartoon artist, and was able to render a hilarious caricature likeness of most of the wrestlers; he was also a master of erotic cartoons that were even more hilarious. He knew that Fred loved Ladies with very large buttocks; the larger the better. He would often draw cartoons of naked Ladies for Fred, exaggerated in a way that really catered to Fred's personal preference. I was with Peter one day when he handed Fred a couple of dozen drawings. Fred snatched them and devoured each one hungrily with eyes that seemed to protrude inches out of his head.

"Oh! – these are great Peter," Fred panted, "Oh, I like that, Oh! – That's the best one yet! - - AAAAAAAGGH!!!!!" Fred screamed and tore all the drawings Peter had given him into confetti and began jumping all over the place.

"SSSSSSSSSSSSS!!!" Laughed Peter.

The reason for Fred's sudden distress was depicted in the last drawing; it was a caricature of Fred at the time when he was in jail for massacring the West Indians in the basement of one of Rachman's buildings. It pictured a naked Fred, bent over sniffing at a flower he held daintily between the thumb and forefinger of one huge hand. While the West Indian that Fred had chewed on, equally naked and massively endowed was mounting him from behind. Then the icing on the cake was a narrative bubble coming from Fred's mouth that read,

"Fuck me harder Percy – or I'll bite your other ear off!!!"

The drawing must have upset Fred for days, but for some reason it seemed that Peter Rann was immune from reprisal and never fell foul of Fred's terrible temper. I am certain that if anyone else on earth tried the same trick, Fred wouldn't have been content in merely ripping off an ear with his teeth, he would have eaten the perpetrator whole.

One of the worst and most cruel tricks Peter played concerning Fred, didn't actually cast the ferocious ear-bitter in the role of the victim; on this occasion that role was amply filled by a Lady named Sadie. Sadie was a middle-aged wrestling fan, who had been a 'special friend' of the wrestlers for years. She conveniently had her own house in London, where she would happily and sportingly take on all comers any time of the night or day. Sadie's only co-resident was a pet Monkey, who would often amuse Sadie and her Lady friends when they visited by vigorously 'spanking the Human' while they all sat around its cage, cheering it on, while drinking their afternoon tea.

Peter who lived and breathed for mischief had noted that Sadie was built just the way 'Mad' Fred liked his women. So one day he took Fred around to Sadie's house and introduced them to each other. The horrid trick that Peter played on poor Sadie was that he convinced Fred that Sadie really fancied him in a big – big way. Sadie was far too terror-struck to contradict him, so 'Mad' Fred Rondell moved in with Sadie lock-stock and barrel.

In Fred's line of work he was apt to keep very late hours, with the result he usually slept in. He was awoken one afternoon by loud whoops and cheering, and got out of bed in order to investigate. Unfortunately for all concerned, Fred's entrance coincided with the Monkey's 'grand finale' – Fred took one look and fled! Sadie didn't see Fred for a few days and prayed that she would never see him again. But Fred suddenly reappeared, and a day or so later the Monkey disappeared, never to be seen, cheered at, or heard from again. Sadie did once attempt to bring up 'The case of the missing Monkey' but only got an undecipherable grunt in response. So the case will go on file with 'whatever happened to Freddy Mills' and other such mysteries.

If Sadie's pet Monkey had been a Female, Fred would have

had no problem with it at all, but homophobic Fred was very skittish around anything Male. He even had problems with Sadie's Baby Grandson when she was asked by her Daughter to Baby sit for her. Sadie once made the mistake of placing the Baby on the bed where she and Fred slept, and Fred declared that not only was she never, under any circumstances to do it again, but he made her turn the mattress over and change all the sheets and pillowslips before he would go anywhere near the bed himself.

So Fred was back with Sadie, and he was there to stay, and to say he cramped Sadie's style was an understatement and then some. As even the roughest, toughest, horniest wrestler would think twice before he risked grazing on 'Mad' Fred Rondell's pasture. Now that he had a permanent abode Fred decided it was time to get back into training in earnest. He got the wrestling twins from Malta, Tony and Ignatius Borg to get him a huge sand filled bag, that he could kick and punch. It was so heavy that Fred had to help the two twins hang the monstrosity in the hallway of Sadie's home. As soon as Fred attacked the heavy bag, he realized something was missing, and just like in 'Goldilocks', Baby-Bear's bed it was too soft. Superhumanly strong Fred unhitched the huge sandbag himself, carried it out into the back yard, and emptied out the sand then refilled it with a mixture of the sand, rocks and broken house-bricks. Satisfied with its extra weight and solidarity, Fred carried the bag back indoors, and unaided hung the monster back in place. Now Fred really had something he could get his teeth into and he beat the bag until he all but smashed the bricks and rocks it contained into dust. Unfortunately for Sadie who forgot the bag was hanging there, she got up in the middle of the night for a piss one night, walked into the bag in the dark and knocked herself out.

GO NORTH YOUNG MAN

When Baby Adrian was about 6 months old I had bought a movie camera, and by the time he was 2, my Son was a seasoned movie Star. Every time I had a day off, if the weather permitted, we would spend our time in Kew Gardens, Regent Park Zoo, in the countryside around Brynmawr, at the Seaside, or just romping around Tooting-Beck Common. As the Summer of 1964 drew nearer and we began to look forward to more flowery scenery as a backdrop, Jean announced that by the beginning of the next year, little Adrian was going to have a tiny co-star. This exciting news had its downside, as we were already cramped in our little 2 roomed flat, and I had made very little progress in my quest to save enough money for a deposit for our own home. We had had enough problems getting somewhere to live when Jean had been pregnant with our first child; I wondered how much fun we would have looking for somewhere to live with 2 children.

Immediately I tackled Jack Dale for more money, but wasn't surprised to once again draw a blank. So I decided at long last to play my Ace card, which I had held to my chest now for almost 3 years.

"Mike," I told my Manager, "I have just found out that I will soon have another mouth to feed. I've asked Jack for a raise, but he won't give it to me, so I'm sorry, but I won't be able to afford to pay you any more money out of my wages."

I was fully expecting Mike to point out that as I had signed a 7 year contract, which entitled him to 10-percent of everything I earned as a wrestler for that period, and that I would have no choice but to continue paying him for another 4 years. I was ready to counter this claim by announcing that I had not been legally old enough to sign the contract in the first place, but fortunately I didn't have to.

"Okay." Mike agreed, but suggested a compromise. He told me that he had almost saved enough money for the deposit on a large house that he was going to buy, and if I would agree to carry on paying him for another 3 or 4 months, it would help him to reach his goal. I thought about it, and suggested a compromise of my own.

"I'll agree to that on one condition," I told Mike, "and that is, if I can rent your flat after you move into your own house." I had made my mind up that I was not going to pay Mike Dimitre another cent out of my wages, but this compromise had far too much going for it for me to even consider any other alternative. Firstly, it would take all the time and stress out of trying to find a flat in the area, that any Landlord would willingly rent to a couple with 2 Children. The new flat would be plenty big enough, as it consisted of three bedrooms, a lounge, a kitchen/dinning room – and last but certainly not least, our own bathroom. The first bathroom that I wouldn't have to share with other tenants since before I had first moved to London 7 years earlier. It would also mean saying goodbye to our present Landlord, Mr. Sikorski and that too would be very nice.

The flat was located in Beechdale Road, which was just off Brixton Hill and was much nearer to Dale Martin's Office than where we were now living. In fact it would cut the distance in half. That in itself would have been reason enough to want to make that move, but there was more - much more. This would not only be a move to a bigger and better flat, it would be a career move, one that would propel me to bigger and better things in the wrestling business.

The advantages that I have listed were more than sufficient for me to want very much to make that move, but the greatest advantage of all was that the house in Beechdale Road belonged to George De-Relwyskow, of Leeds in Yorkshire. He was one of Joint Promotion's biggest Northern Wrestling Promoters. I fully realized that if I was renting a flat from a Landlord who lived more than 200 miles away, in order for him to be certain of collecting his rent promptly, it would be an advantage to him to employ me in his capacity as a Wrestling Promoter. My whole scheme worked – and that was how, and why I was contacted by Relwyskow and Green Wrestling Promotions, who asked me to wrestle for them.

I had wrestled up North before for Wryton Promotions, for Billy Best's Wrestling Promotions and for Jack Atherton and Frank Woodhouse's Promotions. I had only wrestled for Norman

Morrell's Promotions on his Southern shows. But Morrell, as well as running his own Promotion, also ran some shows with Relwyskow, and with another fellow Yorkshire Promoter Ted Beresford who ran Global Promotions out of Huddersfield. I was certain that if I got a start up North for Relwyskow, it would only be a matter of time before I would wrestle up North for all the rest - History would prove my assessment to be correct.

My first match for Relwyskow and Green Wrestling Promotions, was a 'Spectacular' in Leeds, Yorkshire, on December 14th 1964, when I wrestled against, and defeated a genuine Spaniard named Vincente Castella. The Main Event was The Yorkshire Hardman, Les Kellett, versus the great American Ballet Dancer and wrestler, Ricky Starr. The super charismatic Ricky Starr was a fantastic performer, and as well as being a fully-fledged, professional Ballet Dancer, a great wrestler with an excellent amateur background, and also an ex-professional Boxer, who, in his time had knocked out the very tough 'Razor' Ruddock. I watched Ricky's match from beginning to end and was very impressed and inspired by both his charisma and his skill.

My own opponent Vincente was also a very skilled wrestler; he spoke very good English, and was a very polite and likeable person. I wrestled him again the next night in Hull, the night after that I wrestled Heavyweight, Irish Frank O'Donnell in Scunthorpe and then with Vincente once more in Rotherham.

Within a few months I was wrestling for all of Joint's Northern Promotions, for anywhere from a couple of consecutive night's matches to a whole week for each of them. With the result that very soon it was unusual for me to wrestle for Dale Martin's for more than 2 weeks out every month. There were a number of advantages wrestling for the Northerners, for one they were paying me a couple more pounds a match, even for preliminaries. But the fact that I was regarded as a seasoned veteran, with a unique image, I found myself more often than not in semi-main event matches, which meant a better pay-day still. Then there was the advantage of 'absence makes the heart grow fonder,' brought about by the fact that Dale Martin's no longer had an exclusive, and I soon found that the less access they had to a commodity the more they desired it. I asked Jack Dale for a raise in wages and this time I got it, that prompted me to immediately ask for more money from all the other Northern Promoters and I got that too.

What was less desirable was being away from my young Son and pregnant Wife. Not that I got to see very much of them when I had wrestled exclusively for Dale Martin's, as I was on the road most every day from morning, or afternoon, till late at night, or early morning the next day. But, wrestling up North meant sometimes not seeing them at all for as much as a week or two at a time.

Another disadvantage, and one that was almost as undesirable as the one I have just described was that wrestling up North – especially in Scotland brought me right into the very backyard of 'The World Lightweight Wrestling Champion' George Kidd.

****

In spite of being so much more comfortable in our new apartment, I had not lost sight, or the desire to one day own my own house. I was getting more money from wrestling, thanks to my Northern Odysseys, but the more I managed to save, the more inflation kept the property carrot dangling further and further from my nose.

Also our new apartment was an unfurnished apartment, which now meant that we would have the expense of buying everything from new furniture to new carpets. Mike Dimitri sold us a few items that he didn't want to take with him to his new house, including a large plate glass mirror. He also had connections with a furniture store owner who gave us a good deal on furnishing and carpeting for the whole apartment, although I was certain that Mike had his own little deal going with him too. A hefty deposit on our furnishings made a considerable dent in our savings, not to mention the monthly installments which would have to be paid over the next 30 months for the carpets and furniture. I would be making more money wrestling, but spending much more money on rent and furniture etcetera, and spending much more time away from home. I desperately needed a way of making more money if we were ever going to be able to afford a house of our own.

A drop sized solution in the ocean sized dilemma presented

itself as if on cue when Kalman Gaston came to call, and brought with him a large, black, rubber dildo which he banged down on the kitchen table and asked me,

"Can you make a mould of this?!" Needless to say I could – and did, so that was how Kalman and I went into the dildo business.

Becoming dildo merchants was not unique in the wrestling business, as both MC Bobby Palmer, and wrestler Pasquale Salvo had been in the rubber Dick trade for years. As well as dealing in those naughty rubber sculptures, Salvo also sold pornographic photographs and 8mm Blue Movies in order to bolster his earnings as a wrestler and promoter. Making the mould out of Kalman's prototype was easy, finding the correct type of rubber in order to make the castings in were not, we searched everywhere and tried everything, but no dice. Its amazing how we didn't set ourselves on fire, blow ourselves up, or suffocate ourselves on the smoke or toxic fumes, we didn't have a clue, but that did not prevent us from persevering. Eventually our perseverance paid off, but not anywhere as lucratively as we wished, as the cost of the rubber left an incredibly scanty profit margin. After more experimenting than I care to recall, I had found a store called 'Tirantti's' not far from the YMCA which carried all kinds of craft materials. They had a bright yellow rubber that was very rigid, and a bright blood red that was very soft and jelly like. The two mixed and melted together was just the right consistency, even though the resulting color made a very improbable luminous neon orange. Although Kalman and I were now business partners, I would sell him all the dildos he wanted at a fraction over cost, as he had his own customers and I had mine. Amongst whom Karl Denver of the British version of 'The Lion Sleeps tonight' fame was my best. Every time I wrestled in the Manchester area, all I had to do was give Karl a phone-call and he would tell me how many I should bring up North for him.

Kalman's best customer was an Austrian Aristocrat named Irena who owned a very large house in Earl's Court, and a very large stable of girls who lived, and conducted their business from there. Irena loved men - the more the merrier, in fact there was only one thing in the World that Irena loved more than men, and that was her girls. On one particular visit to my home, Kalman brought Irena with him, who wanted to order a new custom built design,

"I vahnt a big one darlink!" she told me.

"No problem, darlink!" I told her, and out came the modeling wax to begin molding her larger than life Ladies pacifier, while Irena and Kalman looked on admiringly. Well she said she wanted 'a big one' and the result was quite frightening, but when I asked her if that was what she had in mind, she told me,

"Bigger – Bigger – it must be Bigger – I vahnt to be Quveen Dick darlink!" she purred.

"Or King Kock!" I suggested.

"No – Quveen Dick, darlink!" she insisted.

"Okay, Queen Dick it is," I conceded, "but are we invited to the Coronation darlink?!" I wanted to know. The main problem with Irena's new gigantic design was, that its early production coincided with a considerable increase in the price of rubber from Tirantti's. I had already estimated that it would take about two and a half times more rubber to produce, than Kalman's original prototype that we had been producing up until that time. If we were going to keep our prices competitive I needed to find a new, and cheaper source of rubber. Once again I eventually lucked out and I acquired a new source that was less than half the price. It was a darkish semi-translucent honey color, a little on the too rigid side. in fact if you hit someone with one of the finished products, it could have really done some serious damage. Mind you, I thought that if they were used for the purpose for which they were designed and intended the same thing could very well apply.

'Talk about penis envy!' I thought. I was happy enough with that solution until a few weeks later when I was wrestling on the same card as Kalman,

"Thank goodness I've got chance to warn you!" he told me excitedly.

"Warn me about what?" I inquired.

"You've got to watch your back," he told me, and be really careful where you go in London!"

"Why!" I asked him impatiently.

"IRENA HAS GOT A HIT OUT ON YOU!" he replied.

BLOOD BOOTS

Master of ceremonies, Sammy King, as a result of a birth defect had one arm that was only about one third the length of the other one; although very few of the wrestlers believed that the short arm was really the result of a birth defect. They claimed instead that his arm had gradually shrunk over time in order to prevent him being able to reach too far into his pockets, when it was time to pay his wrestlers during the very many years the 'Short Fat Sammy' promoted his own wrestling shows. Skinflint Sammy still promoted a number of shows for Dale Martins, including Cardiff. I was wrestling there one night, against Leon Fortuna and once more I was scheduled to emerge triumphant, but instead, thanks to silly Sammy, my triumph turned into a total fuck-up.

I had bullied Leon horribly from the sound of the first bell, but towards the end of the second round, Leon rallied heroically to the sound of great rejoicing, and he took the first fall on me. Usually when a pin-fall or submission was scored by either contestant, Sammy would signal the Timekeeper to ring the bell loudly, which would add to the drama. And then from ringside he would announce who had scored what on whom. This time however, there was no bell ringing, or announcement made, as 'Short Fat Sammy' was laying face down on the timekeeper's table fast asleep. Only after he had been shaken vigorously by the timekeeper did he give the signal to ring the bell. Instead of announcing Leon's first fall from ringside, Sammy struggled out of his seat and into the ring. This he would normally do only, at the very end of a match in order to announce the final result of the contest. After grabbing the microphone and staggering to the centre of the ring, Sleepy Sammy made his announcement,

"Ah, Ladies and Gentlemen, after Leon Fortuna gained the first pin-fall in the second round, and then with Adrian Street gaining a knockout in round 4, by way of a dropkick which sent his opponent flying right out of the ring, the win goes to ADRIAN STREET!" That was what was 'eventually' supposed happen – we hadn't got that far yet!!!! But that stupid git, Sleeping Beauty, had been snoring instead of paying attention. With the result, that he gave the finish away as he thought that it was already the end of the match. Obviously we couldn't do my big knockout finish now, and I was furious. I had really been looking forward to performing it, and anything else would be an anticlimax and much less spectacular, as well as less to gloat about. Now, I had to think of something else entirely, in order to win the match, or it would be a sure way of proving to everyone present that the contest was fixed.

Just a couple of weeks later I was wrestling Leon again, this time at The Colston Hall, Bristol, and once again Leon was going to pin me in the second round, and I was going to knock him out with a dropkick in the fourth. That was what was supposed to happen, but what did occur was almost an action replay of 'The Cardiff fiasco', but on this occasion we couldn't blame Sammy King.

Everything was going great, right up to Leon gaining the first fall. Then as the bell rang to sound the beginning of the third, I rushed out of my corner as though intent on avenging Leon's early advantage. But, instead of attempting to defend himself against the fury of my impending attack, Leon just wandered right by me in a complete daze. He got out of the ring, via my corner, and strolled all the way back to the dressing-room, leaving me standing bewildered in the middle of the ring and still waiting for our match to continue. But continue it didn't, by the time I realized that Leon wasn't coming back, and I followed him back to the dressing room, he had already undressed and was taking a shower.

"What the fuck was that all about, Leon?!!!!!!" I wanted to know, Leon looked at me in wonderment,

"What?!" he replied. Leon was completely bewildered, and he hardly even remembered being in the ring with me less than 10 minutes earlier, let alone fucking up the match. I was told by the other wrestlers that he had been wandering around in a stupor for days. Leon had always been amongst my favorite opponents, as I was always guaranteed to have a very satisfying, entertaining and action packed match every time I stepped into the ring with him. But from that time on there was definitely something missing.

Even though Leon was a couple of years younger than I was, with a couple of years less experience. I had felt from the first time I wrestled against him, that he was ahead of me in his understanding of what professional wrestling was really all about. Also the 'Friendly Islander' from Tonga, had great ring presence, he was a terrific wrestler, and had a great 'Look.' Very exotic, good looking, and crowd appeal second to none, especially where the Women and young Girls were concerned. They were all in love with Leon. With all that going for him it was so easy for the villain to get heat with him, all they had to do was give him a nasty look and the fans would scream the house down. But now something was wrong with Leon and that was a fact, and over the next couple of days I got the whole gory story that fully explained the nagging mystery.

Leon had had the great misfortune to wrestle against Keith Martinelli in Bolton's Wryton Stadium, and Bolton was Keith Martinelli's home town. Very tough, extremely strong and wilder than a Hurricane would describe Keith. But none of these adjectives could come anywhere close to describing him, when Keith was in the ring surrounded by a loud cheering audience – especially if the ring and the audience happened to be in Keith's home town of Bolton. A description that was much more appropriate was coined in the nickname given to him by another victim of Keith's wrestling ring rampages, the 'Strongman' Alan Dennison, when he dubbed him 'Blood-Boots'.

Alan claimed that every single stitch that he had ever had to suffer, that had been necessary to close a gash in his face, or head, had been inflicted courtesy of Blood-Boot's. In fact according to Alan, he had never, ever wrestled in a contest against Keith Martinelli when he didn't leave the ring covered in his own blood. Alan's own tag-team partner, Sid Cooper was so impressed by Keith Martinelli that he decided to dub himself with a similar nickname, and began calling himself 'Hell-in-Boots.' Unfortunately for him, I began calling him 'Helen Boots' and even though he tried to counter it when he again changed his nickname to 'Cyanide' Sid Cooper, he was still forever to be affectionately known as 'Helen'.

When Leon had wrestled against 'Blood-Boots' in Wryton

Stadium, not only had he been beaten savagely from the time the bell sounded to start the contest. He was smashed from one corner-post to the other before being hurled headfirst over the top rope, where he crash landed headfirst on a row of solid chairs that were bolted to the floor of the stadium. Leon's crash-landing brought a premature ending to the contest, and in my opinion an ending to that certain, indefinable quality that would have very soon rocketed Leon to wrestling 'Superstardom'. Leon was still an excellent wrestler, and a great opponent, especially for a villain. But I have always felt that that match he had with 'Blood-Boots' robbed both Leon and wrestling of something very special.

They say that 'forewarned is forearmed', so when I wrestled 'Blood-Boots' in Bolton's Wryton Stadium, I did have some idea as to what to expect as I waited for my opponent to make his entrance. The Bolton crowd's roar hit a crescendo as Blood-Boots hit the ring, and I could tell by his general demeanor and insanely rolling eyes that I could be in for a very long night, or, a very short one, if I was unlucky enough to emulate Leon Fortuna's famous Swan-dive. All too soon, the bell rang and to say my opponent was a trifle over exuberant would be like saying Dale Martin's transport was uncomfortable. He was surfing on a tidal wave of pure adrenaline, and wrestling with Blood-Boots was like wrestling with a rabid Pit-bull, who possessed the strength of two Gorillas.

Well they do say that 'A faint heart never fucked a Pig', so I decided to 'fight fire with fire', I was determined to give as good as I was sure to receive, and 'attack being the best method of defense' turned out to be the best way to survive Blood-Boot's Blitzkrieg. WE HAMMERED THE CRAP OUT OF EACH OTHER – MY FEET HURT FROM KICKING – MY FISTS HURT FROM PUNCHING – MY ELBOWS HURT FROM SMASHING AND I COULD TELL BY THE WAY MY BELL WAS CONTINUINGLY RINGING THAT HIS FEET – FISTS AND ELBOWS MUST HAVE BEEN IN AGONY TOO!!! – But hey, it turned out to be one Hell of a match!

The final victory went to the local boy, but the crowds reaction demanded a re-match, which took place the very next month – and damn me if we didn't do it all over again!!! But, the hard blows I received must have really rattled my brain, because, believe it or not, I liked Blood-Boots and I liked wrestling with him. Even in Wryton Stadium, in his home town of Bolton! The reason was, I was addicted to enthusiastic reaction – and boy-oh-boy you certainly got it when you tussled with Blood-Boots in his own backyard!

Very soon after, I wrestled him again in a town in North Wales, and even on this occasion when I was cheered on to victory our match still contained the same bone jarring intensity. I had traveled to the show all the way from London the same day, so by the time the matches were over I was almost too exhausted to eat anything before making my way to our hotel and flopping into bed. I must have been snoring before my head even hit the pillow, but I didn't sleep for long!

SQUEAK – BANG – SQUEAK – BANG – SQUEAK – BANG – SQUEAK – BANG!!!! I thought I had woken up in Ancient Rome, when the Vandals were battering down the city gates. The squeaking sounded like someone had stamped on a rubber squeaky toy and the banging was shaking the wall behind my bed and all the furniture in the room which included my bed. I banged on the wall with the edge of my fist, which did nothing at all to curb the squeaking and banging, so I banged even harder with the same result. I was really pissed off, so I leapt out of bed and into my pants before bursting out of my room and walloping the door next to my own with a huge forearm smash. The door flew open so I stepped inside, drew a huge lungful of air before bellowing my complaint, when the sight before me completely arrested my bellow before its issue, and froze me with an enormously expanded chest and enormously popping eyes.

All I could see of the Lady was her legs that were dangling over 'Blood-Boot's' shoulders, Blood-Boots, who was as naked as the day he was born was hammering away with the same intensity he had displayed in his matches in Wryton Stadium. When he withdrew it was with such force that the bed slid backwards a yard away from the wall. And when he thrust forward it was with the same velocity he had employed when he had hurled poor Leon over the top rope headfirst into the hard unyielding chairs. It was the impact behind his thrust that forced the loud squeak out of the poor Female, a split second before the head of the bed crashed into the wall behind it. So devastating was his assault that pieces of plaster were cracking off the ceiling and dropping onto Blood-Boots head, shoulders and back like a snowstorm. But it would take a lot more than a hotel falling down around his ears to cause the mighty Blood-Boots to miss one single beat.

TALK ABOUT SEX AND VIOLENCE!!! The first time I got a good look at the Lady was next morning at breakfast, and to my surprise, apart from having bags under her eyes that were as big as her tits, she didn't look the worse for wear. Wrestler's groupies were bloody tough – damn, they had to be!

In spite of the fact that Keith Martinelli and I had become great friends, I still thought that he deserved to be punished for disturbing my sleep the night before. So, when all the other wrestlers were assembled in the dressing the next night, I decided to embarrass him in the time honored wrestlers tradition by describing in detail, Blood-Boot's antics from last night. As I imagined, they all thought the story very funny and everyone laughed a lot, but, none more than Blood-Boots himself, instead of being embarrassed, as I had meant him to be, Blood-Boots thought it was the best wrestler's tale he had ever heard.

MAN-MOUNTAIN

On another trip to the Manchester area, I was in the company of Stefan Milla who had been making the trip for years and knew every place of interest there was to know. First we had a lunch of Salt-Beef sandwiches and Lemon-Tea in the best Kosher restaurant in Manchester. Then we had a drink of something a bit stronger in 'The Chez Joey' which was one of Stefan's favorite watering-holes and then best of all, we visited another Club owned by ex-wrestler, the legendary 'Man-Mountain' Benny.

The 330 pound, Bearded Behemoth, 'Man-Mountain' Benny, was one of the old time greats, and one of the first British wrestlers that I had ever heard of. He was a giant star in both fame and frame, decades before television, and was equal in stature to Jack Pye, Bert Assirati, Norman the Butcher, Francis St. Clair Gregory, 'Bull-dog' Bill Garnon, 'The Bearded Monarch' Ken Davis, Hassan-Ali-Bey and Black 'Butcher' Johnson. There was very little that interested me as much as listening to tales told by wrestling legends of a bygone era, and some of Benny's stories were great. BUT, I don't know if he was missing the palate in the roof of his gob, or if it was caused by his badly broken, little nose, or a combination of both, that punctuated his entire narration with the sound as though he was continually scrapping his throat whilst showering both Stefan and I with an odd bucket-full of spittle. Another serious distraction was the fact that Benny's club was a Strip-joint. And the Lovely Ladies in various states of undress cavorting delightfully on the stage behind Benny's pale, freckled face, straggly bearded and red haired head guaranteed keeping my head and face in his direct line of fire and didn't help to keep my face dry. When a really shapely black stripper began her act Benny drew our attention towards her in particular, as she had recently became Benny's latest conquest,

"Sucks like a junior Hoover," he told us proudly and then added, "She's gonna be the death of me." As it happens, Benny prophesized his own demise, as that was exactly how the 'Man-

Mountain' met his end. Well if you've got to go, I for one can't think of a better way, always a great professional, he certainly knew how to make grand entrance – but a grander exit would be very hard to imagine.

Then as we made ready to leave I shook hands with 'Man-Mountain' Benny, as Stefan fished in his pocket and pulled out a handkerchief which he used to dry his be-spittled face,

"We should have brought a fucking umbrella with us!" he grumbled.

"Is it raining?!" Benny asked.

"Just spitting!" I told him.

Our last match before returning home to London was in Birmingham, I was wrestling against Stefan in a preliminary match, whilst the main event match was the German, Axel Deiter wrestling against the Russian, Ivan Josef Zaranoff. Both of the main event contestants had traveled up from London that day in Zaranoff's car, and both Stefan and I were delighted when we were both offered a ride back to London with them instead of having to travel back by rail. After the matches were over, instead of driving straight home, Ivan made a slight detour to a very large pub, which was just outside the outskirts of Birmingham. I had heard of this pub and of its Host and Hostess, who had an open invitation for any of Joint promotion's wrestlers to go there and eat free of charge after the matches were over. This arrangement had proved to be very beneficial to both Hosts and wrestlers, as on wrestling nights in that area it would always bring grappling fans to the pub in droves who wanted to rub shoulders with any famous mat stars who might be there taking advantage of the free repast.

Although I had heard of this arrangement, owing to the fact that I didn't own a car, or even know how to drive one, I had always used a train to get home and as a result had never before been in a position to take advantage of the invitation. Well the food was well worth the detour, a very large steak each, cooked to perfection, in my case oozing with blood, and keeping it company was a big baked potato and a hillock of grilled mushrooms, plus all the free booze that I cared to consume. The free booze turned out to be our host's biggest mistake. Now I like a drink with a meal, and I would be lying if I told you that I didn't take full advantage of the price tag. But Stefan, who was an alcoholic, was made to look like Temperance Activist 'Mother' Eliza Stewart in comparison with the gluttonous German and our dizzy, designated, Russian driver.

Things began to take a turn for the worse when a fresh faced teenage boy asked us all for our autographs. He told us he was a huge wrestling fan and seemed particularly smitten by the presence of the big Russian Heavyweight. Ivan, who thanks to his possessing a typical wrestler's sense of humor, began to tease him by pretending that he had taken a fancy to him, the boy looked so horrified that we all laughed a lot at his discomfort. This caused Ivan to intensify his act somewhat. In fact Ivan's act intensified to such a degree that I began to feel distinctly uncomfortable myself, and I began to wonder if the Russian superman might genuinely be more than a little strange.

Zaranoff grabbed hold of the boy and forcibly sat him on his lap. The boy who was by now totally embarrassed, countered by back-elbowing Ivan in the eye, and the next thing that happened was the poor kid getting bitch-slapped, and thrown right across the pub. He bounced off someone's table, sending bottles and glasses in all directions and continued on his journey to land arse first in the roaring flames of the pub's fireplace. Ivan was after him like a shot, not to help prevent the kid getting burned, but to continue battering him unmercifully.

It was only the shout going up that the police had been called and were on their way that arrested the big Russian's onslaught, and decided him to get the Hell out of Dodge. But now the big German was nowhere to be found. I imagined that with the amount of food and drink he had consumed, he would most probably be in the toilet throwing it all up, but he wasn't. After checking, I thought that he might be doing something similar outside, but as I was passing the kitchen I decided to take a quick glance inside, and there was the greedy Teutonic Twat raiding the refrigerator. I was almost as disgusted with him as I was with Zaranoff.

Well, we all exited the pub posthaste and dived into Zaranoff's car and after a few precious minutes first getting lost, and then eventually hitting the highway we were off like the wind, a Hurricane force wind! I had never in my life been in a car that traveled that speed, in fact I didn't know that cars were even capable of going that fast. I was not unnerved by the speed we were traveling at, but was more than a little unhappy concerning the sobriety of the driver. There turned out to be merit in my concern, when Zaranoff swerved right across the road as we were passing an 18-wheeler that was hurtling along, and we hit it broadside. The car bounced off the huge lorry, hit a bank roadside and bounced right back into the lorry, and almost under it. We all thought that that was it, but we tore ourselves free, and slammed back into the bank which brought us to an abrupt halt, as the 18 wheeler sped on, seemingly unconcerned.

We all leapt out of the car to inspect the damage, which was extensive but not debilitating. Zaranoff who was still wobbly, but paranoid that the police might still be giving chase herded us back into his vehicle. We were soon hurtling along at the same breakneck speed we had attained before the accident had occurred. Further down the highway we turned into the car park of a Motorway café, and petrol station and pulled up right next to a Truck-driver, who was standing next to his 18 wheeler and inspecting the damage on the left side of his vehicle. Zaranoff was out of the car and on the truck-driver in an instant; Stefan and I were out fast enough to dive in between them before the Russian could inflict any damage, and then had to restrain the staggering German from taking over from the furious Russian. Getting that close to the truck-driver was another bad mistake on the part of Zaranoff,

"You've been drinking!" the truck-driver accused, and then beat a hasty retreat back into his vehicle, but not before making a note of the registration number on the boozy Russian's car. We eventually arrived back in London without further incident, and I for one was very happy that our journey was at an end.

A few weeks later I received a phone call from Zaranoff,

"I want you to come to court with me as a witness." He informed me, and told me the date on which the court case was to be held. It was not for the incident in the pub, but he had been reported by the truck-driver.

"No chance," I replied, "I'm wrestling on that day."

"This is a lot more important than you wrestling!" he told me.

"To you maybe," I answered, "but not to me."

"I could have you subpoenaed." He warned me.

"Ivan," I told him, "you've already made a number of mistakes, but that would be the worst one yet, I know that I can be forced to come to court, and forced to give evidence, but I can't, and won't be forced to commit perjury for you, if I do give evidence, I will tell the truth, the whole truth and nothing but the truth, so help me God!"

With that I slammed down the phone, and that was the end of that. I was not surprised that I was never again invited by Ivan Josef Zaranoff to ride in his car, but believe it or not, I would not have accepted an invitation if it had been offered.

Talking of invitations the Host and Hostess of the pub never ever invited the wrestlers to partake of freebies at their pub again either – I wonder why?!

****

It was the 5th of December 1964 and I was sitting in my favorite seat in my most un-favorite transport,

"It's my Birthday today John." I told Johnny Yearsley, who I had been chatting to since we had began our journey in one of Dale Martin's dreadful vans.

"How old are you?" John inquired.

"24." I replied.

"Oh my God! – How are you going to cope?! He wanted to know.

"What do you mean, how am I going to cope?" I asked him.

"You're 24 years old – right?!" Do you realize that you are now in your 25th year? – That's a quarter of a century – can you imagine what it's going to be like for you in another 25 years? – you'll be 50 – old and ugly – you won't be a good looking young boy anymore, I don't think you'll be able to cope with that!"

"Actually I'll be 49," I told him, "and unlike you John, I do know what it's like to be good looking – and I suppose that if I am old and ugly in another 25 years, I'll know then what you feel like now."

To say that Johnny Yearsley had rugged features would be the biggest compliment that he could ever hope to receive, in truth even the ancient Stone-carvers of the giant monoliths on

Easter Island would have rejected the countenance that Yearsley possessed. John was so self conscious of the very pronounced turn in one eye, that he always kept it closed, which was the reason he was nicknamed 'The Cyclops' by all the other wrestlers.

He also reveled in being the voice of doom and gloom, instead of just wishing me a Happy Birthday, or congratulating me, he preferred to rain on my parade.

"Okay, I'll admit I'm not the best looking guy, but at least I'm not going to lose my good looks like you will – just think what its going to be like for you when you're 50 years old!" he insisted.

"John," I replied, "you are 12 years older than I am, so when I'm 50, you'll be 62 – how are you going to cope with that?!"

In spite of the fact that Johnny Yearsley could be a spiteful, and aggravating twat, I did like him a lot, and unfortunately, we never got the pleasure of teasing each other in another 25 years, as John died about 14 years after my 24th Birthday.

****

The ring in Liverpool Stadium was absolutely enormous, and I estimated that you could probably have fitted about 4 smaller sized rings inside it. It had been designed more for Boxing than Wrestling, the surface was as solid as I have ever encountered in a ring of any sort. On wrestling nights the overly solid surface was covered with an overly thick padding, which overly compensated for the solidarity. One could be excused for thinking that for a wrestler's comfort when taking the horrendous bumps that we took every contest, that there could be no such thing as over-padding. But they would be very wrong indeed. Just walking across the ring was like trying to walk through a couple of feet of heavy snow, and made no sound at all when we collided with it. Then to make things worse, the rounds were also set up automatically for Boxing, and only lasted 3 minutes. The bell would ring, and by the time my opponent and I had trudged through the thick padding all the way to the middle of that huge ring, it seemed it was almost time to turn back around and make our way back to your corner. If you hoped to reach it by the time the bell sounded to end that round. Also the thickness of the padding seemed to prevent our feet from turning properly.

I was wrestling against the Polish Middleweight Champion, Josef Ski on January 22nd 1965 when I began sniping at his legs with my vicious thigh kicks. But as I delivered one of them it was my leg that gave way, and dropped me to the canvas like a ton of bricks instead of my opponent. What had happened was that as I had twisted around and shot out the kick, the padding was so thick and clinging that instead of sliding around as it was supposed to, my supporting foot just stuck where it was imbedded, and twisted my knee out. I writhed on the canvas in agony. The only thing that motivated me to get up, bite the bullet, and get on with the match was that I really wanted to complete my victory over the Middleweight Champion of Poland. I did and I was victorious, but I really hated that ring from that time on.

VINCE

It was late afternoon on the 6th of February, and we were at home in Beechdale Road, when Jean thought that it might be a wonderful time to call the Midwife. The Midwife arrived in plenty of time, in fact it was almost a day later that we were still all waiting, and still no new Baby. By now it wasn't only Jean who was completely exhausted. By early afternoon on the 7th the Midwife called for an ambulance, and we all ended up in a Hospital somewhere near The Oval Cricket Ground. The time dragged on and on. It was now dark, and both Mother and Baby were exhausted, and still struggling. They told me that the Baby's heartbeats were getting weaker, which immediately made my own heart all but stop dead. I had never been so panic stricken in my life, I didn't know how I was going to cope with the situation, and if it hadn't been for the complete feeling of unreality, I don't think I could have. I wanted to do something, but found that I was as helpless as my new unborn child, and probably just as bewildered. I couldn't imagine what Jean must be going through; it was a horrible nightmare from which I was unable to awaken. They told me they were going to do something to induce the progress or something – whatever it was I didn't understand what they were talking about, and still the time dragged on and on. 26 hours had passed since the Midwife had arrived at our home, and Jean had first gone into labor and we were still waiting, I thought that I would go completely insane – but then a Nurse told me,

"Mr. Street, you have a Son!"

We named him Vincent Gary, Vincent because I have always liked the name Vincent since I first heard Gene Vincent sing 'Blue Jean Bop' and Gary after my Brother, Terence Gary. He was another little treasure, But I knew that I also needed to earn a little treasure if I was ever going to keep us all in the custom to which I was determined to eventually become accustomed. Once again as if on cue I walked right into another possible source of extra income.

I hadn't been aware that Mickey Muldoon, the ex-training

instructor who I had met at the Universal Health Studio in Brixton lived just around the corner in Fairmount Road. Which ran parallel with Beechdale Road where we lived. I met him one afternoon as he was coming out of a small grocery shop which was also just around the corner from where we lived. Mickey accompanied me back into the shop, and we chatted as I was getting served, he then accompanied me back home, and we chatted some more over a sandwich and coffee.

Mickey admired 'Alexander the Great' and asked me if I had ever done any sketching, I told him that I had, and showed him drawings that I had sketched of a Cheetah, a Rhinoceros, an Elephant, a Tiger and a Lion's head. Also a number of pin-up Girls, which interested Mickey a lot more than the animals did,

"I'll just pop around the corner and get some of my own drawings to show you." Mickey told me and off he popped. He was back within minutes, and I have to say that I liked Mickey's pin-ups better than my own,

'He must have taken lessons from Freddy mark-2's kinky girlfriend.' I thought, although they were not quite as delightfully disgusting as her's had been. I told Mickey about the drawings that Freddy's girlfriend used to send him when we were both slightly incarcerated. Also about her own weird escapades – whenever she had a suitable partner, and an enthusiastic audience, and Mickey immediately wanted to know if I had any way of contacting her,

"Sorry," I told him, "I haven't got a clue who she is, or even what she looks like."

"Shame," he replied, "she could have earned some money with those kinds of talents going for her." The mention of earning money always grabbed my attention, so I immediately asked him to explain himself.

"I would have paid her for her drawings if they were any good," he explained, "and also for posing for photographs, I'm in the pornography business now." He added proudly. A picture of Mick's naked Wife, Sandra, in the photos he had shown me flashed through my mind.

Talking of pornography, according to Kalman Gaston, Irena, with my help had indeed established herself as 'Quveen-Dick' Darlink, but in the process I had unintentionally all but ruined her business. The cheaper, sub-quality rubber that I had used to save myself money whilst producing her gigantic custom made prototype pricks, just melted into a runny, tacky, toffee like substance, whenever it got hot and wet. Apparently, I had inadvertently gummed up all Irena and her Girl's tools of the trade, with the result that they were now all temporarily out of work. It's no wonder she had a hit out on me – Darlink!

****

I had achieved my goal, wrestling full time for Joint Promotions. I had recreated my image and transformed myself from a card filler to an arena filler - Who could want more - Well I could actually - A LOT MORE! Wrestling up North may have been a great career move, but it took me right into the back garden of my biggest enemy in Professional wrestling - World Champion George Kidd. But if you think that I was keeping rough company inside the ring, you should see what I encountered outside - hostile Police in Spain - Prison in Paris - sex and violence in London.

If you've survived my journey of a lifetime through book 1 - 2 and 3, who knows, you may just be tough enough for book 4. My story continues in - **'SADIST IN SEQUINS.'**

PHOTOS

Me at Dale Martin Wrestling Promotions, 1961.

Me vs. Al Miquet, 1961.

Lucky Somonovich, Arab, Al Miquet, Linde Caulder, Bruno
Elrington, Me, Ian Campbell, and Promotor, 1961.

Joe Cornelius and Me, 1961.

Me with Tony Scarlo at Dale Martin, 1961.

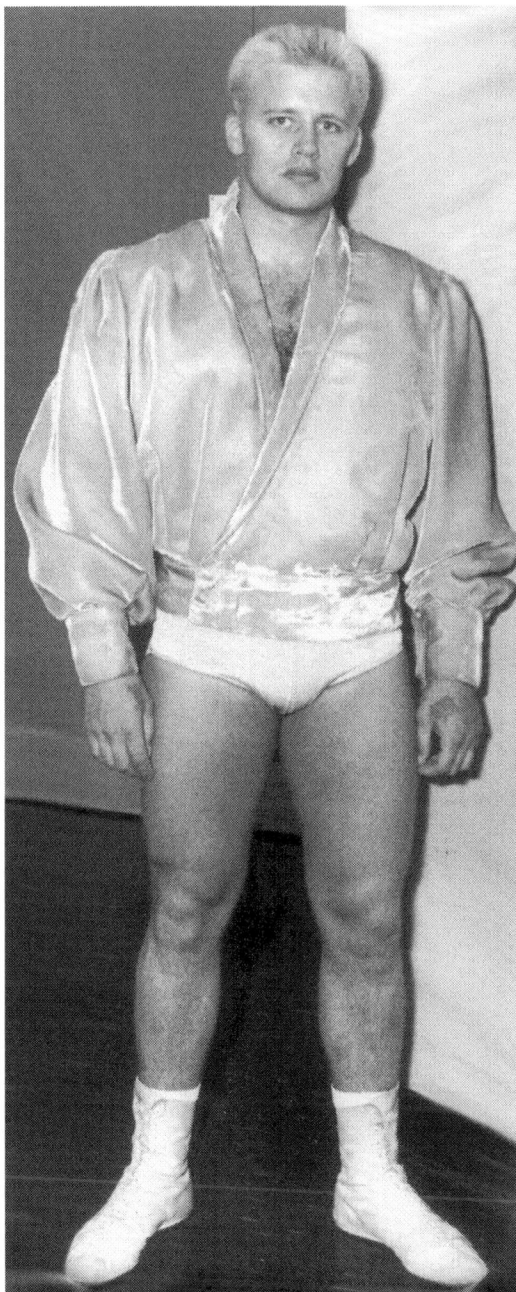

Blue Velvet. 'The Look' that started it all, 1962.

Cowboy Jack Cassidy, Pietro Chapelle, and Me, 1962.

Terence, Pam, Me, Jean, and Shirley on Wedding Day, 1962.

Jean in her wedding dress, 1962.

Me and Jean on our wedding day, 1962.

Me vs. Leon Fortuna, 1962.

Me with baby Adrian, 1963.

Me vs. Dick Conlon, 1964.

Me in 1965.

Me vs. Mick McMichael, 1965.

Me vs. Mick McMichael, 1965.

Me vs. Mick McMichael, 1965.

Me with private tailor, Jack Robinson, 1965.

Spartan Army, 1965.

Me vs. Vic Faulkner, 1965.

Me vs. Vic Faulkner, 1965.

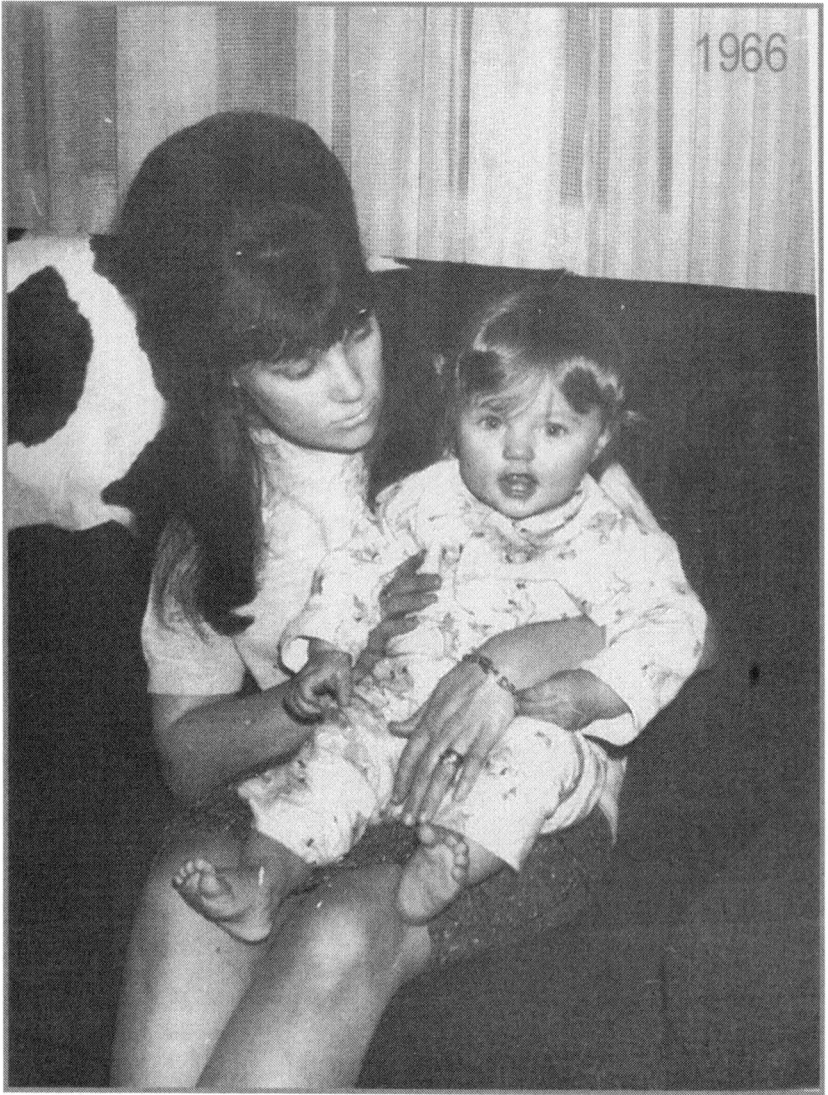

Jean with baby Vince, 1966.

Printed in Great Britain
by Amazon